TEA
WITH
MRS SIMKINS

DELICIOUS RECIPES FOR MAKING A MEAL OUT OF TEA-TIME:
CAKES, PASTRIES, BISCUITS AND SAVOURIES

TEA
WITH
MRS SIMKINS

DELICIOUS RECIPES FOR MAKING A MEAL OUT OF TEA-TIME:
CAKES, PASTRIES, BISCUITS AND SAVOURIES

Tea Notes kindly supplied by Clipper Teas

SPRING HILL

For David
David and Edie

Published by Spring Hill, an imprint of How To Books Ltd.
Spring Hill House, Spring Hill Road
Begbroke, Oxford OX5 1RX
United Kingdom
Tel: (01865) 375794
Fax: (01865) 379162
info@howtobooks.co.uk
www.howtobooks.co.uk

How To Books greatly reduce the carbon footprint of their books
by sourcing their typesetting and printing in the UK.

British Library Cataloguing in Publication Data
A catalogue record of this book is available from the British Library.

ISBN: 978-1-905862-43-6

Cover design by Mousemat Design Limited
Produced for How To Books by Deer Park Productions, Tavistock, Devon
Designed and typeset by Mousemat Design Ltd
Printed and bound in Great Britain by MPG Books Group, Bodmin, Cornwall.

NOTE: The material contained in this book is set out in good faith for general guidance and no
liability can be accepted for loss or expense incurred as a result of relying in particular circumstances
on statements made in the book. The laws and regulations are complex and liable to change, and
readers should check the current position with relevant authorities before making personal
arrangements.

CONTENTS

ACKNOWLEDGEMENTS

I would like to thank my family and friends and everyone who helped with the making of this book.

Special thanks to Moira Blake of Dorset Pastry, Deidre Hills and all the members of the Marnhull Mothers' Union, Adrian Curtis (Family Butcher), Clive Mellum of Shipton Mills and to Claire Tuck, Daniel Parr and everyone at Clipper Teas.

As ever, thank you to Fanny Charles and everyone at the Blackmore Vale Magazine.

And finally, a huge thank you to everyone at How To Books.

Thank you all very much indeed.

INTRODUCTION

I've always had a bit of a thing about tea time so I have *really* enjoyed myself writing this book.

The overwhelming majority of recipes are brand new of course, but there are also a few familiar favourites from *Cooking with Mrs Simkins*. This is because you can't have a proper book about teas without recipes for scones and teacakes, sponges and fairy cakes and so on.

There are, however, several new variations of these recipes. Plus rather than relying totally on self-raising flour being completely fresh in order for sponge cakes to rise, there are also instructions for using plain flour, bicarbonate of soda and cream of tartar instead. You'll find it works a treat!

And in case you are thinking that this book is entirely about cakes and sweet things, don't worry: there are plenty of delicious and interesting savoury recipes too.

Oven Temperature Conversions

Mark 1	275°F	140°C
Mark 2	300°F	150°C
Mark 3	325°F	170°C
Mark 4	350°F	180°C
Mark 5	375°F	190°C
Mark 6	400°F	200°C
Mark 7	425°F	220°C
Mark 8	450°F	230°C

Please be aware that individual oven performance varies tremendously.

Measurements

Both metric and imperial measurements are given for the recipes. Follow one set of measurements, not a mixture of both, as they are not interchangeable.

Helpful Equipment

Here are the most useful sizes of baking tins, most of which are used in this book. Heavier, better quality baking tins conduct heat more efficiently than anything thin and flimsy. They also have a longer life.

Large baking tray

A baking tray that just fits comfortably inside your oven can be used for all kinds of bread and biscuits and scones.

Standard 20cm (8in) square brownie tin

This is a really useful size and shape for brownies and small tray bakes.

12-cup muffin tin

As well as muffins this is perfect for buns, rolls, fairy cakes and deep filled tarts.

12-cup mini-muffin tin

A couple of these are useful for tiny cakes and tarts.

12-cup tart tins

It's useful to have a couple of these for tarts, mince pies, small quiches and for steadying crispy cakes.

Loose-bottomed cake, sandwich and flan tins

It's handy to have the following sizes:
18cm (7in) cake tin; pair of 18cm (7in) sandwich tins; 20cm (8in) cake tin; 20cm (8in) flan tin; 23cm (9in) cake tin – particularly if you make your own Christmas cake.

Loose-bottomed 10cm (4in) tartlet tins

Often sold in packs of six, these are perfect for elegant individual fruit tarts and also for individual quiches and savoury flans.

Mini loaf tins

Often sold in packs of four, these are brilliant for sweet, dinky, little loaves of bread and bar cakes. It's useful to have 12, but they're not cheap so it's worth knowing they hold the same amount of mix as the cup of a 12-cup muffin tin – enabling you to make a mixed batch.

Look after them carefully to keep them in good condition: instead of scrubbing them in hot soapy water or throwing them in the dishwasher, it's usually possible to clean them perfectly well by wiping with kitchen paper.

Ceramic baking beans

Treat yourself to some proper ceramic baking beans: two tubs would be ideal. Ceramic baking beans conduct the heat more efficiently than dried peas or beans when baking pastry flan cases blind. They help to conduct heat to the inside of the pastry case as well as weighing it down and supporting the sides.

ALL KINDS OF TEA TIME OCCASIONS

Afternoon Tea and High Tea are both such British institutions but they reflect two completely different ways of life. There is often confusion between the terms 'Afternoon Tea' and 'High Tea'. High Tea *sounds* very grand with connotations of 'high society', but nothing could be further from the truth.

Afternoon Tea had very aristocratic beginnings. Although tea drinking started in Britain in the 17th century, sitting around, drinking tea with cakes and delicate little savouries came later.

By the 19th century, among the upper classes, lunch was served at midday and, for various reasons, dinner had become a very late meal: 8 o'clock at the earliest, with nothing in between. Ladies were obliged to order a pot of tea during the afternoon along with a little something to keep them going. Eventually, friends and family were invited and the concept of Afternoon Tea began. And so it became a convivial opportunity for the ladies of the house and their friends to relax together and chat as well as to stop their blood sugar levels from plummeting!

A kettle would be boiled on a small spirit stove near the tea table and the lady of the house would make the tea in a silver or bone china teapot. The food would be very delicate and refined: thinly cut bread and butter, cucumber sandwiches made with the slenderest slivers of peeled cucumber, dainty cakes on a pretty cake stand and possibly something toasted in a covered silver dish during the cold days of winter.

High Tea, on the other hand, came about out of necessity, once the Industrial Revolution had turned the majority of working people away from their home-based jobs and into the factories and mills. It was a substantial meal for the whole family at the end of a hard working day, as hearty as funds would permit, and brought to the table with the minimum of effort and accompanied by cups of strong tea.

Most of the family members would very likely have been working all day and would arrive home tired and hungry with little energy or inclination, or even a hot stove or fire, to cook.

During the 19th century tea had come down in price and was first drunk by the working classes as a precious treat, but as prices fell even more it turned into a household staple and was drunk at every mealtime, and often in between as well.

Afternoon Tea is so called because it is based around cups of tea taken in the afternoon, but why is High Tea called *High* Tea? It may very well be because whereas Afternoon Tea was taken whilst sitting in low easy chairs and sofas, with everything set out on small tables, High Tea was eaten whilst sitting 'up' at a full size table on a hard chair or bench.

Maybe, it was because the plates were piled high as working people tucked into their main meal of the day!

Afternoon Tea is usually served earlier in the afternoon, towards 4 o'clock. It is based around 'finger food' although special little cake forks can be used for creamier cakes and pastries. You may also have small 'tea knives' if toast and the spreading of sweet or savoury toppings is involved.

High Tea is served much later, from 5 o'clock, but usually around 6 o'clock. It is partly based around food eaten with a knife and fork: in fact High Tea is sometimes referred to as a 'Knife and Fork Tea' or a 'Meat Tea'. Typical dishes served for High Tea, depending upon the household budget, could be: cold meats, particularly ham, and meat pies such as pork pie or pasties, often served with pickles or relishes, or fish, maybe fried fish or kippers, or dishes with cheese or eggs, and plenty of bread in the form of thickly sliced bread and butter, rolls or toast or toasted crumpets, muffins and fruit breads. There might be a cake component to round off the meal. Later, tinned fruit and tinned fish became popular as well.

For some of us, the last meal of the day is still thought of as 'tea'. Others may call it dinner, supper or the evening meal.

MIL or MIF? Milk in First? Milk in Last?

This is a complete minefield. Many people feel that the tea should be poured first with milk added afterwards, and this is *the only* civilised way to serve tea. Some of us feel that the milk should be poured into the cup first and the tea poured on top, as this way the milk and the tea 'blend' better and you can tell instantly 'if the colour is right'. There is also talk of the hot tea slightly 'scalding' the milk when you do it this way; some people say this improves the taste, others say it doesn't.

There is also the possibility of the hot tea cracking the (usually surprisingly robust) bone china cups, which could become very cold in the unheated houses of the 19th century and therefore vulnerable to the action of the hot tea upon them. In some cases this view could lead to milk in first to prevent the cup from cracking. In others, possibly, it could be milk in last, to show that a few cracked cups here and there were of little consequence as you could buy new ones whenever you felt like it!

Which Milk?

If you are taking milk in your tea, now that we have so many types to choose from, which milk *should* you choose? Many of us feel that full cream or whole milk is too creamy, skimmed milk is too watery and semi-skimmed milk is just right.

Who's Mother?

Generally, the woman of the house is in charge of the teapot and pours everyone's tea for them. If there is no woman of the house or tea is taken out, in a tea shop or hotel perhaps, somebody will be chosen to pour the tea and be 'Mother'. That person will then be in sole charge of the teapot throughout the meal and nobody else should try to pour from it. 'Mother' should be on the alert to the possibility of the others in the party wanting their cups refilled and should be the one to add more hot water to the teapot as necessary.

PICNIC TEA

A picnic is really any kind of combination of food and drink enjoyed outside. It can be a grand affair with enormous wicker hampers and proper china and glassware, but it is more usually fairly informal and simple. It's more likely to be sandwiches and cake with flasks of tea and bottles of soft drinks eaten on a rug spread on the ground.

The great British picnic conjures up childhood memories of sandy sandwiches on the beach sheltered by a stripy windbreak – not so much to protect you and your food from the wind but from all the beach balls whizzing about.

People tend not to be quite so determined to picnic at the seaside, whatever the weather, these days. When I was a child, once you had packed the picnic, got in the car and started on the journey if it rained you just carried on, parked the car 'on the front' and ate your picnic in the car whilst peering out of the steamy windows through the lashing rain at the sea. Some mums even took their knitting – my mum never actually embraced knitting herself, although incidentally, I have: once we had to stop en route to the beach and find a wool shop (never easy) as I'd left one of my needles at home.

And then there were the childhood country picnics seated on scratchy woolly rugs with wasps in the jam. There would be Thermos flasks of distinctive tasting 'picnic tea' and pork pies with tubes of mustard, little cakes and apples, which for some reason your mum would always have polished to a high gloss. There are also impromptu picnics where you might sit on someone's coat with a package of hurriedly put together sandwiches or even something just bought from the nearest shop.

These days, you can arm yourself for a picnic with every type of equipment you could possibly want: cool boxes and freezer blocks, a staggering array of bright and cheerful unbreakable cups and plates, wide-necked flasks, folding chairs that aren't too heavy and are actually comfy, little pop-up tents and sun shades, waterproof rugs and, instead of the old soapy flannel in a plastic bag, you can take wet wipes and hand gels.

Unsurprisingly, on seaside outings, it is usually Mum who is in charge of carting all this paraphernalia to the beach. You often see mums, bent double under the weight of it all, slipping and sliding down the path whilst everyone else runs happily ahead each carrying just a single bucket or a spade.

TV TEA

Although slobbing out in front of the TV for every meal is definitely not to be encouraged, there is something very cosy and relaxing about a companionable family tea in front of the TV. The key is that you watch a programme or film that you all enjoy, the tea things spread out on the coffee table within easy reach.

If it's winter, you might have a fire to sit round as well. When it's chilly and dark outside and you are all tucked up inside with the curtains drawn, toast and toasted crumpets are a particularly welcome treat. There is nothing to stop you bringing the toaster in on a tray rather then dashing backwards and forwards to the kitchen.

You might like to try some savoury spreads and potted meats: the **Amazing Cheese Spread** is fabulous on crumpets, the **Potted Meats** and **Fish Pastes**, great on hot buttered toast.

If you had a casserole the night before or a roast for lunch, you might like to make some of the **Little Pies** in the Savouries section.

CRICKET TEA

The gentle thwack of leather on willow, perfect blue summer skies, stripy deck chairs, players in cricket whites alternately standing around expectantly or breaking into a sudden run, the pavilion in the distance with the promise of tea…

Unfortunately, the beautifully laid out tea in the pavilion is mainly for the benefit of the players. If you are spending the afternoon watching cricket you will probably have to take along your own picnic tea. Alternatively, you can always put on your own cricket tea in the garden. Set up a game of cricket (or rounders) and lay out a spread you can all enjoy. Unless you have a massive garden just don't use one of those insanely hard balls!

A typical cricket tea is intended to be eaten milling around with a plate in one hand and might consist of: plates of sandwiches cut into triangles and resting on their backs – maybe garnished with tomatoes cut into quarters, possibly some miniature Melton Mowbray pork pies or some really good sausage rolls, scones split in half with jam and a dollop of cream already on them, chocolate cake, lemon cake and fruit cake – all cut into slices, and some mixed pastries such as jam and lemon curd tarts.

If you are providing ham sandwiches and pork pies don't forget to put some mustard on the table.

CREAM TEA

The cream tea is such an English tradition: lovely light scones, thick cream (preferably clotted) and strawberry jam, all served with a generous pot of tea.

The way a cream tea is served is practically as important as the food itself. It should be very traditional, either at a refined tea table with a silver or bone china tea pot and delicate cups and saucers, or cottagey and countrified with pretty, mismatched china and a jug of garden flowers on the table, all jostling for space with the little glass dishes of cream and jam. And if the weather is nice, what could be more perfect on a summer's day than a cream tea served outside in a (wasp-free) country garden?

A Note on Jam

The quality of the jam is just as important as the scones and cream. Many a cream tea has been a bit of a let down when a jellified blob of something, corresponding to no known fruit, lurks in the jam dish.

Strawberry jam, preferably homemade, is the most traditional choice. A few sliced strawberries on the side, freshly picked and still warm from the sun, are always appreciated.

Splits

Sometimes, instead of scones, you might be offered a couple of very fresh, soft, round, flour-dusted bread rolls called 'splits' instead. These are mainly found in Devon (Devonshire Splits) and Cornwall (Cornish Splits) and are lovely: see **Milk Splits**.

STRAWBERRY TEA

There's nothing like a strawberry tea in the garden on a balmy day in early summer. It's like a kind of super cream tea with added strawberries. You can serve plenty of **Scones**, or **Milk Splits**, with **Strawberry Jam** and cream with bowls of strawberries as well.

BLACKBERRY TEA

Sometimes, you don't quite want to let go of the summer: even though the school holidays are just about over and the strawberries are long gone, you might fancy a bit of a tea party in the garden before autumn sets in. What you can do is have a blackberry tea.

If you are near a blackberry patch you can start off the proceedings by going blackberrying and then come back to a tea with a bit of a blackberry and early autumn theme.

Instead of strawberry jam with your scones, you could have blackberry jelly or crab apple jelly and make a sponge cake filled with blackberry jelly and lemon buttercream. An apple cake would also go down well. With any luck you'll catch some late summer sunshine!

RELAXED CHATTY TEA

This is mainly a fantasy as, in the real world, all the people you would like to get together for tea and cakes and plenty of undisturbed talking one afternoon are all far too busy. You are probably far too busy yourself.

Anyway, in this fantasy, all your favourite friends are gathered together, without a care in the world, all chatting away and eating delicious cakes and drinking tea. You'll have all your best crockery out and there'll be flowers on the table. No one will be on a diet or have a food allergy and no one will have to rush off. If there are any children in the party, they will be sweet and funny and behave beautifully and any babies will sleep peacefully, waking up occasionally to gurgle adorably for a few moments before snoozing off again.

Here are some suggestions as to what to serve in case you ever do manage to pull off such an event. You never know, it could happen – on a special birthday or anniversary perhaps!

You may just want to have tea and cakes or you may want some delicate little savouries as well. Make sure you provide your friends' favourite things but you may like to include some of the following:

- Delicate, crustless sandwiches cut into triangles – possibly **Egg and Cress**, **Smoked Salmon**, **Cucumber** or **Cream Cheese and Cucumber**
- Something chocolatey – a large **Chocolate Cake** to cut at, **Little Chocolate Cakes** or **Chocolate Butterflies**, **Brownie Buns** or **Simple and Sneaky Millionaire's Shortbread**
- Something lemony – a large **Lemon Cake** to cut at, **Lemon Drizzle Cake** or **Lemon Curd Tarts**
- Strawberries during the summer – either in little bowls with a jug of cream to pass round, or simply arranged on a plate with any larger ones cut in half, or **Strawberry Tarts**
- You may also like to include some **Scones**, already split and spread with jam and a dollop of cream, or possibly a few **Pastries** or some **Homemade Meringues**

- You can have a large pot of tea on the go: Earl Grey, perhaps, and put out an array of fruit or herb teas in the kitchen and let people make their own if they prefer something else.

Tea in the Garden

If you have a fairly secluded plot there is nothing nicer than tea in the garden on a summer's day: lazing around, with tea and cakes and cooling drinks, chatting to family and friends, the birds singing away in the background. Sometimes, during the darkest days of winter, you might imagine yourself having tea in the garden practically every day when summer finally comes. In reality, the weather can prevent you doing this very often at all, so at the very first sign of any sunshine in late spring get out there with your teapot and make the most of it!

Nursery Tea

The late Victorian and Edwardian eras were the golden age of Nursery Tea with Nanny. It conjures up a cosy picture of clean, happy children tucking into wholesome boiled eggs with soldiers and mugs of milk, a dappled grey rocking horse and a row of dolls and teddies not far away.

Before Queen Victoria came to the throne, childhood could be very short and after babyhood children were often treated as young adults. Working class children would work to help the family as best they could and children from more privileged backgrounds would be expected to adopt the manners of their elders. Whatever you feel about nursery life possibly being segregated from the rest of the household, at least it meant children were more able to be children: to have their own space to play and learn in and interesting toys and more light-hearted books. Not all parents left their children with nannies all the time and Nursery Tea was often an opportunity for parents and children to be together.

Although Nursery Tea is an upper and middle class institution, the food has more in common with the working class High Tea. It is the last meal of the day. This is a 'tea' where no actual tea is served: although Nanny and visiting parents would no doubt have taken the opportunity to have a cup of tea, the children would have drunk milk or water.

The children would have eaten a more substantial lunch and tea would be a lighter but still sustaining meal of something like boiled eggs and soldiers or bread and butter, little sandwiches (with the crusts left on, to make your hair curl), bread and butter and jam, buttered toast, currant buns and maybe a little cake or biscuit.

Today, if we use the term at all, we just mean a meal at the end of the day for small children whose bedtime is still relatively early. Mum and Dad will probably eat their meal together later.

Children's Birthday Tea Party

Quite often a birthday party at home is for a fairly large group of very young children or a smaller group of older ones. Sometimes, for a few birthdays in between, children may go through a stage of preferring to be taken out for a 'treat' instead.

Younger children

Parties at home are great fun and always appreciated, but they can be hard work. Young children probably won't actually eat a great deal. They will be too excited to concentrate on very much food and can be heart-breakingly fussy, so don't knock yourself out by going overboard. Try to aim for a ratio of three quarters savoury to a quarter sweet and keep it fairly simple. Remember, homemade food is far better for young digestions than mass produced stuff full of additives. Also you definitely don't want a houseful of toddlers high on junk food to contend with! If you are aiming to eat half way through the party, have some drinks on hand from early on as children can get very thirsty if there is a lot of activity going on.

Don't forget the hungry mums and dads!

Parents often stay at parties for younger children and since parties are normally held over the lunch or tea-time period, parents will be feeling a bit peckish themselves, so make sure you have made enough to feed them as well.

Suggestions include:
- **Little Sausages on Sticks** (avoid sticks for very young children)
- **Easy Sausage Rolls**
- **Little Cheese Tarts**
- **Sandwiches:** cut the crusts off and cut into four. Thinly sliced cheese, wafer thin ham, egg mayonnaise, Marmite, and jam, honey or marmalade all go down well for younger children
- **Cheesy Biscuits**
- **Light Cheesy Buns**
- **Mini-Loaves and Duck Rolls**
- Salady bits, grapes, strawberries
- Bread sticks are popular and not as salty and fatty as crisps. Lightly salted taco chips are also appreciated

As well as the birthday cake you can also have a selection of biscuits and small iced cakes and buns available. Most mums and dads agree: it is usually better to bring out the cakes after most of the savouries have been eaten!

Older children

Older children, on the other hand, can get very hungry indeed and eat an enormous amount. Popular choices might be a big pot of chilli or curry with plenty of rice, lasagne, shepherd's pie, spaghetti bolognese, homemade pizza, homemade hamburgers with plenty of salad and relishes, toasted sandwiches or piles of sausages and mash. Crusty bread or garlic bread on the side is usually a good idea as are bowls of salad, grapes and taco chips.

Ice cream is usually a good choice for afterwards and it's nice to have the traditional birthday cake with candles. Alternatively, you might have a chocolate cake or a pyramid of fairy cakes or even brownies (try the **Chocolate Brownie Buns**) with candles stuck in them.

✓ **A Note on Plates**

Paper plates can be a bit flimsy and food can slide off too easily, especially in the hand of an excited toddler. It's better if you can to lay in a stock of cheerful coloured plastic plates that you can wash and use again and again for parties, picnics and in the garden.

If you are having a themed party and are hankering after novelty paper plates, what you can do instead is have plain plastic re-usable plates, as above, but buy coloured and patterned paper napkins.

✓ **A Note on Allergies and Health Issues**

This may sound obvious, but do make sure you know all about any allergies that some of your small guests may have, particularly if parents aren't staying. Also, if someone suffers from asthma, for example, be sure his or her inhaler is available and that they are able to use it. Plus, of course, with very young children whose parents aren't staying, be sure to have a contact phone number. Young children can get very excited at parties and conditions normally well under control can be exacerbated by all the fun.

CHRISTMAS TEA AND CHRISTMAS HOLIDAY TEAS

On Christmas day itself, all you may want to do at tea time is collapse into a chair with a cup of tea and a modest slice of Christmas cake, possibly followed a little later by a satsuma.

Since the Christmas holiday, strictly speaking, lasts for 12 days, only *beginning* on Christmas day, there will be plenty of other opportunities for festive teas. Here are a few suggestions to bear in mind over the holiday period:

- **Christmas Cake**
- **Mince Pies**
- **Christmas-spiced Apple Pies**
- **Plum Loaf**
- **Gingerbread People**
- **Little Sausages on Sticks**
- **Little Sausage Rolls**
- Cold Cuts – served with plenty of fresh salad or in sandwiches
- **Orange Jelly**, served with Greek yoghurt, possibly sweetened and flavoured with a little sugar and vanilla
- Satsumas and walnuts – more fruit, in the form of grapes and highly polished fragrant Cox's Orange Pippins would also be welcome.

EASTER TEA

Easter is such a lovely time of year: the weather is starting to look a bit hopeful, the flowers are putting on a good show, birds are tweeting and lambs are gambolling in the fields. Easter Sunday is a good time to have family and friends round for tea in the afternoon and with none of the pressures of Christmas entertaining!

After all the Easter eggs and Easter egg hunts it is possibly wise not to go overboard with chocolate for tea as well, although the odd mini-egg is almost bound to make an appearance.

Eggs and fresh greenery are topical so dainty egg or egg and cress sandwiches would work well, and possibly some baby quiches served with some spring salad leaves on the side. **Hot Cross Buns**, although strictly speaking meant for Good Friday, make a welcome bridge from the savoury part of the tea to the sweet.

You could make some iced **Fairy Cakes** and decorate them with sugar-coated mini-eggs or with some spring flowers from the garden: arrange them on the cakes just before serving. Stick with something you know is harmless such as primroses, pansies or violas. Sit them on kitchen paper first for a while if they are a bit damp and inspect closely for insect life. Be sure not to use anything that has been sprayed or is close to an exhaust-fume laden road.

You may like to have some **Easter Biscuits** as well, either cut in the traditional fluted round shape or into Easter chicks, eggs and bunnies.

A **Simnel Cake** could be your main cake. Even though originally it used to be eaten on Mothering Sunday, it seems to have become more of an Easter tradition. You could decorate it with the traditional 11 balls of marzipan or with some fresh flowers, as above – or you could do both!

Children, and the young at heart, may appreciate an **Easter Bunny Custard Blancmange** and a jelly.

You could set the table with pretty pastel colours, spring flowers and fluffy chicks. You might even want to get a bit arty with twigs, either just as they are, or sprayed white and hung with little eggs and Eastery bits and pieces.

CHRISTENING PARTY

Christenings are usually held in the morning, so you are probably more likely to have a lunch rather than a tea-time meal, but if you are having an informal buffet style gathering and a christening cake at home, it can seem a bit more like a tea.

In any event, christenings are happy joyful occasions, with the emphasis on new life, children and families. There is likely to be a complete mix of age ranges, from the youngest baby to the most senior grandparent and all ages in between. Consequently, there needs to be a mix of food to appeal right across the age range whilst still keeping everything fairly simple (to keep preparation and clearing up to manageable levels).

If the party is held during the summer, the weather is fine and you have enough space, it's nice to be able to go into the garden. It's quite a good idea to set the food and drink up inside the house so that people can come in and choose what they want and take it outside. This way the food is protected from extremes of weather and it's easier to clear up afterwards. This also hopefully leaves the house itself fairly free for any older relatives to have a quiet sit down and for any very young children and babies to be settled down for a nap.

Drinks

You will probably want to serve Champagne or something similar plus tea and coffee, juices and soft drinks, with possibly sherry for older guests. One bottle of Champagne for every four or five guests should be ample for a christening tea, unless you a going for a full blown 'wetting the baby's head' version, in which case, you'll need to allow a bit more. Unless you have a huge amount of people at the party, one bottle of sherry, with a second tucked away in reserve, should be plenty.

The Christening Cake
A fruit cake, covered with marzipan and icing, like a Christmas or wedding cake is the most traditional. Some people may have followed the old tradition of keeping the top tier of their wedding cake for the christening of their first child. Usually, the icing will have yellowed slightly; if this is the case, a professional cake decorator should be able to take off the old icing and replace it with sparkling fresh white icing.

If no-one is very keen to have a fruit cake, you could have a chocolate one but it can get very messy if there are lots of children. One good idea is to have a pile or tower of **Fairy Cakes**. This looks really lovely, is usually very popular with children and adults, and there is no nerve wracking and time consuming slicing involved. If you want to go mad you could always put a few (not too many) celebratory candles on the top few cakes.

Food
Lots of little sandwiches usually appeal to all ages and other savouries that can mainly be eaten with one hand are welcome. Little quiches, sausage rolls and individual pork pies are usually good. Salady bits such as cut up sticks of celery, red and yellow pepper, cucumber, carrot and cherry tomatoes (cut in half, otherwise they can be a bit squirty) are all welcome. It's nice to have little cubes of cheese and so on, on sticks, but if there are a lot of mobile toddlers in the party, it's best to do without the actual sticks to avoid accidents. Bread sticks and crispy things are usually popular, also olives and cocktail onions. Have some mayonnaise and mustard on the table.

Cakes and sweet things
Iced fairy cakes and butterfly cakes are always popular and look pretty. If it is summer you could set out little individual bowls of strawberries with spoons and provide sugar and cream. Fruity ice lollies are good for children – you could hand them out in plastic drinking cups (with the wrappers already removed if they are bought ones). A few little pastries as well are nice, and are popular with older guests.

Balloons, banners, bunting and flowers
This is an occasion where you can really go to town with balloons and maybe a banner or some bunting and flowers in the house. If you have been sent masses of cards they look great hung on lengths of narrow pastel ribbon hung along a wall or across the ceiling.

FAREWELL TEAS
At some time, or several times, in our lives we may need to arrange a funeral tea for a dear friend or relation. This is never easy: if the person who has died has lived a long and happy life, it is just about

bearable and can even turn into a joyful celebration of a life well-lived, but if it is for a younger person it is hard to find any kind of consolation anywhere.

As with arranging the funeral service itself, planning the refreshments that follow can give a focus to the first stunned days of grief and be a specific task to be done for the deceased. The lunch or tea is an important continuation of the funeral as it creates an opportunity for everyone to be together to talk about the person who has died and to comfort each other.

There are several points to bear in mind when arranging such an occasion.

Some people may be so distraught or in such a state of shock that they may be unable to eat anything much at all. They may also feel very parched or faint. Have plenty of cool water and glasses available.

Other people may have travelled long distances, may have missed meals and may actually be ravenously hungry and in need of nourishment. It is particularly important for people who have travelled long distances and are driving to have something inside them, to revive them and keep them going on the journey back. Older relatives, who perhaps wouldn't normally travel very far, may have made a special effort and need particular consideration. Equally, there may be children in the party who will need to be catered for.

Usually, at a funeral tea, people won't be sitting down at a table but taking a plate of food and sitting somewhere else or just standing. Therefore, the food must be easy to pick up and to eat with one hand. It also needs to be fairly compact and neat (no oozing cream cakes or overfilled egg sandwiches) as people will most likely be wearing their best clothes and trying to talk to other guests: they need food they can pick up and eat neatly.

Another practical point to consider concerns where the tea is to be held. If it is in your home or a fully equipped hall with access to a fridge the choice of food will be wider. If the tea is going to be laid out sometime beforehand, particularly if the weather or indoor temperature is warm, you must avoid anything that is likely to spoil and become a breeding ground for bacteria. In this latter case, cold meats, smoked salmon and so on are completely out of the question.

The food needs to be nourishing but easy to digest and there should be plenty of reviving hot tea and coffee, jugs of water and juice.

It's good to have sherry or something similar for a toast but, as this is a tea rather than a wake, alcohol probably won't figure much more largely than that: people may be driving or just not feel like drinking much. Older guests in particular, however, might appreciate a little tot of whiskey or brandy or something similar in their tea. If you feel that might be the case, have a bottle standing by.

Sandwiches, savouries and cakes

It can be a nice idea to include, if it's practical, some of the deceased's favourite foods. Alternatively, this may be unbearably poignant and, if so, it's best not to. Traditionally, you might provide something like ham sandwiches, cheese sandwiches made with thinly sliced cheese, smoked salmon sandwiches and lightly filled egg mayonnaise sandwiches.

This may be sufficient with some cake or you may like to add some more savouries such as baby quiches, little sausage rolls, or miniature Melton Mowbray pork pies, cut in half. You might like to add a small amount of salad already prepared in bite-sized pieces such as small leaves of lettuce, slices of cucumber cut in half, halved cherry tomatoes or quartered larger ones and so on. You could also provide some mustard and possibly some mayonnaise.

Buttered buns or buttered slices of fruit loaf, fruit cake, sponge cake, little iced cakes and jam or lemon tarts are all good choices.

If the funeral is just before lunch and more seats are available, something more substantial may be called for. A ploughman's-style lunch can work well, provided keeping the food fresh and cool is no problem. The sight of some attractively laid out cold meats and cheeses, fresh bread and butter, salads and relishes can sometimes lift everyone's spirits a little. As well as the traditional crusty baguette-type bread, provide some softer rolls as well, particularly if older people and young children are present. Also, for those who have no appetite for anything hearty, include tea and coffee and biscuits.

Simple tea and cakes

If all the guests are very local, and the funeral is in the afternoon, you may prefer to have just tea and cakes. If there are any bakers among the proposed guests, they will in all likelihood be only too pleased to make a cake to contribute, so don't be afraid to ask beforehand. It's nice to involve other people as they are often desperate to help but don't quite know what to do, and it also spreads the load a bit.

Tea and biscuits

Sometimes, the immediate family will want to be alone after the service but there may be a wider group of guests not included in this, who may be longing for a restorative cup of tea and a chance to talk. What you can do in this situation is to arrange for tea and biscuits to be served after the service whilst the immediate family slip away. This can be arranged in a local community hall, church or village hall, or some churches have a specific refreshments area within the church building. Nobody will mind if there is no family representative present. Ask a friend or neighbour to take care of this or someone from the church may be able to help. The family can then have something at home in private.

Buying the funeral tea

It may be that nobody can actually face preparing sandwiches and cakes, which is completely understandable. What you can do is buy just a few nice things ready-made to keep everyone's strength up.

Choose some sandwiches from a reputable store, or ask someone to go in and do it for you. Try to do this or phone a few days before: you may be able to order in advance or at least give them some warning, as they may need to order extra.

Get someone to collect them on the day, in good time for the tea. Take them all out of the wrappers, cut each one in half to make two dainty triangles and arrange them on large plates or trays. They look nice if you arrange them in lines, resting on their backs. If you are up to it, arrange some halved cherry tomatoes around the plate (halved, because they can be too 'squirty' whole, with seeds shooting out as you bite into them) or buy a punnet of cress and snip some over the top.

Buy a decent fruit cake or two, cut into slices so that people can help themselves more easily, and anything else along those lines that you think people might enjoy and will be easy to serve and eat. Don't get too much, just a couple of cakes altogether should be enough unless it's a very large party.

Grapes are easily digestible and refreshing, so buy some and have a couple of dishes of them on the table. Provide some plain biscuits as well, particularly if there are older people in the party: Digestives and Rich Tea are popular choices. Again, you won't need many, unless there are a large number of guests.

Flowers on the table

If you can, and it's practical, try to have a few flowers on the table. A funeral without flowers can make people feel even bleaker than they do already. As well as a tribute to the person who has died, the flowers are there to lift the spirits of the people who are left and to offer a symbol of hope. In the same way, it can be helpful to have flowers at the funeral tea.

Don't forget to provide paper napkins. A box or two of tissues is helpful.

FARMHOUSE TEA

A farmhouse tea immediately conjures up pictures of good wholesome simple food: lovely crusty bread – very possibly a cottage loaf, freshly churned golden butter, brown, boiled, new laid eggs, a big ham, rich fruit cake, a pot of homemade strawberry jam and so on. All served with plenty of freshly brewed tea in an enormous brown teapot with jugs of creamy milk for the children.

It's the kind of spread that is so well described in children's storybooks, and as a consequence is the type of tea that many of us aspire to and feel nostalgic about. Happily, it's fairly easy to put together and if everyone can manage a bracing walk in the fresh air beforehand, to work up a hearty appetite, so much the better.

TYPES OF TEA

Never underestimate the restorative power of a nice hot cup of tea. Much like having a hot bath, most things seem at least a little bit better after a cup of tea. Usually, you might not really think about it, but next time you are feeling a bit ropey and having a cup of tea take the time to notice how you feel – you are almost certain to experience a slight lifting of mood or easing of symptoms afterwards!

Tea itself is a fascinating and complex subject. Here is an initial overview of just some of the main tea types written by Daniel Parr, Technical Manager of Clipper Teas.
All tea, whether it's Green, Black, White or Oolong comes from the same plant, the Camellia Sinensis in which caffeine naturally occurs. Good quality tea – Green, Black or Oolong – starts out with two leaves and a bud.

Black Tea

For the production of Black Tea the leaves are deliberately put through a fermentation process otherwise known as oxidisation, which causes the green tea leaves to turn dark brown. This helps develop the tannins, flavours and characteristics of Black Tea.

The broad stages of Black Tea manufacture are as follows:

1. Plucking
2. Withering
3. Rolling/Cutting
4. Fermenting (oxidising)
5. Drying
6. Sorting and Grading
7. Packing into bulk containers and packaging

Green Tea

The main difference between the production of Green Tea and Black Tea is that Green Tea does *not* undergo the deliberate fermentation process. Like an apple, when tea leaves are bruised or cut this damages the cells and exposes them to the air and enzyme activity will naturally turn them brown. Therefore, as opposed to Black Tea, with Green Tea the target is to *stop* as much fermentation from naturally occurring as possible, so that leaves remain as green and fresh as the process allows.

To support this, Green Tea manufacture includes a specific process step that can be referred to as 'fixation'. This effectively involves a short and sudden heat treatment in order to kill or halt enzyme activity.

Depending on the origin and the factory, fixation is generally done by either pan frying i.e. 'dry heat' or by steaming i.e. 'wet heat'. The leaves then undergo a further drying stage as do all other teas, to reduce moisture and to act as the final fixation stage prior to grading and sorting.

Like Black Teas, it is a combination of bush varietals, origin, climate, and processing methods and skills that provides such a wide range of styles, flavour profiles and different qualities.

The broad stages of Green Tea manufacture are as follows:

1. Plucking
2. *Withering
3. Steaming/**Pan frying
4. **Rolling/Cutting
5. Drying
6. Sorting and Grading
7. Packing into bulk containers and packaging

*Not all producers will choose to wither green tea
**Steps 3 and 4 are interchangeable in sequence depending on the producer
   Green Tea should always be served without milk.

White Tea

White Tea is produced in a very similar manner to Green Tea in that the leaves are not fermented and are intended to stay green. White Tea is said to be one of the least processed teas, which is true when taking into account the number of process steps.

Two important factors that set White Tea apart from Green Tea are the bush varietals used for plucking, and the processing. Bush varietals selected to produce White Tea have a higher level of the small white hairs on the back of the tea leaf, known as 'white hairy down' and this helps to give White Tea its unique character.

White Tea is also *always* withered and has a much longer, or more severe, wither than Green Tea, which also contributes to its unique character and smooth mellow and rounded flavour.

White Tea is traditionally from high grown areas in the Fujian province in South East China, and although other provinces also now commonly produce this tea on a commercial level, Fujian is still one of the main producers.

The broad stages of White Tea manufacture are as follows:
1. Plucking
2. Withering
3. Sorting and Grading
4. Drying
5. Breaking/Cutting*
6. Packing into bulk containers and packaging

*Only if producing tea bag grades
Like Green Tea, White Tea should always be served without milk.

Redbush

Redbush, also known as Rooibos, isn't strictly speaking a tea at all as it is produced from the plant *Aspalathus linearis*, a broom-like member of the legume family of plants that only grows in the Western Cape of South Africa. Unlike normal tea, Redbush is not plucked; instead it is harvested by being cut at approximately half a metre from the ground and the entire cutting is processed, including the leaves, bark and stem.

Like Black Tea, Redbush is deliberately fermented, although by a different method, which helps to develop its reddish-orange colour. Redbush is an excellent substitute for Black Tea, as it's the non-*camellia sinensis* product that is closest in character to normal Black Tea: both in terms of how the brewed tea is in appearance and colour, as well as how it tastes, although clearly it has its own unique flavour and characteristics.

Redbush has a fresh, clean woody taste and, if it is of a good quality, will have a distinctive caramel-like character.

Like Black Tea, Redbush can be enjoyed equally well with or without milk, yet it has the benefit of being naturally caffeine free.

Darjeeling

An exceptional, light, golden tea with a delicate taste from one of the world's finest growing regions, Darjeeling is regarded as the Champagne of teas.

Darjeeling Black Tea is typically light and delicate, with a fresh, vibrant and distinctive muscatel character that is unique to Darjeeling. For the connoisseur, Darjeeling is best enjoyed black due to its light and delicate nature.

Darjeeling is situated in North West India in the foothills of the Himalayan Mountains. On a clear day Mount Everest can be seen in the distance. Darjeeling is a recognised origin by geographical position, and controls are in place to avoid teas from other nearby areas falsely claiming to be Darjeeling's. Darjeeling is set at 6,000 feet above sea level and enjoys a cool climate as a result, which enables the tea to grow slowly, which in turn means the leaves have longer to develop the natural chemical make-up that helps contribute to its distinctive flavour.

Most of the tea bushes in Darjeeling are grown from the China-type bush: *Camellia sinensis var. sinensis*. These China-type bushes have smaller leaves and are better suited to colder climates than the *Camellia sinensis var. assamica*-type bushes that are commonly found in other areas such as Assam or Africa. They tend to be used more for CTC production (cut, tear and curl), as they tend to produce teas with a fuller, richer and heavier taste and liquor whereas the China-type bushes tend to deliver lighter, more fragrant and delicate teas.

Darjeeling Black Teas undergo a much lighter and more delicate fermentation process compared with other Black Teas: the leaves are almost semi-oxidised which can often be seen by the mixture of black, golden and light brown leaves with hints of green noticeable in a fine quality Darjeeling.

The growing of Darjeeling is seasonal and the quality and price of the tea produced depends greatly on the time of year. Typically, the season runs between April and October.

Assam

Assam is the world's largest tea-growing region in North East India, lying on either side of the Brahmaputra River. The Brahmaputra valley lies approximately 120 miles east of Darjeeling, and also borders with Bangladesh, Burma and China.

This part of India experiences high precipitation (or rainfall) during the monsoon period: as much as 10 to 12 inches of rain per day. The daytime temperature rises to about 102°F, creating greenhouse-like conditions of extreme humidity and heat. This tropical climate contributes to Assam's unique malty taste, a feature for which this tea is well known. Owing to the climate and geographical location, like Darjeeling, Assam tea production is very seasonal.

Assam produces many varieties and qualities of both orthodox, and CTC (cut, tear and curl) Black Teas, with the finer quality orthodox teas being produced at the beginning of the season from the first and second flush (or first and second tea crops). The largest part of the season's production takes place between July and September.

CTC (cut, tear and curl) production, mainly for the tea bag market, can be produced all season with the better quality teas coming from July production. However, for those tea factories that produce both orthodox and CTC, the focus of production at the quality time at the start of the season will be leafy orthodox teas as these will command the highest value.

A typical good quality Assam will be bright, rich, full-bodied and have a distinctive malty character.

Ceylon

Ceylon teas are basically Sri Lankan teas. The teas are still described in the tea industry as 'Ceylon', as this is how they were traditionally termed when the country was known by its former name of Ceylon. Ceylon produces mainly orthodox teas. Some Estates attempted to convert to CTC (cut, tear and curl) teas in the past, however stiff opposition from India and East Africa, particularly Kenya, meant that many of them switched back to orthodox.

Ceylon produces mostly Black Tea and is traditionally considered a Black Tea producing country. Black Tea is what is talked about mostly when the quality of Ceylon tea is described. However, Ceylon is also capable of producing very high quality Green Teas and as Green Tea's popularity grows in different markets, more producers are starting to diversify into Green Tea as well as Black Tea.

Most of Ceylon's tea production takes part in two areas in the South West of the country at between 3,000 and 8,000 feet above sea-level or elevation. Tea production does occur all year, and is less seasonal than, say, Assam. However, the time of year does impact on the quality being produced. Generally, the best quality teas are produced in the periods from the end of February to the middle of March in the western parts, and from the end of June to the end of August in the eastern parts.

Ceylon produces a vast array of different qualities and styles and these are linked to the different tea-growing regions and elevation. There are six main regions in Sri Lanka: Galle, Dimbula, Uva, Nuwara Eliya, Ratnapura and Kandy. Generally the finer, better teas are high-grown and the lesser quality teas are low-grown.

- **Low-grown:** 1,500–1,800 ft above sea level – these are of general good quality, colour and strength but lacking in distinctive and vibrant flavour and character.
- **Mid-grown:** 1,800–3,500 ft above sea level – these are of general better quality than the low-grown, with good colour and rich flavour.
- **High-grown:** 3,500–7,500 ft above sea level – these are the best quality teas with a golden colour and highly refined, intense and distinguished flavour.

In general terms, a good quality black Ceylon tea will deliver a bright golden colour and a brisk, crisp taste with a reminiscence of citrus. Ceylon tea is excellent as a single origin tea or for use in a blend. However, due to the more recent higher cost of production and therefore purchase price, in Sri Lanka versus other big Black Tea producers such as Kenya and Assam less and less Ceylon tea is being used in blends being offered by UK tea brands.

China

Tea was discovered in China, and is believed to have been cultivated since before the birth of Christ. Owing to the long history of tea production in China and the sheer size of the country and distribution of tea production, throughout so many different areas with different cultural backgrounds, China has developed the widest range of teas in the world. They can also be considered some of the finest teas and the most expensive. In fact, there are several thousand different varieties of tea in China so it is impossible to go into any real detail here.

The best tea is grown in the mountains at higher elevations; however, tea is also grown at lower elevations on flatter land as well. Tea is grown in many different provinces, mainly in the South East part of the country: some of which include Fujian, Zhejiang, Hubei, Yunnan and Hunan.

The type of production in China is orthodox although techniques vary dramatically between different producers, depending on the area and on the teas being produced. In fact, many speciality teas are still made by hand, as the delicate nature of the teas can be difficult to replicate using machinery.

In general, China produces the following main tea types: Green, White, Yellow, Oolong, Black, Pu-erh and Lapsang Souchong. Traditionally, and generally, Chinese people do not drink their tea with milk, and therefore have developed the teas in this way. Even the Black Tea China produces was not developed to be drunk with milk, although it may be drunk this way on occasion: if used in Europe to produce an Earl Grey product, for example. However, Chinese Black Tea would not be suited to an English breakfast-style product, based on its characteristics.

China is one of the only tea-producing countries in the world where the most expensive teas are generally sold into the domestic market and the less expensive teas are exported. This is a direct reflection of how important Chinese people regard tea to be.

Earl Grey

'Earl Grey' is a fancy name or descriptive term for a certain type of tea blend, whereby Black Tea is blended with Bergamot oil or flavouring. Depending on the brand, the quality and taste profile of Bergamot will differ.

However, in general terms, Bergamot provides a deeply refreshing citrus flavour that can also carry some slight floral notes. The tea used in Earl Grey, whether loose leaf or tea bags, is generally always selected to give a light and delicate liquor and colour, so as to compliment the Bergamot, rather than compete against it.

For this reason, orthodox teas are almost always used rather than CTCs (cut, tear and curl) with origins such as China, South India and sometimes Sri Lanka being common.

English Breakfast

'English Breakfast' is a fancy name attributed to a certain type of tea blend based on its quality characteristics, rather than any particular requirements over blend make-up or tea origins.

A good English Breakfast tea will generally be a premium quality Black Tea suited to the typical English market: it will be of good strength, have a rich and full flavour and be bright in colour ideal for drinking with milk.

On this basis, many English Breakfast products will be blends of Assam, Kenya (sometimes other East African countries such as Rwanda or Uganda) and sometimes Sri Lanka.

BRING BACK THE TEAPOT!

Although the usual method of making tea these days seems to be to give a tea bag a quick dunk in a mug of hot water, you can't beat making it in a teapot for flavour. It's also a small, calming ritual in what may otherwise be quite a frantic day.

If you frequently make tea for one, it's worth investing in a one-cup teapot. If you try to make a small amount of tea in a larger pot, by the time the tea has brewed it will have lost too much heat and won't be hot enough.

Use a small pot and fill it to the top with water. By the time it has brewed it will be just the right temperature. Bag-in-a-mug tea tends to be scalding hot with a thin and papery flavour, unless you have flattened the bag on the side of the mug with a spoon, in which case it can taste a bit 'stewed'.

Making the perfect cup of tea in a pot takes barely any more time and is less messy, as it doesn't involve trailing the dripping bag across the kitchen balanced on a teaspoon!

Boil the kettle using freshly drawn water.

Take a little water from the kettle before it boils and warm your teapot, swilling the water round and discarding it.

Put in your tea bag(s) or loose leaves.

Take the teapot to the kettle, so that when it boils there is no delay and the water doesn't go off the boil.

Fill the teapot with the boiling water and leave to steep or brew for 3–5 minutes before pouring.

✔ Lie Down and Relax with Two Teabags
Squeeze the excess tea from a couple of used teabags and put them in the fridge to chill. Lie down for ten minutes (longer if possible) with a chilled teabag over each eye. It's incredibly soothing and relaxing.

Highly Recommended Tea-Time Treats from the book: *Cooking with Mrs Simkins*

Slightly Restrained Elevenses Brownies
Light Apple Cake and Buns
Strawberry Cake and Buns
Apple and Cinnamon Buns
Flapjacks: Plain, Fruit, Apricot
All Kinds of Crispy Cakes
Virtuous Cake
Chocolate Biscuits
Orange Biscuits
Lemon Biscuits

SANDWICHES

Tea-time sandwiches are dainty, delicate little morsels rather than a substantial meal in themselves like a lunch-time or a breakfast sandwich. Traditionally, the crusts are cut off, and each round of sandwiches is cut into four: triangles are the classic way but you can also cut them into appetising little squares or fingers.

Which Bread?

It's important to have *really* fresh bread for sandwiches: anything the *slightest* bit dry makes a very disappointing sandwich indeed.

Brown and white bread are both good choices for tea-time sandwiches but anything wholegrain usually seems a bit too hearty for the tea table. Some fillings seem to go better with white bread – egg mayonnaise, for example, others such as smoked salmon are a natural partner for brown. A lovely soft milk loaf works well with sweeter fillings such as jam or lemon curd. If you are making several varieties of sandwich, use both brown and white bread for variety.

Which Spread?

The idea is to spread the bread with something that will contribute to the flavour and also waterproof the bread so that any moist fillings don't make it soggy. Equally, something like a single slice of meat can be a little dry without something spread on the bread first.

Butter gives the best flavour and mayonnaise can work well with certain fillings. The fun can go out of making sandwiches quite quickly if you are trying to spread butter straight from the fridge, so either soften it by putting it in the microwave for about 20 seconds or use one of the butters available that are mixed with a little oil and spread much more easily – take it out of the fridge for half an hour or so beforehand unless the weather is very hot as it can still be a little firm when it's fridge-cold.

Making Lots of Sandwiches

Making sandwiches can be a bit of a logistical nightmare if you have quite a few to make and several different fillings. Here are a few pointers to help make it as painless as possible.

Bear in mind that people usually make too many sandwiches, and there are usually some left over, so don't go overboard. If you are serving a variety of other foods as well, one round per person (four little sandwiches) is usually ample, as some people won't eat as many as that and the hungrier eaters can then take more than their share.

It's better to err on the side of caution and not do quite enough and then, if possible, be prepared to make another couple of rounds later should the need arise.

Make the sandwiches as close to the time of eating as you can so they are really fresh. Once they are made, arrange them on the serving plates and cover with foil, tucking it under the plates to secure: foil will keep the sandwiches fresh and you can remove it carefully afterwards and re-use it. You can soon drive yourself mad with cling film as it sticks everywhere except where you want it!

If there is going to be a slight delay and the room is warm, make sure any sandwiches filled with meat or fish are in the fridge. You may need to 'rationalise' your fridge in readiness beforehand.

Whatever your feelings about sliced bread normally, you can't beat having ready-sliced bread if you are making lots of sandwiches. Also, make sure the butter isn't hard (see above).

Before you start, make sure your working area is completely clear and you have plenty of elbow room.

Make one kind of sandwich at a time: butter the bread, put in the filling, stack them up no higher than four rounds at a time, remove the crusts and put them aside (see below), cut the stack in four, arrange on the plates and cover.

Clear the fillings away from that batch and then move on to the next.

Sometimes, it can seem like a good idea for several of you to have a kind of production line going: one butters the bread, one does the fillings and so on. This *can* work but often, unless you are working in a very large kitchen, you may prefer to take it in turns to make a batch each from start to finish instead, as it's very easy to start falling over each other in a smaller kitchen!

One slight exception to this is if you are making a large number of egg sandwiches: it's much easier if one person has the single responsibility for shelling the eggs and preparing them.

What to do with All Those Crusts?

What do you do with all those crusts? If you are cutting the crusts off quite a few rounds of sandwiches the wastage can be quite alarming but don't worry, they do have a use.

Just put all the crusts onto a flat tray out of the way somewhere and cover lightly with a clean tea towel or greaseproof paper to allow them to dry out a little.

1. When you have a moment, break up the crusts into smaller pieces and whiz them in batches in the food processor to make breadcrumbs. Store in a plastic bag or box in the freezer. Take out what you need each time and reseal. They are useful for stuffings and coatings or to add to meatballs. You can also fry them in a little butter or oil and scatter over pasta dishes.

2. Alternatively, snip your crusts into small pieces with sharp kitchen scissors to make croutons and store in a plastic bag or box in the freezer. Take out what you need each time and reseal. These are

very handy for scattering over savouries, salads and pasta dishes or even for a quick lunch with baked beans instead of toast.

To make croutons, heat some oil in a pan and spread a single layer of croutons across the bottom. Turn and coat in the oil and then lower the heat to moderate. Fry, turning occasionally, and keeping an eye on them, until they are crisp and golden.

Please note: during the summer it's always best to pack any kind of sandwiches for a picnic in a cool box with freezer blocks, but if you are taking sandwiches filled with meat or fish it is *absolutely essential* **if the weather is the slightest bit warm.**

Sandwich Fillings

AMAZING CHEESE SPREAD

Make delicate little cheese sandwiches with brown or white bread, a light smear of butter and a fairly generous layer of **Amazing Cheese Spread**. If you have any herbs in the garden, a few snipped chives or a little chervil work well scattered over the spread.

ANCHOVY PASTE

The **Homemade Anchovy Paste** makes an excellent sandwich: delicate in appearance, yet robust in flavour. Use brown bread, real butter and spread thinly. You may like to add some very thinly sliced, peeled cucumber (see **Cucumber Sandwiches**).

BANANA

You can make banana sandwiches with mashed banana for small children – don't fill them too full – but normally it's better to slice the banana. Thinly sliced brown or white bread, spread with real butter, and some fairly thinly sliced banana make a great sandwich. Make them just before you want to eat them to avoid the banana going soggy and brown.

BANANA AND HONEY

As above but spread one slice of buttered bread with honey: set honey or runny honey both work well.

THINLY SLICED ROAST BEEF WITH HORSERADISH OR MUSTARD

Butter some brown or white bread, or this may be a rare tea-time occasion for granary bread, and spread one slice with a light dab of horseradish sauce or mustard. Add the thinly sliced roast beef and serve with some delicate cocktail gherkins and silverskin onions.

HOMEMADE POTTED BEEF

Spread **Homemade Potted Beef** fairly generously on white or brown buttered bread. Some people may like to add a little trace of mustard. Again, cocktail gherkins and silverskin onions would be welcome.

CHEESE

When making a cheese sandwich, especially for tea time, slice the cheese *very* thinly into wafers – either with a sharp knife, one of those hand-held cheese slicers or use the slicing side of a box grater. It's much nicer to have several overlapping delicate little wafers of cheese rather than one great thick wodge.

MINIATURE CHEESE SANDWICHES

Make delicate little cheese sandwiches with brown or white bread, lightly buttered and filled with wafer thin cheese, as above. Cut the crusts off and cut each round into nine little squares. This makes them very appealing for children. Alternatively, make some using brown bread and some using white. Spear three sandwiches on a cocktail stick to make little nibbles, alternating the brown and white bread.

CUCUMBER

Cucumber sandwiches are the classic afternoon tea sandwich. Prepare the cucumber properly by peeling it first and then cutting it into wafer thin slices. Lay the slices on a double thickness of kitchen paper and sprinkle lightly with salt – a light grinding of Maldon Salt is perfect. Lay a couple more layers of kitchen paper on top and leave for a while. This draws out excess moisture from the cucumber and adds to the flavour.

Sandwich between slices of soft white bread, lightly buttered, and be sure to cut the crusts off and cut the sandwiches into dainty triangles!

THINLY SLICED CHEESE AND CUCUMBER

Cheese and cucumber go beautifully together. Prepare the cucumber and slice the cheese thinly as above. Sandwich together as above. Mayonnaise, spread on the bread instead of butter, works well with cheese and cucumber if you fancy a change.

THINLY SLICED ROAST OR POACHED CHICKEN WITH MALDON SALT AND MANGO CHUTNEY

Butter some brown or white bread and cover with thinly sliced chicken. Grind a little Maldon Salt lightly over the top and dab on a little mango chutney: the kind made with smaller pieces of mango works better.

PLAIN CHICKEN AND MALDON SALT

Sometimes, all you want is a perfectly plain chicken sandwich with just the *lightest* sprinkling of salt. Make as above but without the mango chutney.

CHICKEN, LEMON MAYONNAISE AND WATERCRESS

Spread some brown bread lightly with mayonnaise into which you have stirred some very finely grated lemon zest and a small squeeze of juice. Cover with the thinly sliced chicken and add some sprigs of fresh watercress.

COLD SAUSAGE PICNIC SANDWICH

These are fantastic eaten in the open air. Cook some really good butcher's sausages the day before, cool quickly and refrigerate. To make the sandwiches, slice the bread (brown or white) more thickly than usual for tea-time sandwiches, and butter. Slice each sausage length-wise: either in half or try to cut three thin slices. Lay between the slices of bread and cut each one in half. Take brown sauce and mustard with you; the ones in squirty bottles and jars are useful.

CREAM CHEESE AND CREAM CHEESE AND CUCUMBER

You may like to butter some brown or white bread very lightly first or you may prefer to spread the cream cheese directly onto the bread.

Cucumber goes beautifully with cream cheese. Prepare the cucumber as for **Cucumber Sandwiches**, and lay on top of the cream cheese.

CREAM CHEESE WITH GARDEN HERBS

Fresh garden herbs work well with cream cheese: snipped chives and/or chervil are excellent.

CREAM CHEESE AND NASTURTIUM SANDWICHES

Nasturtium leaves and flowers, and the flower buds, have a mustard cress-like flavour: mild at first but then with a peppery explosion on your tongue!

They also look gorgeous with their traditional glowing jewel-like reds and oranges or the newer varieties of yellow, pale creamy lemon or deep wine red shades.

They make a beautiful dainty little sandwich: use brown bread and spread with just a little butter and some cream cheese.

You need 4–6 completely bug free, unsprayed youngish leaves per round of sandwiches. Fold each leaf in half, cut along the fold, and then roll it up and snip over the cream cheese once you have spread it over the bread.

When you have made your sandwiches, cut the crusts off and cut the sandwiches into dainty triangles. Serve garnished with more leaves and some of the flowers. (You can put some flowers and flower buds in the sandwiches as well, if you like.)

Just perfect for a lazy afternoon tea in the garden.

EGG MAYONNAISE

Most people are partial to a classic egg mayonnaise sandwich. Don't over boil the eggs and then leave them sitting in the cooling water, otherwise they will be as rubbery and bouncy as little balls with nasty dark rings and a noticeably unpleasant smell! Boil for the time suggested below and then whip them out and get them into cold water as fast as you can.

To hard boil the eggs: bring the water to a fast boil and add the eggs once the water is boiling, and then set the timer and boil for 7–8 minutes *only*. Remove from the heat *immediately* and plunge into cold water. Roll the eggs briskly on a flat surface and peel off the shell.

Don't forget: use eggs that are several days old for hard boiling, as if they are very fresh they are a nightmare to peel – you'll find yourself peeling away chunks of white with the shell.

Once they are cool, chop roughly with a sharp knife and then mash with a dinner fork, adding just enough mayonnaise to bind them together – you don't need a huge amount. You might find it easier to work on a board rather than using a dish: you can get a better angle with the fork on a board and it's a lot simpler.

Lightly spread some white bread (which is more traditional), or brown if you prefer, with either butter or mayonnaise and spread with the egg mixture – don't go mad with the filling as it can all drop out again when some unwary person tries to eat it.

Egg and Cress

Proceed as above but snip some old fashioned cress from a punnet (or grow your own) into the sandwich on top of the egg.

Growing Cress

Get yourself a saucer or something similar in size and shape – plastic plant pot saucers are perfect – and arrange three or four thicknesses of kitchen paper on top. Soak the paper with water and scatter the seeds fairly thickly over the paper. Put the saucer somewhere light, not too cold and draught free. Choose somewhere you can keep an eye on it and water regularly.

Keep the paper moist but not dripping wet. Until the seeds start to sprout, lift up the edge of the paper and water carefully underneath or you will wash all the seeds away from the middle. Once the seeds have sprouted you can use a small watering can with a fine rose.

When the tiny seedlings are approaching eating size, snip with scissors. Sow a batch every week for a continuous supply.

Lightly Curried Egg Mayonnaise

Make as for **Egg Mayonnaise** but stir a small amount of curry paste or curry powder into the mayonnaise before you mix it with the egg.

Homemade Fish Paste

Any of the **Homemade Fish Pastes** make great sandwiches, either on their own or with some thinly sliced cucumber. Butter the bread lightly first.

HAM

Home-baked ham, cut as thinly as possible, or ready-cut wafer thin ham, are the best choices for a tea-time sandwich. If everybody likes mustard, spread a little lightly over one of the buttered slices of bread; if not, offer mustard separately.

HAM AND CHEESE

Wafer-thin ham and wafer-thin cheese together make a good sandwich.

HAM AND MARMALADE

This may sound a bit strange, but it's a great combination and works particularly well eaten in the open air as part of a picnic. If you are fond of mustard, a dab goes beautifully with both the ham and the marmalade.

POTTED HAM

The **Homemade Potted Ham** makes a good sandwich. Butter brown or white bread and spread the potted ham fairly generously. Again, a dab of mustard works well. Tiny cocktail gherkins and silverskin onions are appropriate for the tea table but feel free to take the full size versions on a picnic.

HONEY

Lovely, soft, fresh bread, brown or white, spread with butter and honey make a welcome sandwich for a child or an adult. Both set and runny honey work well but, for some reason, runny is usually more popular with children. Eat with a banana for a picnic tea.

JAM

This is a classic child's sandwich, or one for nostalgic adults. Soft, very fresh, white bread such as milk loaf works really well. Strawberry jam is the classic choice but also try apricot conserve, raspberry seedless jam or a jelly such as crab-apple or bramble.

Lemon Curd

This is more popular with older children or adults. A sandwich made with really fresh white bread and homemade lemon curd is so delicious, you won't need any cake!

Marmalade

Marmalade sandwiches are not just for well-known bears. If you have some really fresh white bread and are packing a quick picnic, marmalade sandwiches are a good thing to take if you haven't much in the way of cake or biscuits in the house. Generally speaking, a lighter marmalade with thin shreds of peel works best, but it's really a question of personal taste – you might prefer a granary bread with chunky marmalade. Whichever you choose, don't skimp on the butter.

Marmite, Marmite and Cheese, and Marmite and Lettuce

If you are a Marmite fan, there is nothing easier and tastier than a Marmite sandwich. Brown or white bread both work well, and don't skimp on the butter. *Do* skimp on the Marmite, however, and spread it nice and thinly.

A tiny smear spread over one buttered half of a cheese sandwich works well and Marmite and crisp fresh lettuce are a wonderful combination. Why not go mad and have Marmite, Cheese *and* Lettuce!

Sand Sandwiches

These aren't really made from sand, of course, but brown sugar! Butter some very fresh bread, brown or white, making sure the butter isn't too soft, but still quite 'shiny'. Sprinkle fairly lightly with soft brown sugar and cover with another buttered slice. Leave the crusts on and cut into two or four. These are popular as an occasional treat for children and nostalgic adults.

Smoked Salmon

If you are pushing the boat out, this is the sandwich to serve. Thinly cut, lightly buttered, fresh brown bread, delicious smoked salmon with possibly the *lightest* touch of freshly ground black pepper, served in little triangles garnished with wedges of lemon. Perfect. If it's a really special occasion, you can pretend you are at the Ritz and treat yourselves to a glass of Champagne as well!

ALTERNATIVE SMOKED SALMON

Make as above but instead of butter, spread the bread with mayonnaise – don't go mad with it but don't be too mean either. Add a touch of freshly ground black pepper and garnish with lemon, as before.

SMOKED SALMON, CREAM CHEESE AND BLACK PEPPER

This is the sandwich version of the classic bagel filling. Spread brown bread lightly with butter or just with the cream cheese, grind a little black pepper lightly over the top and add the smoked salmon. Serve with wedges of lemon.

SMOKED SALMON WITH A TOUCH OF HORSERADISH SAUCE

Admittedly, this sounds strange but it works really well: the flavours complement each other beautifully. Spread brown bread lightly with butter and dab a little horseradish sauce on one side, then add the smoked salmon. Serve with wedges of lemon.

TINNED SALMON

Tinned salmon, pink or red, makes a great sandwich. Drain the liquid from the salmon, mash with a fork and bind together with a little mayonnaise – alternatively, if you are going down the nostalgia route, use a dab of salad cream.

A little squeeze of lemon juice and a light grinding of black pepper are nice additions to the salmon and mayonnaise mixture.

Sandwich between brown bread – either lightly buttered or lightly spread with mayonnaise. This is good just as it is or with some thinly sliced cucumber. Much like egg mayonnaise: don't overfill.

TINNED TUNA

Drain the liquid from the tuna, mash with a fork and bind together with a little mayonnaise. Add a little squeeze of lemon juice and a light grinding of black pepper. Sandwich between brown bread – either lightly buttered or lightly spread with mayonnaise. This is good just as it is or with some thinly sliced cucumber. As above: don't overfill.

TUNA AND COTTAGE CHEESE

This sounds *extremely weird* but tastes surprisingly good! Mix together equal quantities of drained, mashed tuna and cottage cheese. Sandwich between lightly buttered brown bread.

FLAVOURED BUTTERS

You can make flavoured butter very easily and use it to add an extra special touch to sandwiches. Choose the butter to complement the filling.

- **Lemon Butter**: Stir a little finely grated lemon zest into softened butter and use with fish, chicken and salady fillings.

- **Curry Butter**: Stir a little curry powder or curry paste into softened butter and use with egg, plain chicken or beef, tuna or salad.

- **Chilli Butter**: Stir a little curry powder or finely chopped fresh chilli into softened butter and use with cheese, plain chicken, beef or sausage.

- **Herb Butter**: Stir some finely chopped or snipped 'soft' herbs, such as chives, chervil, mint, parsley, dill or French tarragon, into softened butter and use with egg, cheese, cream cheese or chicken.

- **Cinnamon Butter**: See Bath Buns

Tea and Sandwiches Are Not Just for Tea Time

In the traditionally-run British home, trays of tea and sandwiches always used to (and still do in some areas) appear in times of slight, but not absolutely desperate, crisis: the neighbours are locked out and waiting for the locksmith, someone has broken down outside your house, a mum has gone into labour and gone to hospital and so on. Pots of tea are made and brought into the sitting room and someone will be in the kitchen cutting sandwiches. It's a way of rallying round and offering hospitality and *doing something* whilst you wait for help or news to arrive.

Incidentally, coffee and sandwiches can paint a different picture altogether. You might order coffee and sandwiches (and very possibly a glass of brandy) if you arrive at a hotel late at night when you are starving hungry but the kitchen has officially closed.

SAVOURIES

EASY SAUSAGE ROLLS

In contrast to some of the readymade pasty pink sausage and greasy pastry combinations you can buy, homemade sausage rolls, fresh from the oven, are delicious and welcoming. Instead of fiddling around with sausage meat, buy good quality butcher's sausages and readymade, ready-rolled, all-butter puff pastry: preferably Dorset Pastry.

No precise quantities are given – each sausage will make 1 large sausage roll or 4 small ones.

Quantities to suit of:
Good quality butcher's sausages
Good quality all-butter ready-rolled frozen puff pastry, defrosted in the fridge until pliable

You will need a large, greased baking tray.

Preheat the oven to 200°C (fan oven) or equivalent.

Roll each sausage in a blanket of pastry and cut from the roll with a sharp knife, brush along the cut end with a little water and seal the edge. Lay each sausage roll join-side down on the prepared tray.

Make 2 or 3 little slits with the point of a sharp knife along the length.

For delicate little bite-sized sausage rolls, cut each pastry-rolled sausage into four with a sharp knife and make a couple of slits in the top.

Bake on a greased baking tray for approximately 20 minutes until puffed and golden.

If you prefer, you can peel the skin off each sausage first – this sounds like a bit of a faff, but it is actually relatively easy! You may also like to brush the sausage rolls with an egg beaten with a teaspoon of water, before they go into the oven, for a glossy professional finish.

LITTLE SAUSAGES ON STICKS

It can be quite difficult to find really good cocktail sausages. Instead, buy good quality chipolatas and gently squeeze each one in the middle and twist to make two smaller sausages, and then cut them apart with kitchen scissors. Bake in an un-greased baking dish, at 180°C (fan oven) or equivalent, for approximately 20 minutes, turning halfway.

Prick each sausage gently to release surplus fat and drain on kitchen paper. Spear with cocktail sticks and serve with a selection of mustards.

LITTLE CHEESE TARTS

These can be a little bit of a fiddle to make but they are so delicious it's worth it. They are great for picnics and parties. There is no need to bake blind: as they are so small the filling and pastry can cook together.

You will need a greased 12-cup tart tin and a 6cm (2½in) plain cutter.

Preheat the oven to 180°C (fan oven) or equivalent.

Sieve the flour carefully into the bowl of your food processor and add the butter, vegetable shortening and salt. Whiz into fine crumbs. Add the water and whiz again. Once it is starting to form big crumbs and clump together, turn it out onto a lightly floured board and knead it gently into a ball.

Roll it gently with a lightly floured rolling pin and cut into rounds. Press them gently into the tart tin. (If you have a second tart tin it would be useful, otherwise bake a separate part batch.)

Peel and slice the onion fairly finely. Fry until soft and barely coloured. Drain on kitchen paper. Grate the cheese.

Beat the egg and egg yolk gently together with the mustard powder (stir it through a tea strainer with a teaspoon to prevent it clumping together) and pepper. Add the cream and whisk in lightly.

Spread the onion evenly over the bottom of the pastry case and pour the cream and egg mixture over the top. Finally, scatter the cheese evenly over the surface. Bake for 15 minutes or until risen and until golden. Serve warm or cold.

Makes about 16

For the pastry
160g (6oz) plain flour
40g (1½oz) butter, cold
   and cut into small pieces
40g (1½oz) block vegetable
   shortening, cold and cut
   into small pieces
Pinch of salt
2–3 tablespoons cold water

For the filling
1 small onion
A little oil
75g (3oz) cheese
1 egg
1 egg yolk
Pinch of dry mustard
   powder
Freshly ground black or
   white pepper
6 tablespoons cream
   (single or double, but
   not extra thick)

LITTLE CHEESE AND BACON TARTS

Make these in exactly the same way as the **Little Cheese Tarts** but also fry **2 or 3 rashers of lean bacon**, cut into small squares or matchsticks. Add a little oil to the pan if necessary. The bacon should be cooked through but not crisp. Drain on kitchen paper and scatter over the base of the flan with the onion.

Spoon the filling into the unbaked cases, as above, and bake for around 12–15 minutes or until the pastry is cooked and the filling is risen and golden. Eat warm or cold.

SAVOURY GARDEN TARTS WITH ALL-BUTTER PASTRY

These elegant summery tartlets are just right for a light high tea in the garden. Serve with a leafy salad, some boiled new potatoes and fresh bread and butter.

The recipe below will give you your foundation. You can then top the light, cheesy, savoury custard with a few extra vegetables, either from the garden or whatever you happen to have in the fridge.

Suggestions – use singly or mix together:

- Asparagus – thin spears or fatter ones sliced vertically
- A few fresh peas or small mange tout
- Baby spinach leaves, torn slightly and incorporated into the savoury custard
- Small florets of broccoli
- Thinly sliced bell pepper
- Baby sweetcorn – whole or sliced in half vertically – or sweetcorn kernels
- Light scattering of 'soft' herbs such as: chives, chervil, dill, basil or French tarragon

See recipes for **Garden Salad** and **Homemade Salad Dressing** accompanying the **Lavender and Honey Bread** in the **Bread** section.

You will need 8 greased, fluted, loose-bottomed 10cm (4in) tartlet tins, and a baking tray, plus baking beans (preferably ceramic) and greaseproof paper.

Preheat the oven to 180°C (fan oven) or equivalent.

Cut out 8 circles of greaseproof paper using one of the loose bottoms as a template, and put your baking beans into a jug with a good pouring spout for ease of use.

Making the pastry
Sieve the flour and salt carefully into the bowl of your food processor and add the butter. Whiz into fine crumbs. Add the water and whiz until the mixture is starting to come together. Turn it out onto a floured board and knead it lightly until it forms a ball.

Divide the pastry into 8 equal pieces.

Working with one piece at a time, form it into a ball and roll out gently, keeping it circular, on a very lightly floured board with a lightly floured rolling pin, to a thickness of just less than ½ a centimetre.

Drape the pastry circle over the prepared tin and lower gently into position. Firm the pastry lightly into the fluted sides and coax it into shape. Smooth your hand carefully over the top of the tin so the fluted edges cut through the excess pastry and trim it away or gently roll your rolling pin over the top.

It is really important that you don't stretch the pastry: if you do it will ping back down the sides of the tins during baking like overstretched elastic!

For ease of use, arrange the tartlet tins on a baking tray. Put a little circle of greaseproof paper in each one and fill almost to the brim with baking beans.

Bake for 12–15 minutes or until crisp and golden.

Leave to settle and cool in the tin.

Once cool, remove the baking beans from the pastry cases. The easiest way is to pick up each pastry case and tip the beans out carefully into an empty washing up bowl or something similar. Peel away the greaseproof paper circles.

Making the savoury custard
Beat the egg and egg yolk gently together with the mustard powder (stir it through a tea strainer with a teaspoon to prevent it clumping together) and pepper. Add the cream and whisk in lightly.

Scatter the cheese over the base of each baked pastry case. Pour in the cream and egg mixture. Arrange your garden or fridge bits and pieces over the top.

Bake for 15 minutes or until risen and until golden. Serve warm or cold.

Using the pastry trimmings
Re roll the trimmings and use them to make some little jam tarts. The re-rolled pastry is fine for small tarts but a little bit over-worked for anything larger.

For the pastry
160g (6oz) plain flour
Pinch of salt
80g (3oz) butter, cold and cut into small pieces
3 tablespoons cold water

For the savoury custard
1 egg
1 egg yolk
Pinch of dry mustard powder
Freshly ground black or white pepper
6 tablespoons cream (single or double, but preferably not extra thick)
50g (2oz) cheese, grated

Plus: garden herbs and vegetables of your choice (see above)

BAKED EGGS

Baked eggs are a lovely light dish for tea-time and perfect to tempt invalids or anyone feeling a bit feeble: in fact, they are just the thing to eat tucked up in bed with a hot water bottle if you are a bit poorly but able to eat eggs and dairy.

The point of baking eggs, rather than poaching or boiling them, is that you can fancy them up a bit: with a little splash of cream and maybe some gently cooked mushrooms, a few snips of smoked salmon or some ham and what have you. The cream stops the egg drying out as well as giving extra flavour and lusciousness.

Butter, for greasing
1–2 very fresh eggs per
person
Salt and freshly ground
black or white pepper
1 tablespoon double
cream per egg

You will need a ramekin for each egg: approximately 7.5cm (3in) in size is ideal, plus a fairly shallow baking dish.

Preheat the oven to 160°C (fan oven) or equivalent.

Butter each ramekin and crack an egg into each one. Season with a little salt and a couple of grinds of white or black pepper. Spoon a tablespoon of cream on top: try to cover the whole surface of the egg. A tablespoon of cream is plenty: more will make the eggs too rich.

Put the ramekins into the baking dish and pour in some recently boiled, but not actually boiling water, to come about halfway up the ramekins.

Bake for 10–12 minutes until the white is set, the yolks are still runny and the cream is looking a little bit golden in places.

Put the ramekins on serving plates with a teaspoon and some dainty fingers or triangles of lightly buttered toast or some fresh white bread and butter. Eat immediately.

As with many other dishes, you are at the mercy of your own oven and it may take a couple of attempts before you time your eggs exactly to your liking. Keep notes and persevere: they are well worth it!

Variations

You can make your egg a little bit more substantial by putting one of the following in the buttered ramekin first and cracking the egg on top:

- A few lightly cooked sliced mushrooms – drain briefly on kitchen paper first – and possibly a few snipped fresh herbs such as chervil, chives and parsley
- Some wafer thin snippets of ham or snips of smoked salmon

Spread the Word

Here is a selection of delicious and nostalgic savoury spreads for piling onto hot buttered toast or slipping into sandwiches. You can choose from old-fashioned **Potted Ham** or **Potted Beef, Mrs Simkins' Amazing Cheese Spread** (**Original** or **Red Hot Chilli**) and a variety of **Fish Pastes**. All are made in the food processor and you can whip up the cheese spreads and fish pastes in record time.

Potted Meats

Potted meat may sound a bit old fashioned and uninspiring but, actually, it is a lovely treat spread on toast or crusty bread or made into tea-time sandwiches. Usually, modern potted meat recipes rely quite heavily on butter, both mixed in with the meat and in another layer on top. These lighter versions are made instead by whizzing the cooked meat in the food processor with some of the stock it was cooked in. If you wish, you can seal it with a thin layer of clarified butter.

POTTED HAM

You don't come across potted ham very often these days but it is seriously nice. As well as tea time, it's great for a weekend lunch or supper. You can also serve it as a starter (it's very economical!) for an informal dinner or take it on a picnic, as long as you can keep it cool. Try it in sandwiches, with crusty bread or rolls, or on hot buttered toast. Add possibly a dab of mustard and a crisp pickle (silverskin onion, gherkin or plain mixed pickles or piccalilli are all good) on the side. Some leafy green salad also goes well.

Sometimes, you see recipes for potted ham involving quite a lot of butter mixed in with the ham, which can be a little rich. Here, the potted ham is made in the food processor with some of its own stock and is much plainer altogether.

You can certainly seal it with a thin layer of clarified butter (see below) if you like, to keep the flavour and moisture in and any bacteria out, but you really don't have to, provided you cover it well with cling film or foil and eat it within a couple of days. However, it does add a nice professional touch. If you are serving it as a starter seal each pot with butter and then press a single whole bay leaf gently into the surface – very impressive!

Instead of leftover ham, this recipe involves boiling a ham knuckle, which you can buy from your local butcher for about the same price, or a little less, than half a dozen eggs.

Ham knuckle, also known as ham hock, is the same cut as the one traditionally used for thick pea and ham soup. It is so delicious and affordable it is also worth cooking for the ham alone, which can be stripped from the bone using a dinner fork to produce succulent, thick shreds of meat, great for chunky sandwiches or served hot with a fried egg and some home-fried potatoes on the side.

POTTED HAM *continued*

SERVES 6

1 ham knuckle
1 large onion, sliced
1–2 carrots, peeled and
  cut into strips
2–3 sticks of celery,
  trimmed and cut into
  strips
1 bay leaf
A few black and/or white
  peppercorns

✓ Note on hygiene
Make sure your
hands are *scrupulously*
clean as you remove the
meat from the bone: if
you can, it's better to do
the whole operation with
a dinner fork and a
short-handled sharp
knife and avoid handling
it at all.

You will need 6 small 7.5cm (3in) ramekins.

You may need to soak your ham knuckle overnight if it's very salty. Check with your butcher.

Put the ham into a large saucepan with the onion, carrot, celery, bay leaf and peppercorns. Pour over enough water to cover: this will probably be about 3 litres (6 pints) or so. Bring to the boil, skim off any froth and simmer fairly briskly for 2 to 3 hours, or until the ham is virtually falling off the bone. Check from time to time, adding more water if necessary.

Once cooked, take the ham from the stock, cover with foil and leave to rest in a warm place for 20 minutes or so. Reserve the stock and keep in a cool place (not the fridge as it will be too hot at this stage).

Use a dinner fork to take all the ham off the bone, once it has rested. Remove and discard as much fat as you can: don't worry about the odd tiny bit here and there as it will add to the flavour and texture.

You should have about 225g (8oz) of meat or thereabouts. Put the meat into the food processor and add a couple of tablespoons of the stock or cooking water. Whiz and then add a couple more tablespoons of stock. Repeat until you have added about 10 tablespoons in all and the ham is the texture of smooth pâté and is slightly clumping together. Add a spot more stock if it seems too dry. You shouldn't need any further seasoning at all as the flavour is already delicious: you definitely won't need any salt and pepper isn't really necessary either.

Divide the mixture between 6 small 7.5cm (3in) ramekins. Alternatively, you can use 4 larger ramekins or 1 large dish or container: it doesn't have to be round, a rectangular one looks good, and white china looks particularly attractive against the rosy pink colour of the ham. Once the ham is all potted, take a teaspoon of the cooking liquid at a time and pour 1 teaspoonful over the surface of each ramekin of ham to add extra moisture: adjust quantities accordingly if you are using larger containers.

Cover with foil or cling film, or clarified butter, if using. Store in the fridge and use within 48 hours.

CLARIFIED BUTTER

Clarified butter is very pure, clear, golden, melted butter that has been separated from the milk solids that butter contains. When you cook with normal butter it can burn quite easily, which is why a mixture of oil and butter is sometimes recommended for frying rather than butter on its own. The solids are the part that burns and once they have gone, you can cook with the butter on a much higher heat. Ghee, which is used in Indian cooking, is unsalted butter that has been clarified or 'made clear'.

Unsalted butter is normally used for clarifying. This is only because once the butter is clarified some of the salt may be removed at the same time as the milk solids.

It's really easy to clarify butter. 225g (8oz) will give you enough clarified butter to seal your potted ham or potted beef with some left over for cooking. You can use slightly less if you like, say 175g (6oz), but don't go below that, or by the time you have removed all the solids you will have hardly anything left!

Cut the butter into small pieces.

Heat gently in a heavy bottomed saucepan over low heat until it spits and cracks and bubbles.

Remove the pan from the heat and very carefully skim off the froth from the top with a tablespoon.

Pour the clear, golden liquid butter carefully through a nylon sieve into a container, taking care not to include the solids on the bottom of the pan. If you have some clean muslin or a brand new disposable dish cloth to line the sieve, so much the better. (It's tempting to just pour the whole lot through the sieve, but don't, because the milky solids will get through!)

Cool slightly and pour over your finished ramekins of potted ham or beef. Store what's left, in the fridge in a clean jar with a lid, and use it for frying: it gives everything a beautiful flavour.

Always make sure it is stored covered in the fridge. Uncovered butter soon reacts with the air or oxidises and starts to taste 'stale' and 'airy'.

You can also freeze clarified butter.

POTTED BEEF

As with the **Potted Ham**, above, you don't see potted meat or potted beef very often and, if you do, it is likely to be a rich mixture of finely minced, cold cooked beef blended with butter. This is a plainer, lighter version with much more flavour. Like the Potted Ham, this is great in sandwiches, with crusty bread or rolls, or on hot buttered toast. Mustard and pickles, particularly piccalilli and gherkins, are all good served on the side, and some fresh, crisp salad also goes well.

Chuck steak, blade or skirt, are all really economical cuts and they respond well to long, slow cooking and are full of flavour. Don't try to remove any slight bits of membrane or connective tissue before cooking as this all helps with the flavour.

Leave the meat in its original pieces and don't cut them any smaller before cooking; similarly don't cut the vegetables any smaller than suggested. This is so you don't have too many pieces to strain out of the stock at the end: if the pieces are too small and bitty it's difficult to strain all the precious stock out properly.

If you are lucky, once you have made the recipe, you may be left with a useful quantity of very nice beef and vegetable stock as a bonus – perfect for enhancing a stew, casserole, soup or gravy. If you won't be using it over the next day or two, make sure you freeze it as it's much too good to waste.

SERVES 6

225g (8oz) chuck steak, blade or skirt (ask your local butcher)
A very little oil, for frying
1 large onion, cut into 4
1–2 carrots, peeled and cut in half length-wise
2–3 sticks of celery, trimmed and cut in half length-wise
Approximately 1½ litres (2½ pints) hot water
1 bay leaf
1–2 tablespoons Worcestershire sauce
1 scant level tablespoon soft dark brown sugar
A little salt

You will need 6 small 7.5cm (3in) ramekins.

Brown the beef in the oil. Put the prepared vegetables into a clean pan and add the water, bay leaf, Worcestershire sauce and brown sugar. Stir and add the browned beef – including all of the beefy residue from the pan, so be sure to scrape it all off. Bring everything to the boil and then simmer gently, partially covered with a lid, for 2–3 hours until the beef is falling apart and very tender. Check from time to time, adding more water if necessary.

Once cooked, remove the pieces of beef from the stock, and transfer to a warm plate. Cover with foil and leave to rest in a warm place for 20 minutes or so. Strain and reserve the stock and keep in a cool place (not the fridge as it will be too hot at this stage).

Put the meat into the food processor and add a couple of tablespoons of the stock. Season very lightly with salt. Whiz and then add a couple more tablespoons of stock. Repeat until you have added about 10 tablespoons in all and the beef is a fairly smooth, pale paste and is slightly clumping together. Add a spot more stock if it seems too dry.

Check for seasoning: you may need the slightest touch more salt.

Divide the mixture between 6 small 7.5cm (3in) ramekins. Alternatively, you can use 4 larger ramekins or 1 large dish or container. Once the beef is all potted, take a teaspoon of the cooking liquid at a time and pour 1 teaspoonful over the surface of each ramekin of beef to add extra moisture: adjust quantities accordingly if you are using larger containers.

Once cold, cover with foil or cling film, or clarified butter, if using. Store in the fridge and use within 48 hours.

Once any remaining stock is cold, store in the fridge and use within 48 hours or freeze.

Mrs Simkins' Amazing Cheese Spreads

Isn't it amazing what you can do with a food processor in your own kitchen! Who'd have thought you could make something quite so delicious from a bit of cheese and a splash or two of milk and oil?

This spread is just fabulous on toasted crumpets for a cosy Sunday tea tucked up in front of the fire on a winter's afternoon. It's also lovely on toast, on fresh bread and butter or on digestive biscuits. It is good as a dip with slices of celery or apple, although don't go too mad obviously, as it's quite rich.

If you can lay your hands on a few chives try the spread on fresh bread and butter or a buttered roll with a few snipped chives on top.

You don't need any extra seasoning: you just want to taste the beautiful flavour of the cheese. The exception is the Red Hot Chilli version where the chilli complements the cheese and gives an exciting bite.

ORIGINAL CHEDDAR SPREAD

110g (4oz) cheddar cheese
1 tablespoon semi-skimmed milk
3–4 teaspoons rapeseed oil (or similar mild oil)

Cut the cheese into smaller pieces and whiz in the processor until it becomes rather bumpy grated cheese. Add the milk and whiz briefly. Add a teaspoon of oil and whiz again. Add the rest of the oil and whiz until smooth.

RED HOT CHEESE SPREAD WITH CHILLI

110g (4oz) Cheddar cheese
1 tablespoon semi-skimmed milk
3–4 teaspoons rapeseed oil (or similar mild oil)
Small piece of fresh red chill or ½ miniature chilli (alternatively, use a pinch of chilli powder to taste)

Snip the chilli into small pieces with sharp kitchen scissors.

Cut the cheese into smaller pieces and whiz in the processor until it becomes rather bumpy grated cheese. Add the milk and whiz briefly. Add a teaspoon of oil and whiz again. Add the rest of the oil, the snipped chilli (or chilli powder) and whiz until smooth.

Fish Paste

Fish paste possibly sounds even more drab and miserable than potted meat, but again, it tastes great. These homemade versions of the stuff in little jars are really easy and much tastier and more substantial than the readymade variety *and* they go further. Try to think 'spread' rather than 'paste' if it helps! Unless you have a bit of a thing about bones, buy tins of salmon and sardines complete with the skin and bones, not the 'skinless and boneless' varieties. The bones are a terrific source of calcium and are completely harmless – they are soft and edible because the fish is pressure cooked at high temperatures.

All of the following fish pastes are fabulous spread on hot buttered toast with or without an extra squeeze of lemon. Alternatively, use in sandwiches or on buttered rolls, with possibly some thinly sliced cucumber.

Each of the following recipes will make sufficient to fill, or almost fill, a large ramekin measuring 8.5cm (3½in) in diameter.

You will need a food processor to make these fish pastes. Try them once and you'll be hooked!

SARDINE AND TOMATO PASTE

This paste is a bit like the loaves and the fishes: it seems to make a single tin of sardines go much further than usual. This recipe makes more than enough paste for two, whereas a tin of sardines on toast normally seems barely enough for one.

Empty the sardines and tomato sauce into the bowl of your food processor. Add the oil, pepper and lemon juice. Whiz until smooth, stopping a couple of times, and scrape the paste down from the sides of the bowl with a flexible spatula. Check for seasoning. Refrigerate and use within 24 hours.	120g tin sardines in tomato sauce 2 teaspoons mild oil Freshly ground black or white pepper to taste Squeeze of lemon juice to taste

TUNA PASTE

Empty the tuna into the bowl of your food processor. Add the oil, pepper and lemon juice. Whiz until smooth, stopping a couple of times, and scrape the paste down from the sides of the bowl with a flexible spatula. Check for seasoning. You may need a touch of salt. Refrigerate and use within 24 hours.	185g tin tuna in spring water, drained 2 teaspoons mild, flavourless oil Freshly ground black or white pepper 2 teaspoons lemon juice – or to taste

TUNA AND MAYONNAISE PASTE

185g tin tuna in spring
  water, drained
2 teaspoons mayonnaise
Freshly ground black or
  white pepper
2 teaspoons lemon juice –
  or to taste

Empty the tuna into the bowl of your food processor. Add the mayonnaise, pepper and lemon juice. Whiz until smooth, stopping a couple of times, and scrape the paste down from the sides of the bowl with a flexible spatula.

Check for seasoning. Refrigerate and use within 24 hours.

SALMON PASTE

You can use either pink or red salmon for this recipe.

212g tin salmon, drained
2 teaspoons mild,
  flavourless oil
Freshly ground black or
  white pepper
2 teaspoons lemon juice –
  or to taste

Empty the salmon into the bowl of your food processor. Add the oil, pepper and lemon juice. Whiz until smooth, stopping a couple of times, and scrape the paste down from the sides of the bowl with a flexible spatula.

Check for seasoning. Refrigerate and use within 24 hours.

SALMON AND MAYONNAISE PASTE

This is lovely and luscious.

Empty the salmon into the bowl of your food processor. Add the mayonnaise, pepper and lemon juice. Whiz until smooth, stopping a couple of times, and scrape the paste down from the sides of the bowl with a flexible spatula.	212g tin salmon, drained 2 teaspoons mayonnaise Freshly ground black or white pepper 2 teaspoons lemon juice, or to taste
Check for seasoning. Refrigerate and use within 24 hours.	

What is the difference between red and pink salmon?
They are different species. Red Sockeye salmon is larger and more deeply flavoured than pink Humpy or Humpback salmon (which develops a hump on its back once it leaves the sea and swims upstream to spawn). Red salmon is not as plentiful as pink salmon so it has more rarity value, which is why it is more expensive.

ANCHOVY PASTE

This isn't the most handsome and appetising of spreads to look at, but it tastes delicious and is fabulous spread thinly on hot buttered toast. The quantities given are for a very small amount but you won't need very much as it's rather powerful.

Whiz the anchovies, including their oil, and the lemon juice, cayenne and black pepper together in the food processor or pound together in a pestle and mortar. Alternatively, mash everything together with a dinner fork.	50g tin anchovies in oil Squeeze of lemon juice Tip of a teaspoon of cayenne pepper Freshly ground black pepper
Once you have a smooth paste, transfer it to a small dish or ramekin, cover and store in the fridge. Serve spread thinly on triangles or wide soldiers of hot buttered toast.	

FRIED PLAICE

Plaice has a beautiful, delicate, distinctive flavour and is a really traditional choice for a knife and fork tea. It has always been a great favourite for high tea at old-fashioned tea shops, particularly those near the coast where it can be served freshly caught.

Plaice is termed as a flat fish and its smooth skin is deep steely grey with bright orange spots on its upper side, and pearly white with no spots at all on the under side. When you buy your plaice at the fish counter you will probably be given a mixture of both, there is a very slight difference in taste and texture and they are equally delicious. The flavour of the upper side of the fish is a little stronger and the texture fractionally meatier; the underside is more subtle.

Even a whole plaice isn't very thick and a plaice fillet is half the thickness of the whole fish, so consequently a plaice fillet will cook in a flash – 5 minutes in the pan should be more than enough, it will probably be ready after 4 minutes.

SERVES 2 BUT EASY TO DOUBLE QUANTITIES

75g (3oz) bread, preferably on the dry side

Oil for frying

1 rounded tablespoon plain flour

2 plaice fillets

1 egg, beaten

Tear the bread into rough pieces and, using a food processor, whiz into fine crumbs. Tip into a dry frying pan (no oil) and heat on the hob over a moderate heat for a few minutes, stirring constantly with a wooden spoon or spatula. This is to dry out the crumbs and crisp them up a bit.

Once the crumbs are ready, tip them onto a flat plate and heat some oil in a frying pan over a moderately high heat.

Put the flour into a shallow dish and coat the plaice in the flour. Have the beaten egg ready in another shallow dish.

Dip the floured plaice into the egg and then into the crumbs.

Fry the plaice briefly, turning the heat down to moderate. Turn it over after a couple of minutes, until the plaice itself is no longer translucent in appearance, but opaque and cooked and the coating is golden. This should take no more than 5 minutes at the most, check after 4. Sit the plaice on kitchen paper for a few moments to absorb any oil.

Serve with a wedge of lemon and chipped potatoes or plain, boiled, new potatoes and some peas: petit-pois are nice and dainty with plaice. You may like some tartare sauce on the side as well, plus a slice or two of fresh, thin, bread and butter and a pot of tea.

SKINNY CHIPS IN JACKETS

These are very yummy and very quick to prepare and cook. Since they are cooked in the oven, there is no need to wrestle with boiling hot pans of seething oil. The skinniness of the chips means they cook through quickly and thoroughly; the skins add extra deliciousness and texture. (Some chips will have quite a bit of skin on them: others will just have a little top and bottom.)

You will need a large baking tray (or 2 baking trays if you are cooking for several people).

Preheat the oven to 200–220°C (fan oven) or equivalent.

Scrub the potatoes and cut into quarters. Lie each quarter flat-side down on a board and cut into thin slices about ½ a centimetre wide. Cut each flat slice into strips about a centimetre wide. Spread them out onto a clean teacloth and pat them as dry as you can: if you are making quite a few, you can spread them out on one teacloth and lay another across the top.

Put them onto a baking tray and spread the oil over them, using your hands to make sure they are all coated. Spread them out in a single layer and put them into the oven. Bake for about 10–15 minutes until they are cooked through and lightly golden.

Turn them over halfway through the cooking time: when you do, take the tray out of the oven and put it on a flat surface, closing the oven door to keep the heat in. Once they are ready, you may need to lay them on kitchen paper to absorb any excess oil, but if you have judged the oil just right, there will be no need.

Serve sprinkled with sea salt: you can buy a special grinder for sea salt flakes or use a pestle and mortar. (You may also want a little tomato ketchup or mayonnaise.)

QUANTITIES GIVEN ARE APPROXIMATE: I MEDIUM-SIZED POTATO IS USUALLY SUFFICIENT FOR CHIPS FOR I PERSON.

Per person:
I medium potato
About I tablespoon mild flavourless oil such as sunflower or rapeseed
A little sea salt, such as Maldon Salt, to serve

SKINNY CHIPS IN JACKETS WITH ATTITUDE

These are the same as the above but with a little touch of seasoning. You can serve these for High Tea but, actually, they are perhaps more suited to lunch and supper.

Prepare the chips in exactly the same way as above but mix the **tip of a teaspoon (or to taste) of chilli powder (or curry powder)** with the oil. This gives a really good flavour, evenly distributed.

POTATO WEDGES IN THEIR JACKETS (WITH OR WITHOUT ATTITUDE)

Again, these are made in a similar way. Instead of cutting the potatoes into skinny slices, cut them into wedges. The easiest way to do this is to cut the potato in half and put it flat-side uppermost on a board. Cut carefully into wedges, aiming to cut 6 wedges from each potato half.

Continue as above but allow for 15–20 minutes cooking time.

CHIPPED POTATOES

The phrase 'chipped potatoes' really just means chips, but it has a nice, old fashioned, High Tea ring to it, making you think of long ago cafés, where the waitresses wore black dresses and frilly white aprons. Once again, these are made in a similar way to the wedges, above, but the potatoes are peeled and par-boiled beforehand.

Small salad and new potatoes work very well during the summer, giving the chips a lovely flavour.

SERVES 2–3	Peel the potatoes and cut each one length-wise into 3–4 slices. Cut each slice into 2–3 chunky chips – you should have about 30 chips in all.
Approximately 450g (1lb) potatoes – this equates to 3 small–medium potatoes	Bring to the boil in a saucepan of water and simmer briskly for 5 minutes.
	Preheat the oven to 200–220°C (fan oven) or equivalent.
Approximately 1–2 tablespoons flavourless oil	Lay a clean tea towel on a board or the worktop, drain the potatoes and arrange on the tea towel in a single layer. Wrap the tea towel (or use a second one if you are making more) around the potatoes and leave until they are cool enough to handle and quite dry.

Put the cooling, dry potatoes onto a baking tray and spread the oil over them, using your hands to make sure they are all coated. (Don't use too much oil. What you are aiming for is a light coating on the potatoes – there shouldn't be any left sloshing round the tray!)

Spread them out in a single layer and put them into the oven. Bake for about 15–20 minutes until they are cooked through and very lightly golden. Turn them over halfway through the cooking time: when you do, take the tray out of the oven and put it on a flat surface, closing the oven door to keep the heat in as you do so.

As before, once they are ready, you may need to lay them on kitchen paper to absorb any excess oil but if you've judged it right there will be no need.

These go perfectly with the Fried Plaice for a good old fashioned tea-shop High Tea or equally well with thick slices of home-cooked ham and fried eggs for Ham, Egg and Chips.

✔ **Useful Note**
Set your timer for halfway through the cooking time if you think you'll forget to turn them over and then re-set it.

BAKED HAM

A home-baked ham is easy to prepare and fabulous hot or cold. Eat it hot with egg and chips for a classic High Tea or with a baked potato and salad. Eat it cold with salad or thinly sliced in sandwiches. Serve it hot or cold with **Three Spoon Sauce and Baby Leaf Salad**.

Buy a piece of **gammon** from your local butcher and bake it with Demerara sugar and hoisin sauce for an extra special flavour. Tell your butcher you want to do this so he will give you a piece with a large enough area of fat for you to work on. Your butcher can advise you on cooking times: it will usually be something like 25 minutes per 1/2 kilo or 1lb. Bake your ham for the required time, but half an hour before it is cooked, take it out of the oven and allow it to cool slightly.

Have ready: **a couple of tablespoons of Demerara sugar** and **a couple of tablespoons of hoisin sauce** mixed together in a bowl. (If you have a very large piece of gammon you may need more.)

Using 2 large carving forks or a large fork and a fish slice, put the ham on a large board or work surface. If you have an old clean tea towel that you can put underneath this will help and stop it slipping.

Using a smallish, sharp kitchen knife rather than a carving knife (too unwieldy) and a dinner fork, slice the skin off the fat so that all the fat is exposed. Don't cut too deeply or you will cut into the meat itself.

Once you have removed all the skin, score some lines across the fat, criss-crossing to make diamond patterns. Smooth the hoisin and sugar mixture onto the exposed fat, with the back of a dessertspoon. You may need to help it along with your finger tips.

Put the ham back into the oven, uncovered for half an hour, or until the sugar is just tinged slightly brown and melting and the ham is fully cooked.

Ham for Tea with Three Spoon Sauce and Baby Leaf Salad

This is a beautifully simple suggestion for an appetising High Tea, yet special enough for guests. It's also perfect for an early summer meal in the garden. The baby-leaves are too delicate to be dressed but if you scoop up a forkful with some ham and dip it into the sauce all the flavours work beautifully together.

Simply serve slices of the **Baked Ham**, above, with **baby leaf salad**, **boiled new potatoes** and some lovely **fresh white bread and butter**. Serve the **Three Spoons Sauce**, below, separately or spoon into tiny individual bowls and put one on each person's plate.

Three Spoon Sauce

Stir the mayonnaise and mustards together and then stir in the water. If you have one of those tiny little hand whisks for whisking hot milk, you can give the sauce a gentle whisking as well.

SERVES 3–4 BUT IT'S EASY TO INCREASE THE QUANTITIES PROPORTIONALLY

- I tablespoon mayonnaise
- I level egg/coffee spoon each of English and Dijon mustard
- I dessertspoon water

Fried Ham – Twice as Nice

Baked Ham is very good sliced and fried the next day. Heat some oil in a pan and once it's hot add the slices of ham. Turn them over and then lower the heat to moderate. Fry until completely heated through. It's lovely with egg and chips, and also with baked beans and a lightly buttered soft bread roll.

Fried Ham is also wonderful for a weekend breakfast.

LITTLE HOT CHILLI PIES

These are great for a warming winter tea by the fire or standing around in a cold garden on Guy Fawkes' night. Give them a chance to cool down a little before you bite into them as they retain the heat for quite a while after they have come out of the oven.

They are perfect to make with leftover chilli when you only have a small amount. You only need a heaped teaspoonful of chilli for each pie, so even if you make two batches, it's still not very much chilli! Make sure the chilli is well flavoured and not too sloppy.

It's more 'correct' to use plain cutters for savoury pies but the fluted ones do make these pies look very appealing!

MAKES 12 PIES

For the pastry
160g (6oz) plain flour
Pinch of salt
40g (1½oz) butter, cold
    and cut into small pieces
40g (1½oz) vegetable
    shortening, cold and cut
    into small pieces

**For the filling and
    topping**
12 generous teaspoonfuls
    leftover chilli
Approximately 25g grated
    Cheddar cheese (grated
    in a brisk up and down
    movement to avoid any
    long strands)

You will need 2 fluted cutters: 7½cm (3in) and a 6cm (2½in), and a greased 12-cup tart tin.

Preheat the oven to 180°C (fan ovens) or equivalent.

Sieve the flour and salt carefully into the bowl of your food processor and add the butter and vegetable shortening. Whiz into fine crumbs. Add the water and whiz until the mixture is starting to come together. Turn it out onto a floured board and knead it lightly until it forms a ball.

Roll it out gently with a floured rolling pin to a thickness of about ½cm.

Cut out 12 circles with the larger cutter (for the pies) and 12 circles with the smaller cutter (for the lids). As you put the larger circles into the tart tins, firm them down gently to give the finished pies a good shape.

Put a generous teaspoon of chilli into each: don't overfill, though, as it can boil out. Brush the edge of each lid with water and press them gently onto the pies.

Top each pie with a little grated cheese, press the cheese down gently into the pastry.

Don't make a hole in the top with the point of a knife or anything: the steam generated inside the pie will help to make sure the chilli is fully reheated and the tops of the pies will have an appealing domed shape. This won't happen if there is an escape hole in the lid.

Bake for about 15–18 minutes or until pale golden. Remove from the tin with a small palette knife and cool on a wire rack. Eat warm, not boiling hot!

SATURDAY NIGHT CASSEROLE, SUNDAY TEA PIES

There is something about a pie that speaks deeply to the British psyche. There is also something about little individual versions of normally larger items that is particularly appealing. These are perfect to make with any kind of leftover casserole when you have only a small amount left. A heaped teaspoonful of casserole is plenty for each pie. Make sure you cut any large chunks of anything into smaller pieces: it's easy to do this using a knife and fork. Make as for the **Little Hot Chilli Pies** recipe above, using **leftover casserole** instead of chilli, but brush each pie with **egg beaten with a teaspoonful of water** rather than topping with cheese.

STEAK AND BLUE CHEESE PIES

If your leftover casserole is a beef one, slip some small cubes of **Stilton or Dorset Blue Vinny** into the pie with the rest of the filling before you put the lids on. These are lovely to offer to guests around Christmas time.

BAKED BEAN PIES

These are fun for older children to make for a weekend or holiday tea but do be careful to let the pies cool down enough before you bite into them.

MAKES 12 PIES

For the pastry
160g (6oz) plain flour
Pinch of salt
40g (1½oz) butter, cold
   and cut into small pieces
40g (1½oz) vegetable
shortening, cold and cut
into small pieces
3 tablespoons cold water

**For the filling and
   topping**
415g tin baked beans
Approximately 25g grated
   Cheddar cheese (grated
   in a brisk up and down
   movement to avoid any
   long strands)

Variations
You can spice up the
beans a bit if you like:
try stirring in some curry
paste or powder to taste
and a few sultanas, or
chilli powder or snipped
fresh chilli. If you don't
want to top the pies with
cheese (maybe not with
curried beans), you could
glaze them instead with
an egg beaten with a
teaspoon of water.

You will need 2 fluted cutters: 7½cm (3in) and a 6cm (2½in), and a greased 12-cup tart tin.

Preheat the oven to 180°C (fan oven) or equivalent.

Sieve the flour and salt carefully into the bowl of your food processor and add the butter and vegetable shortening. Whiz into fine crumbs. Add the water and whiz until the mixture is starting to come together. Turn it out onto a floured board and knead it lightly until it forms a ball.

Roll it out gently with a floured rolling pin to a thickness of about ½ a centimetre.

Cut out 12 circles with the larger cutter (for the pies) and 12 circles with the smaller cutter (for the lids). As you put the larger circles into the tart tins, firm them down gently to give the finished pies a good shape.

Empty the tin of beans into a bowl and stir gently to make sure the sauce is distributed evenly. Put a about a level dessertspoon into each pie – you may not need the whole tin – you are aiming to fill each pie generously but not so much so that everything squelches out when you try to put the lids on.

Brush the edge of each lid with water and press them gently onto the pies.

Top each pie with a little grated cheese and press the cheese down gently into the pastry.

Don't make a hole in the top of the pies with the point of a knife: this will make the tops domed in shape rather than flat. They will be boiling hot inside when they first come out of the oven, so take care.

Bake for about 15–18 minutes or until pale golden. Remove from the tin with a small palette knife and cool on a wire rack. Eat warm, not boiling hot!

LEFTOVER ROAST AND GRAVY PIES

These are such a treat; it's worth making extra gravy at lunchtime so you will have enough.

It's difficult to give precise quantities, as it depends on how much meat and gravy you have left. If you don't have enough to fill all the pies, you can make up the rest of the batch by filling the pies with baked beans (see above). Alternatively, you can make jam tarts or cut out the pastry circles for some more pies and freeze them to use another day.

You will need 2 fluted cutters: 7½cm (3in) and a 6cm (2½inch), and a greased 12-cup tart tin.

Preheat the oven to 180°C (fan oven) or equivalent.

Make the pastry, roll it out and put it into the tart tin, as above.

Cut the meat into small dice: roughly ½ a centimetre or so, and stir into the gravy.

Put about a dessertspoon of meat and gravy into each pie – you need the balance between wanting them to be generously filled, but not so much that the filling oozes out.

Brush the edge of each lid with water and press them gently onto the pies.

You can bake these just as they are, or brush the lid of each pie with an egg beaten with a teaspoon of water for a glossy, professional finish.

As above, don't make a hole in the tops of the pies with the point of a knife: this will make the tops domed in shape rather than flat and the steam will help to ensure the filling is piping hot. They will be boiling hot inside when they first come out of the oven, so take care.

Bake for about 15–18 minutes or until pale golden. Remove from the tin with a small palette knife and cool on a wire rack.

Eat whilst they are warm but not boiling hot!

Depending on what meat is inside your pies, you may like to serve them with a dab of mustard.

Cold roast meat and cold
leftover gravy
Pastry, as above

CHEESY BISCUITS

These are perfect for all kinds of parties and picnics. They are very similar to cheese straws but rolled and cut out as biscuits.

MAKES ABOUT 15 DEPENDING ON CUTTER SIZE

50g (2oz) plain flour
Pinch of dry mustard
    powder
Pinch of salt
25g (1oz) butter, softened
75–110g (3–4oz) grated
    well-flavoured Cheddar
    cheese

You will need a large, greased baking tray and some biscuit cutters.

Preheat the oven to 180°C (fan oven) or equivalent.

Sieve the flour and mustard powder carefully into the bowl of your food processor, sprinkle in the salt and add the butter. Give the mixture a quick whiz to start everything off and add the cheese (the lesser amount of cheese will make a slightly less rich biscuit, the greater amount will be a little cheesier and richer).

Keep whizzing, stopping from time to time to remove the lid and give the mixture a quick stir, until the mixture starts to clump together. Stop the machine, remove the blade and transfer the mixture to a clean board. Gently bring the mixture together with your hands and knead it lightly until it looks and feels like a ball of cheesy marzipan.

Flour the board lightly and, using a floured rolling pin, roll out the mixture to a thickness of just less than a centimetre. Cut out your shapes and arrange on the prepared tray. Re-roll and cut out the rest. If you have any dough left over, roll it into little balls and flatten with your hand or a fork and bake with the others.

Bake for 7–8 minutes, or until they are golden in colour. Remove from the oven and leave to settle for a few moments. Remove carefully with a palette knife and finish cooling on a wire rack. Store in an airtight tin.

TOASTY TEA

A toasty tea can be a cosy Afternoon Tea with plates of hot buttered toast and crumpets, preferably eaten round a roaring fire on a chilly day, or it can be a knife and fork High Tea with something like **Welsh Rarebit** or toast and eggs.

BOILED EGGS

Boiled eggs are very much part of the traditional tea table: soft-boiled eggs with firm whites and runny golden yolks are perfect for a relaxed, light 'High' tea and very popular with children. Serve with fingers of toast for 'boiled eggs and soldiers', sometimes also known as 'dippy eggs'.

Boiled eggs are also gorgeous with fresh, soft bread and butter. Try boiled eggs, brown bread and butter, some fresh watercress and just a tiny bit of Maldon Salt for dipping. Make a pot of tea and have some **Homemade Strawberry Jam** on the table to have with the rest of your bread and butter.

Eggs for boiling should be as fresh as possible and, ideally, they should be at room temperature.

Realistically, 4 eggs are the most you can boil at a time: if they are to be eaten with a soft and runny yolk and firm whites. Bring the water to a boil in a small to medium sized deep saucepan. Put in your eggs: a spaghetti server is a handy tool for the job.

Start timing from the moment they go into the boiling water. An average size egg should take 4 minutes and it's best if you don't actually cut the top off the eggs until you have buttered the toast, which just gives the whites a fraction longer to set. Bantam eggs may only need 3½ minutes. Always eat immediately.

POACHED EGGS ON TOAST

Poached eggs on toast are always a treat: comforting, light and nourishing. Sometimes, two poached eggs, nestled side by side on adjoining triangles of toast are called 'two on a raft'. Poached eggs on a split and a toasted muffin make a lovely toasty tea too. Poached eggs require careful timing so that the white is firm but the yolk is runny enough to run all over the toast when you put your knife in.

Some people prefer to poach eggs the traditional way 'completely naked' in a pan of simmering water, but there is a lot to be said for poaching eggs in an actual egg poacher. You can tell when they are done much more easily. You can see them clearly when you take the lid off and give them a gentle nudge with the tip of a dinner knife. If you can get hold of one, a stainless steel egg poacher with stainless steel cups works brilliantly: non-stick cups are inclined to scratch easily and plastic cups are forever melting when you get them too near the hob by mistake.

Fill your egg poacher half way up with boiling water from the kettle. Put a little dot of butter into each cup and put the lid back on. Once the water has come back to the boil and the butter has melted crack the eggs in. Put the lid on and cook for roughly the time it takes to make your toast: about 3 minutes. Once the egg is cooked the white will be opaque and will come away from the side of the cup easily when nudged with a knife; it will still be quite 'quivery' though. Slip a dinner knife round the edges of the cups (unless they are non-stick) and turn the eggs out onto slices of buttered toast. Always eat immediately.

WELSH RAREBIT

Welsh Rarebit makes a lovely lunch, but it is just as good at tea time. Serve it as a High Tea with some salad and a dollop of coleslaw or, for a more relaxed tea by the fire, cut it into triangles or wide fingers.

Combine the cheese, egg yolk, milk and seasoning in a small, heavy saucepan and cook on a medium heat, stirring pretty much all the time. It will thin down and then thicken slightly again as it amalgamates and starts to bubble gently. Don't take your eye off it or have the heat too high or the egg will split and scramble.

Once the cheese has melted and the mixture is smooth, take it off the heat and set aside: it will thicken even more. Lightly toast the bread and allow it to cool slightly before buttering: this is because the toast needs to be crisp to support the rarebit. Spread the cheese mixture onto the toast and grill until bubbling and golden.

You might like to try adding wholegrain mustard for a change: the flavour is good and the mustard seeds speckled through the rarebit look attractive.

Light and luscious version
This is possibly even more delicious than the original: instead of 2 tablespoons of milk, use a generous heaped tablespoon of half fat crème fraîche.

Blue cheese version
You can make Welsh Rarebit with blue cheese as well. It's particularly good just after Christmas if you have some Stilton or similar left over. Use blue cheese instead of the Cheddar. Be careful not to over-brown it under the grill though or the flavour will be ruined. Lovely with some cranberry sauce on the side, some green salad and a few walnuts.

SERVES 1–2 BUT IT'S EASY TO DOUBLE OR TREBLE QUANTITIES

50g (2oz) mature Cheddar, grated
1 medium egg yolk
2 tablespoons semi-skimmed milk
Pinch of dry mustard or dab of English readymade mustard from a jar
Few shakes of Worcestershire sauce
2 slices of decent bread, brown or white, not too thickly cut
Butter for spreading

HAM RAREBIT

Lay a wafer-thin slice of ham onto the lightly buttered toast and top with the rarebit mixture. Finish off under the grill as usual.

Oven-toasted and Oven-fried Sandwiches

Toasted sandwiches are really delicious and perfect for a toasty tea. They can be fairly chunky and homely, made more substantial with some salad on the side, or delicate tempting little crustless triangles, fancied up with a little cress or baby leaf salad sprinkled round the plate.

Special sandwich toasters usually work well, or you might have an extra attachment for your toaster, but it is very straightforward and easy to make them in the oven, wrapped in foil. You can also make more at a time this way.

OVEN-TOASTED CHEESE SANDWICH

Preheat the oven to 180°C (fan oven) or equivalent.

For each person, **butter 2 slices of bread** and make a sandwich with some **thinly sliced cheese** (Cheddar works well, but you could also try something more oozy, such as Gruyère) and make up a sandwich in the usual way.

Cut the sandwich into 2 or 4 pieces and wrap in foil in a single layer.

Bake for about 10 minutes until the cheese has melted and the bread is toasty. Put it back into the oven with the foil open for a further 3–5 minutes until the outside is crisp. You may like to turn the sandwich over after a couple of minutes to make sure both sides are of equal crispness.

OVEN-TOASTED HAM AND CHEESE SANDWICH

Make the sandwich as above but add some **thinly sliced ham**.

OVEN-TOASTED HAM SANDWICHES

Make the sandwich as above but leave out the cheese: you may like to add **a little mustard**.

Caution!
If you feel like adding a little pickle or chutney to your sandwich, please do, but be aware it will need to cool down slightly before you bite into it, as the pickle or chutney will be *boiling hot* when it first comes out of the oven! Similarly, if you want to attempt a baked bean toasted sandwich (and why not?) the same rule applies: anything liquidy will retain heat for longer than anything more solid.

TOASTING LEFTOVER CHEESE AND HAM SANDWICHES

If you have any sandwiches left over from an earlier meal, you can toast them perfectly well, as above.

OVEN-FRIED SANDWICHES

Another delicious sandwich, croque monsieur, which is the French name for a fried ham and cheese sandwich (although in some cases it may be grilled), can also be made easily in the oven.

If, instead of making the sandwich in the usual way, and buttering the bread on the *inside*, you butter the bread on the *outside*, you will get a richer and more luscious outside to the sandwich, which is much more like a fried sandwich than a toasted one.

DOUBLE DECKER HAM RAREBIT

This makes a very substantial high tea. Make an **Oven-toasted Ham Sandwich** according to the recipe. Spread the top with **rarebit mixture** and put under the grill until golden and bubbling.

INSIDE-OUT TOASTED CHEESE AND HAM SANDWICH

This is another substantial plateful. Make an **Oven-toasted Ham Sandwich** according to the recipe. Spread the top with a fairly generous layer of **grated Cheddar cheese** and put under the grill until the cheese is melted and golden.

TOAST WITH CREAM CHEESE AND HAM

This isn't a recipe as such, but more of a serving suggestion. Cut **a thickish slice of wholemeal or granary bread** and toast: in the toaster, under the grill or, best of all, in front of the fire if you are in a position to. Let it rest for a moment or two and **butter** lightly. Spread with some **light cream cheese**, and top with a tiny grinding of **black pepper** and **a very thin slice of ham**. If you have some **tart jelly** such as crab apple or gooseberry, a little dab would go well.

Quantities given for the following recipes are per person unless otherwise specified.

TOASTED CHEESE

Toasted cheese is a real favourite with most people. Make sure the **toast** has cooled and crisped slightly before you put the cheese on top. Some people butter it first, some don't. Whether or not you butter the whole slice, it's nice to butter the edges of the toast so they crisp up nicely under the grill. A **generous layer of grated cheese** melts more evenly and satisfyingly than sliced, it also goes further.

Crumbly cheeses such as Cheshire, Wensleydale, Caerphilly and Lancashire all toast brilliantly and make a change from Cheddar.

CHEESY CHILLI CRUMPETS

The chilli makes this into quite a bracing tea-time dish. Toast the **crumpets** and **butter lightly**. Arrange some **grated cheese** carefully on top and add **a thin slice or two of red chilli**. Put under a hot grill until golden and bubbling and the chilli is very slightly charred.

CHEESE BEANO

This is perfect for a toasty children's tea.

A small serving of baked
  beans
2 eggs
2 slices of decent bread,
. brown or white
Butter for spreading
Thinly sliced or grated
  Cheddar

Heat the beans, poach the eggs and lightly toast the bread. Cool the toast slightly, butter it and spoon the beans on top. Cover with the cheese and put under the grill until the cheese is bubbling. To serve: top with the eggs and arrange any leftover beans around the side.

✔ **A Note About Toast**
It is very simple to make perfect toast but it can be easy to spoil it. It's essential to have decent bread, preferably from an uncut loaf that you slice yourself. It doesn't really matter whether it is brown or white or whole grain, all make good toast. Also, butter is usually better than spreads and margarines for flavour. Finally, burnt toast is not pleasant: toast should be a lovely golden brown, and it should rest for a few seconds to let the steam escape and stop it from going bendy and soggy. You can leave it in the toaster for a few moments or prop it up against something.

CINNAMON TOAST

This is a lovely nostalgic treat. It's particularly nice on a cold day and very easy to make if someone calls round unexpectedly and you have no cake or biscuits to speak of. Put the kettle on and you can have the cinnamon toast ready by the time the tea has brewed!

Toast the bread lightly, cool slightly and butter (it should be actual butter as this is key to the flavour). Sprinkle the sugar and cinnamon mixture over the top and put under a hot grill until bubbling. Cut into triangles and cool slightly before eating, otherwise you will have the roof of your mouth off!

Quantities to suit of:
Slices from a decent loaf, cut fairly thinly, brown or white
Butter for spreading
Equal quantities of ground cinnamon and unrefined sugar mixed together (caster or granulated sugar are both suitable)

SCONES AND SAVOURY BUNS

Scone Surgery

Make up your own baking powder with two parts cream of tartar to one part bicarbonate of soda. This will give a beautifully light texture to the scones and also avoid that bitter tang of too much bicarbonate of soda you can get with scones sometimes. Try to minimise re-rolling the dough as much as you can, as too much handling will give the finished scones a tough texture. Be sure to warm the milk to assist the raising agents to even greater heights.

Roll the dough out quite thickly: a good half an inch or generous centimetre, otherwise you will have a flat biscuit. Lastly, don't overcook the scones or they will be hard.

Weather Warning

If the weather is very hot and humid you may find your dough is a bit sloppier and stickier than normal and maybe even a bit 'curdled' looking. This makes the dough more difficult to work with but the finished scones will still taste good.

A Conversation about Scones

Friend	Cup of tea?
Mrs S	Oh, yes, *please*!
Friend	And would you care for a scone?
Mrs S	Lovely!
Friend	I hope they'll be all right; it's your recipe. Mostly, anyway.
Mrs S	I'm sure they'll be fine. Mostly?
Friend	Mostly, yes, apart from the bits I remember my Great Aunt Bertha telling me.
Mrs S	Oh, OK. Did your Aunt make really good scones, then?
Friend	Oh, no! They were dreadful: hard as a rock and very bitter.
Mrs S	I see.
Friend	Well, yes, I know, but scones are a very traditional thing, aren't they? You've got to keep these family traditions going! I'm sure these will be fine.
Mrs S	Indeed.
Friend	Anyway, here they are. Help yourself.
Mrs S	Thank you.
Friend	What do you think? Tell me honestly.
Mrs S	They're, um, cooked well, aren't they? Did you, er, time them at all?
Friend	Well, not exactly. I haven't got a clock in here, the timer's broken and I couldn't seem to read the time display on my mobile phone…
Mrs S	Who can?
Friend	And anyway, Aunt Bertha always used to say it was an instinctive thing: you just *knew* when scones were done.
Mrs S	I see. Clairvoyant, was she?
Friend	No, not really, she was totally insensitive as a matter of fact. Do you think they're bitter?
Mrs S	They are a bit. You didn't use the combination of bicarbonate of soda and cream of tartar then.
Friend	No. Aunt Bertha always said the secret of a good scone was plenty of bicarb.
Mrs S	I see. Do you think maybe they are slightly on the thin side, at all?
Friend	Look, I know you said in your recipe to roll them out thickly, but Aunt Bertha said you should always try and make your dough go as far as possible. They look a bit funny and crumpled on top don't they?
Mrs S	A bit, yes. Did you try to re-roll them as *little* as possible, as I suggested?
Friend	Oh! I forgot all about that! I didn't soften the butter or warm the milk either, now that I come to think about it. Would it have made any difference, do you think? Oh! What are you doing? You'll hurt your head banging it on the table like that!
Mrs S	Sorry! Sorry! I don't know what came over me! Better now. Let's have another cup of tea.

PLAIN SCONES AND FRUIT SCONES

Preheat the oven to 200°C (fan oven) or equivalent.

Sieve the flour, bicarbonate of soda and cream of tartar into a bowl large enough to give you room to manoeuvre. Rub in the softened butter, stir in the sugar (and fruit if using). Mix the milk in gradually; an ordinary dinner knife works well.

Knead gently and place on a floured board. Roll out quite thickly with a floured rolling pin to a generous couple of centimetres or three quarters of an inch, and cut out with a 6cm (2½in) cutter, a fluted one looks professional. Re-roll the trimmings and cut out again (these won't be quite as good as the ones you cut out first).

Bake on a greased baking sheet for 8–10 minutes until well risen and golden brown on top. Don't overcook them or they will be too hard. Cool on a wire rack. Eat with butter or strawberry jam and clotted cream.

MAKES ABOUT 8–9 SCONES. IF YOU WANT TO MAKE MORE, MAKE SEPARATE BATCHES, RATHER THAN ONE BIG ONE, IT'S EASIER TO HANDLE.

225g (8oz) plain flour

1 teaspoon bicarbonate of soda

2 teaspoons cream of tartar

40g (1½oz) softened butter

25g (1oz) unrefined caster sugar

150ml (¼ pint) semi-skimmed milk, warmed slightly

For fruit scones
Add 75g (3oz) of raisins or sultanas or a mixture

SCONE BUNNIES

Very young children aren't always keen on scones with cream and jam but they can be partial to a nice 'Scone Bunny' with butter and jam. It's worth cutting out some scones using a rabbit cutter if there are a few children in the party. You can use other novelty cutters if you prefer, but make sure the shapes are fairly simple without any complicated thin little legs and twiddly bits, as they won't work with scone dough.

LAVENDER SCONES

These scones are nice and quaint and cottagey: perfect for tea in the garden. Choose lavender that is still in bud and deep purple, as once the flowers open, it can be a bit 'bristly' in the mouth. Also, be careful not to *over do it* with the lavender: you don't want to feel as if you are eating a bar of soap!

A Word of Warning
Be sure to use only the more common English lavender: Lavandula *angustifolia*, sometimes called Lavandula *officinalis* or Lavandula *spicata*. The tufty French lavender: Lavandula *stoechas* can be toxic.

MAKES ABOUT 8–9 SCONES

225g (8oz) plain flour
1 teaspoon bicarbonate of soda
2 teaspoons cream of tartar
40g (1½oz) softened butter
25g (1oz) unrefined caster sugar
About 10 sprigs of lavender flowers, no more (this will equate to a couple of teaspoons)
150ml (¼ pint) semi-skimmed milk, warmed slightly

Preheat the oven to 200°C (fan oven) or equivalent.

Lay the lavender sprigs on kitchen paper for a while to dry out and allow any passengers to leave. Remove all the florets from the stalks and shake them lightly in a sieve.

Sieve the flour, bicarbonate of soda and cream of tartar into a bowl large enough to give you room to manoeuvre. Rub in the softened butter, stir in the sugar and lavender. Mix the milk in gradually; an ordinary dinner knife works well.

Knead gently and place on a floured board. Roll out quite thickly (see Plain Scones above) with a floured rolling pin, and cut out with a 6cm (2½in) fluted cutter. Re-roll the trimmings and cut out again.

Bake on a greased baking sheet for 8–10 minutes until well risen and golden brown on top. Cool on a wire rack.

Eat warm or cold with butter or clotted cream and jam. A lovely old-fashioned jelly such as bramble, crab apple or gooseberry works beautifully with the light lavender flavour. Alternatively, spread with butter and a creamy set honey. A light, soft, cream cheese also works well.

Savoury Scones

Savoury scones are lovely with a cup of tea in the garden in the summer and they are also a welcome winter treat, served warm from the oven.

HERB SCONES

These are gorgeously savoury: eat them fresh from the oven with butter and possibly some thin slices of cheese.

Preheat the oven to 200°C (fan oven) or equivalent.

Sieve the flour, bicarbonate of soda and cream of tartar into a bowl large enough to give you room to manoeuvre. Rub in the softened butter and stir in the sugar and herbs. Mix the milk in gradually with a dinner knife.

Knead gently and place on a floured board. Roll out quite thickly with a floured rolling pin to a depth of about a centimetre or half an inch, and cut out with a 6cm (2½in) fluted, round cutter. Re-roll the trimmings and cut out again.

Bake on a greased baking sheet for about 10 minutes until well risen and golden brown on top. Cool on a wire rack.

MAKES ABOUT 8–9 SCONES

225g (8oz) plain flour
1 teaspoon bicarbonate of soda
2 teaspoons cream of tartar
40g (1½oz) softened butter
10g (½oz) unrefined caster sugar
About 1 level tablespoon dried mixed herbs or a heaped one of finely chopped fresh herbs
150ml (¼ pint) semi-skimmed milk, warmed slightly

CHEESE SCONES

If you would like to increase the strength of cheese flavour in your scones do this by using the same amount of cheese but choosing a stronger, more vintage variety. If you add extra cheese instead, the texture of the finished scones can be affected and they may well have a slightly greasy feel to them.

MAKES ABOUT 8–10

225g (8oz) plain flour
1 teaspoon bicarbonate of
   soda
2 teaspoons cream of
   tartar
Generous pinch mustard
   powder
40g (1½oz) softened
   butter
10g (½oz) unrefined caster
   sugar
75g (3oz) grated well-
   flavoured Cheddar
   cheese, mature if
   possible
150ml (¼ pint) semi-
   skimmed milk, warmed
   slightly

Preheat the oven to 200°C (fan oven) or equivalent.

Sieve the flour, bicarbonate of soda, cream of tartar and mustard powder into a bowl large enough to give you room to manoeuvre, and rub in the softened butter. Stir in the sugar and cheese. Mix the milk in gradually: a dinner knife is ideal for this.

Knead gently and place on a floured board. Roll out with a floured rolling pin to a depth of a couple of centimetres or three quarters of an inch, and cut out with a 6cm (2½in) fluted, round cutter. Re-roll the trimmings and cut out again.

Bake on a greased baking sheet for 8–10 minutes until well risen and golden brown on top. Cool on a wire rack.

CHEESE AND HERB SCONES

These have a lovely extra savoury flavour: just add both **cheese** and **herbs** to the scones.

✓ **Freezing**
Scones are best when completely fresh but you can freeze them: allow them to cool completely, put in a freezer bag, secure the top and store in the freezer. You can then whip them out of the freezer an hour or two before guests arrive for tea.

PLAIN BROWN SCONES

These have the most beautiful nutty flavour and go really well with cheese. They are also very good with butter and honey.

They are made in exactly the same way as the plain scones but use **half plain and half wholemeal flour** and **cut down the sugar to 10g (½oz)**. Make sure you stir and sieve the two flours together thoroughly first so that they are completely blended.

LIGHT CHEESY BUNS

These light, fluffy, savoury buns are very child-friendly. They are lovely warm from the oven but still good cold. Offer them as part of a tea-time spread, take them on a picnic or tuck them in a lunch box.

*As with the **Cheese Scones**, if you would like to increase the cheesiness of the buns do this by using the same amount of cheese but choosing a stronger, more vintage variety. If you add extra cheese instead, the texture of the finished buns can be affected and they can become heavy and greasy.*

You will need a greased 12-cup muffin tin.

Preheat the oven to 160°C (fan oven) or equivalent.

Whiz the butter and sugar together in a food processor. Carefully sieve in half of the flour, cream of tartar, bicarbonate of soda, mustard powder and salt, and then add the eggs.

Sieve the rest of the flour, mustard and raising agents over the top and whiz briefly. Add the milk, whiz again and then add the cheese.

Whiz until combined: the mixture will remain fairly stiff. Spoon into the prepared tin, dividing the mixture as equally as possible. Bake for about 15 minutes, or until the buns are springy to the touch and a skewer inserted comes out clean.

Leave in the tin for a few minutes, as they are very fragile at this stage, and then ease them out gently with a small palette knife and cool on a wire rack. Cover with a clean tea towel to keep them moist and prevent them drying out as they cool.

MAKES 12

110g (4oz) softened butter
10g (½oz) unrefined caster sugar
110g (8oz) plain flour
2 teaspoons cream of tartar
1 teaspoon bicarbonate of soda
Good pinch mustard powder – around ½ teaspoon
Small pinch salt
2 fresh eggs
4 tablespoons milk
75g (3oz) well flavoured grated mature Cheddar cheese

RED HOT CHEESE AND CHILLI BUNS

Cheese and chilli always go well together. These appeal more to the adult palate. Make the buns as above and add some **chilli**.

You can either:
Add half a teaspoon or so of chilli powder to the dry ingredients at the beginning
or
Fry a red chilli (or a couple of those red-hot miniature chillies you can grow at home) in a small amount of oil, then drain briefly on kitchen paper and add with the cheese. One advantage of using fresh chillies is that they show up attractively in the finished buns.

Proceed as for the main recipe.

Cakes and Buns

The Secret of Cakes

Some of us feel very strongly that de-activated self-raising flour is a major cause of disappointing flat cakes. If you are using self-raising flour for a recipe it needs to be *completely fresh*. It should be well within its sell by date and it also helps if the bag has not been opened for very long.

It must also be stored properly in a cool dry place. If you are wondering why years ago cakes seemed to rise more, possibly more people had cool, dry pantries and larders then, and didn't keep their flour in a warm kitchen cupboard. Possibly also they baked more regularly and used their flour more quickly.

As self-raising flour can be unreliable and lose its raising ability so easily, it may be time to move away from it altogether and find a reliable alternative.

Instead of self-raising flour, you can use plain flour and add a raising agent to it yourself. Baking powder works well for cakes and biscuits that don't need a light fluffy rise, but you need something with a bit of extra oomph for light airy sponges and scones.

For the lighter cake recipes in this book I have used bicarbonate of soda and cream of tartar at a ratio of one part bicarbonate of soda to two parts cream of tartar: it works like magic!

Once you have sorted out the flour, you are well on your way to a successful cake but there are a few other factors to bear in mind as well.

Correct oven temperature and times

Ovens can very tremendously. Even the same oven can vary as it ages. Keep a note of the times and temperatures for your own oven that you have used for particular recipes. It's easiest just to pencil them in by the actual recipes in the recipe book. The notes will then be there for you to refer to when you make those recipes again.

It is worth noting here that fan ovens generally do seem hotter as the hot air circulates round the food: the difference is usually about 20°C.

Eggs must be very fresh

As an egg gets older its composition changes and the components that help the cake to rise deteriorate and eventually stop working. If an egg pops out of the shell with a round yolk like a little ball it is fresh; if it flops out looking very flat, it isn't.

Use warmed, softened butter

Unlike when making pastry, butter must be soft and slightly warm for a successful cake mix. If you try to mix it in when it is cold and too hard the cake will be heavy. An easy way to soften butter quickly is to put it in the microwave on high for 20–30 seconds.

Use the right type of sugar

Unless the recipe specifically gives a choice, use the type of sugar specified. Caster sugar is best for light sponge cakes as it is much finer.

Correct mixing

Generally, with some notable exceptions such as muffins, cakes need to be thoroughly mixed. However, this doesn't mean you should over-mix: be thorough but don't *over do it*. Mix sponge cakes until they look smooth and glossy, then ease the mixture gently into the baking tin(s).

Even if you are using a food processor, try to add the ingredients in the same stages you would if you were mixing by hand, rather than the all-in-one method some people prefer. This means whiz the butter and sugar together first until they are combined and fluffy, then sieve a layer of flour over them, next add the eggs (already beaten lightly with a fork). Finally add the rest of the flour and, after a quick whiz, extra liquid, such as milk, if you are using any.

Sieve your flour

Modern flour is fine and light but it does settle in the bag and you need to aerate it again. This is why you need to sieve it: to let lots of air in so you end up with a light, well risen cake. Hold your sieve quite a way above the bowl if you can.

Icing sugar, on the other hand, needs sieving to remove any lumps, so it is perfectly fine to push icing sugar through the sieve with a spoon, in fact positively *don't* sieve it in the same way as flour as it's much finer and you will be enveloped in clouds of choking sweet dust!

Correct size tins

You must use the same size tin as specified in the recipe. The cooking times have been worked out around a particular tin size so if you use something different it won't cook at the same rate.

Don't open the oven door whilst baking is in progress!

Every time you open your oven door, you lose heat. It is particularly crucial that you don't lose heat when you are baking something that needs to rise like a sponge cake. If you have a window in your oven door, make use of it to check on progress. If you do have to return a cake to the oven because it's not quite done, be aware that it won't be quite as good as if it had been undisturbed for the whole baking time and make a note for next time.

If you are embarking on cake baking for the first time, it's a good idea to start off with fairy cakes. They are much less scary as they almost always rise! Once you have built your confidence up you can then bake a large size cake: you'll wonder what all the fuss was about!

A mountain of fairy cakes makes a perfect birthday cake for any age group. Pile them up and put a few candles on the top ones. They are much easier to serve as well: no slicing!

All Sorts of Fairy Cakes and Butterfly Cakes

The mixture is exactly the same as the sponge cake mixture and the same rules apply: it is best to have everything slightly warm so leave the eggs out of the fridge and warm the butter slightly in the microwave if necessary: 10–20 seconds or so on high is usually just about right.

ICED FAIRY CAKES

You can have fun decorating these with whatever takes your fancy.

MAKES ABOUT 18 CAKES

175g (6oz) butter, softened
175g (6oz) unrefined
   caster sugar

175g (6oz) very fresh self-
   raising flour
or
175g (6oz) plain flour
2 teaspoons cream of
   tartar
1 teaspoon bicarbonate of
   soda

3 eggs
2 tablespoons milk

You will need a 12-cup muffin tin plus paper cases.

Preheat the oven to 180°C (fan oven) or equivalent.

Whiz the butter and sugar together in a food processor until combined and fluffy. Sieve in some of the flour, the cream of tartar and the bicarbonate of soda and add the eggs. Then sieve in the rest of the flour. Whiz again. Add the milk and whiz until smooth and glossy. You may need to scrape the mixture down from the sides a couple of times with a flexible spatula.

Arrange the paper cases in the muffin tin and spoon 2 generous teaspoons of mixture into each case. Bake for around 15 minutes or until risen and pale golden and springy to the touch. A skewer or wooden cocktail stick should come out clean when inserted. Remove from the tin with a small palette knife and cool on a wire rack. Bake the remaining part batch.

Note: This will give you muffin-shaped fairy cakes with rounded tops. If you want a flatter, more cup cake type size, fill each case barely halfway and once in the oven check after 12 minutes or so. You should have enough mixture left over for about another half dozen cakes.

GLACE ICING

The lemon juice takes the edge off the sweetness and if you use the glycerine it will give the icing a lovely, sticky, slightly stretchy quality.

225g (8oz) icing sugar
2 tablespoons lemon juice
   (sieve through a tea
   strainer)
2 teaspoons glycerine
   (optional)

Sieve the icing sugar into a large bowl and stir in the lemon juice and glycerine, if using. Beat with a wooden spoon until glossy.

Spoon over the cooled cakes. You can either spread the icing over the whole top of the cake, or spoon on a little circle of icing in the middle of each cake.

PINK ICING

For pink-tinted icing without using food colouring, add a little **sieved raspberry jam**. For a more lilac-toned pink, use a little touch of **blackberry jelly or sieved blackcurrant jam**.

TEENY TINY FAIRY CAKES

These are exactly the same but half the size. Make up the mixture and icing in exactly the same way but bake in two 12-cup mini muffin tins instead, and then a second batch, using petit four cases. They will take less time to bake, usually about 8–10 minutes.

CURRANT FAIRY CAKES

Make up the fairy cake mixture, as above and once it is all mixed together remove the processor blade and stir in **75–110g (3–4 oz) of currants** (depending on how curranty you want them).

These are lovely plain but possibly even better iced with **Glace Icing** above.

BUTTERFLY CAKES

These little cakes look so pretty and delicate. Make up the fairy cake mixture, as above, filling the cases half full. Make up some **Lemon Buttercream**.

Once the cakes are cool slice the tops off and put to one side. Spoon a little dollop of buttercream onto each cake. Cut each top in half so you have two 'wings' and arrange on top of each cake. Just before you want to eat them, sieve some **icing sugar** over the top: if you do it too soon the icing sugar will eventually sink into the cake.

LEMON BUTTERCREAM

Beat the butter until creamy in a largish bowl. Sieve in the icing sugar, a little at a time. Finally, stir in the lemon juice to loosen it slightly.	50g (2oz) butter, softened 110g (4oz) icing sugar 1–2 tablespoons lemon juice

LITTLE CHOCOLATE CAKES

These are beautifully chocolately and perfect for children's parties.

MAKES ABOUT 18 CAKES	You will need a 12-cup muffin tin plus paper cases.
175g (6oz) butter, softened 175g (6oz) unrefined caster sugar	Preheat the oven to 180°C (fan oven) or equivalent.

175g (6oz) butter, softened
175g (6oz) unrefined
   caster sugar

150g (5oz) very fresh self-
   raising flour
or
150g (5oz) plain flour
1 teaspoon bicarbonate of
   soda
2 teaspoons cream of
   tartar

3 eggs
25g (1oz) good quality
   cocoa powder (not
   drinking chocolate)
2 tablespoons milk

You will need a 12-cup muffin tin plus paper cases.

Preheat the oven to 180°C (fan oven) or equivalent.

Whiz the butter and sugar together in a food processor until combined and fluffy. Sieve some of the flour in a layer over the mixture and then add the eggs. Sieve in the rest of the flour, the cream of tartar and bicarbonate of soda and the cocoa. Whiz again. Add the milk and whiz until smooth and glossy. You may need to remove the lid a couple of times and scrape the mixture down from the sides with a flexible spatula.

Arrange the paper cases in the muffin tin and spoon 2 fairly generous teaspoons of mixture into each case. Bake for around 15 minutes or until domed and risen and springy to the touch. A skewer or wooden cocktail stick should come out clean when inserted. Remove from the tin with a small palette knife and leave to cool on a wire rack. Bake the remaining part batch.

CHOCOLATE GLACE ICING

200g (7oz) icing sugar
25g (1oz) cocoa powder
4 tablespoons milk
2 teaspoons glycerine

Sieve about a quarter of the icing sugar and cocoa powder into a large bowl and stir in the milk and glycerine. Sieve the rest of the icing sugar and cocoa in a bit at a time until it is all incorporated. Beat with a wooden spoon until glossy. Spoon over the cooled cakes. You can either spread the icing over the whole top of the cake or spoon a little circle of icing into the middle of each cake.

CHOCOLATE BUTTERFLY CAKES

The above mixture also makes great butterfly cakes. You can make them with either **Chocolate Buttercream**, below, or **Lemon and Vanilla Buttercream**. It's quite nice if you are having a bit of a party to make half with chocolate and half with vanilla and arrange them on the same plate. If you need to soften the butter quickly, try putting it in the microwave on high for 10–20 seconds.

CHOCOLATE BUTTERCREAM

Sieve the combined cocoa and icing sugar into the softened butter a little at a time, mixing it all together with a wooden spoon. Finally, loosen the mixture slightly with the milk and beat until smooth and glossy.

Once the cakes are cool, slice the tops off and put to one side. Spoon a little dollop of buttercream onto each cake. Cut each top in half so you have two 'wings' and arrange on top of each cake. Just before you want to eat them, sieve some icing sugar over the top: if you do it too soon the icing sugar will eventually sink into the cake.

75g (3oz) butter, softened
25g (1oz) good quality
  cocoa powder
150g (5oz) icing sugar
A little milk to mix

LEMON AND VANILLA BUTTERCREAM ICING

Cream the butter in a bowl large enough to give you room to manoeuvre. Use a wooden spoon. Gradually add the icing sugar, passing it through a sieve. When the icing sugar is all combined, add the vanilla and stir in a squeeze of lemon juice, just enough to loosen the mixture slightly.

50g (2oz) butter, softened
110g (4oz) icing sugar
Few drops of vanilla
  extract or ½ teaspoon
  of vanilla bean paste
Squeeze of lemon juice

CUP CAKES

A cup cake is very like a fairy cake but much more glamorous and opulent. Cup cakes tend to be topped with a swirl of buttercream rather than glace icing and you can really enjoy yourself decorating them and making them look fabulous. Don't hold back: they are *meant* to look a bit extravagant!

You can adapt the basic recipe below to make five more different flavours. You might like to make a mixed batch: home-baked cup cakes are always popular as gifts. You can swap the buttercream icings round if you like: chocolate cup cake with coffee icing or raspberry cup cake with lemon and vanilla icing, for example. Cup cakes are also perfect for celebrations, arranged on a stand for weddings and parties or lavishly and lovingly decorated for Valentine's Day.

These cup cakes are made in paper muffin cases in a muffin tin, so they are a little larger than fairy cakes.

ORIGINAL CUP CAKES

These are lovely and light.

MAKES 12 CAKES	You will need a 12-cup muffin tin plus paper muffin cases.
175g (6oz) butter, softened 175g (6oz) unrefined caster sugar 175g (6oz) plain flour 3 eggs, beaten 1 teaspoon bicarbonate of soda 2 teaspoons cream of tartar 2 tablespoons milk	Preheat the oven to 160°C (fan oven) or equivalent. Whiz the butter and sugar together in a food processor until combined and fluffy. Sieve in some of the flour and add the eggs. Sieve in the rest of the flour, the bicarbonate of soda and cream of tartar. Whiz again. Add the milk and whiz until smooth and glossy. You may need to scrape the mixture down from the sides a couple of times with a flexible spatula. Arrange the paper cases in the muffin tin and, using a dessertspoon, divide the mixture equally between the cases. Bake for around 18 minutes or until risen and pale golden and springy to the touch. A skewer or wooden cocktail stick should come out clean when inserted. Allow to rest for a few minutes and then remove from the tin and cool on a wire rack.

LEMON BUTTERCREAM

Beat the butter in a largish bowl until creamy. Sieve in the icing sugar, a little at a time. Finally, stir in the lemon juice to loosen it slightly.

Assembling the cup cakes
Swirl the buttercream over the top of each cake so that it either completely covers the top or arrange it in a large circle so that there is a narrow rim of cake showing around the edge. You can then go to town with the decorations of your choice.

50g (2oz) butter, softened
110g (4oz) icing sugar
1–2 tablespoons lemon
  juice

VANILLA CUP CAKES

Follow the **Original Cup Cakes** recipe but add **1 teaspoon of vanilla extract or vanilla bean paste** to the beaten eggs before you add them to the cake mixture. Ice with the lemon and vanilla buttercream, below.

LEMON AND VANILLA BUTTERCREAM

Add ½ **teaspoon vanilla extract or vanilla bean paste** to the original **Lemon Buttercream** icing.
   A single chocolate chip (milk or white chocolate) or a sprinkling of crushed nuts make an attractive decoration.

LEMON CUP CAKES

Follow the **Original Cup Cakes** recipe but add the **finely grated zest of ½ a lemon** to the cake mixture. Ice with the original **Lemon Buttercream**.
   A *tiny* amount of *very* finely grated lemon zest or some pale and pretty cake decorations look attractive on top.

RASPBERRY CUP CAKES

These have the most delicious, understated and elusive raspberry flavour and are golden brown in colour. The pale peachy-pink buttercream looks very glamorous and wedding-like.

Use only **110g (4oz) of sugar** in the **Original Cup Cakes** mixture and also add **2 rounded tablespoons of seedless raspberry jam**. Cream the jam with the sugar and softened butter in the usual way.

The raspberry version bakes a little more quickly: test after 15 minutes, but as always, be aware that oven performance can vary tremendously.

Ice with **Raspberry Buttercream**, below.

RASPBERRY BUTTERCREAM

Add **2 gently rounded dessertspoons of seedless raspberry jam** to the original **Lemon Buttercream**.

If you are making these for a wedding or wedding anniversary, gold or silver cake decorations look particularly stylish.

COFFEE CUP CAKES

Add **2 teaspoons of instant espresso coffee powder** to the flour for the **Original Cup Cakes** mixture. Ice with **Coffee Buttercream**, below.

If you can, make the Coffee Buttercream a few hours ahead of time, and keep it cool and covered (preferably not in the fridge as it will set too hard). This gives the coffee flavour a chance to mellow and develop.

COFFEE BUTTERCREAM

50g (2oz) butter, softened
110g (4oz) icing sugar
1–2 teaspoons instant espresso coffee powder
1–2 tablespoons milk

Beat the butter in a largish bowl until creamy. Sieve in the icing sugar and coffee powder together, a little at a time. Finally, stir in the milk: enough to loosen it slightly.

You may like to sprinkle the top of the cakes with cocoa, drinking chocolate powder or even cinnamon to give a kind of cappuccino effect. Alternatively, decorate with grated chocolate, chocolate chips, chocolate bean sweets or chocolate-coated coffee beans. Walnut or pecan halves are also good, giving a traditional 'coffee cake' look to the cup cakes.

CHOCOLATE CUP CAKES

Use **150g (5oz) of flour** in the **Original Cup Cakes** mixture with **25g (1oz) of good quality cocoa powder (not drinking chocolate)** and add **1 teaspoon of vanilla extract.** Ice with Chocolate Buttercream, below.

CHOCOLATE BUTTERCREAM

Sieve the combined cocoa and icing sugar into the softened butter a little at a time, mixing it all together with a wooden spoon. Stir in the vanilla. Finally, loosen the mixture slightly with the milk and beat until smooth and glossy.

Decorate with grated chocolate, chocolate chips or chocolate bean sweets, crushed nuts or anything else you fancy.

25g (1oz) good quality cocoa powder
75g (3oz) icing sugar
50g (2oz) butter, softened
¼ teaspoon vanilla extract
1–2 tablespoons milk

PLAIN AND SIMPLE SPONGE CAKE

This is the classic Victoria Sandwich. Apparently, Queen Victoria herself was very fond of this type of sponge cake 'sandwiched' simply with jam.

175g (6oz) butter, softened

175g (6oz) unrefined caster sugar

175g (6oz) plain flour

2 teaspoons cream of tartar

1 teaspoon bicarbonate of soda

3 eggs

2 tablespoons milk

Good quality jam such as seedless raspberry or bramble jelly (strawberry can be a bit sweet to fill a sweet sponge cake)

Icing sugar, to finish

You will need 2 greased 18cm (7in) loose-bottomed sandwich tins.

Preheat the oven to 180°C (fan oven) or equivalent, see below.

Whiz the butter and sugar together in a food processor until light and fluffy. Sieve the flour in carefully with the cream of tartar and bicarbonate of soda, and add the eggs. Whiz again. Add the milk and whiz until very smooth and glossy and everything is well mixed. You may need to scrape the mixture down from the sides a couple of times with a flexible spatula.

You should now have a dropping consistency. That is to say, the mixture isn't so thick that it won't drop easily off a spoon, but it isn't runny either.

Pour into the prepared cake tins using a flexible spatula to help all the mixture out.

Bake in the middle of the oven for 18–20 minutes until the cakes are risen and golden and a skewer inserted comes out clean.

Allow the cakes to rest for a few moments and then carefully loosen the edges with a small palette knife: they should be starting to contract away from the sides of their own accord.

If the tins are still too hot to handle, stand the cakes, one at a time, on a jar or something similar. Using both hands, protected with an oven glove or tea towel, pull the side of the tin down so the cake is left, still on its base, on top of the jar. Move it closer to your cooling rack and loosen from the base using a large palette knife. Transfer gently (you may need a fish slice as well as the palette knife at this stage) onto the cooling rack. Repeat with the other cake.

Try not to flip the cake over straight out of the tin onto the cooling rack. This manoeuvre will leave you with deep lines or squares indented across the top of your cake which doesn't look very professional: should you ever wish to enter your sponge cake into a baking competition, you would be marked down for this!

Once the cakes are cool, spread one with jam; position the other on top, and sieve icing sugar over it. (White caster sugar is more traditional but it can feel a bit too gritty in contrast with the light texture of the sponge.)

Sponge Cake Temperatures
Suggested temperatures for baking sponge cakes of this type can vary from 160°C to 190°C. If your oven is a fairly steady average performer, set it to 180°C. If you have a very fierce oven, 160°C may be preferable. If the finished sponge comes out of the oven flat and hard, it is likely the temperature was too high and the top cooked before the centre could rise. If the sponge comes out of the oven heavy and not completely cooked, it is likely that the temperature was too low or it wasn't cooked for long enough. It may be that you will have to have a couple of attempts before you get it right, but keep notes and persevere: you will get there in the end!

LIGHT LEMON SPONGE

Add the **very finely grated zest of half a lemon** to the **Plain and Simple Sponge Cake** recipe, above.
Once the cake has cooled, fill with **Lemon Buttercream** as above and sieve some **icing sugar** over the top.

EXTRA SPECIAL LEMON SPONGE

Make the **Light Lemon Sponge** as above. Sandwich together with **Homemade Lemon Curd** from the **Sundries** section. Ice the top with **Glace Icing**, see above.

OLD-FASHIONED BIRTHDAY CAKE

This is a really simple, old fashioned, cake-shaped birthday cake.

Make the **Plain and Simple Sponge Cake** as above. Sandwich with jam and coat the top with the glace icing below.

175g (6oz) icing sugar
3 tablespoons lemon juice
2 teaspoons glycerine

Glace Icing

Sieve the icing sugar into a large bowl and stir in the lemon juice and glycerine. Beat with a wooden spoon until smooth and glossy.

Spoon the icing carefully over the cake: aim to keep it all on top of the cake but if a little drizzles down the sides don't worry, it will just look more traditional, like a cake in a child's picture book.

For Pink Icing, see the Fairy Cakes section.

SPONGE CAKE WITH JAM AND BUTTERCREAM

Again, make a perfectly **Simple Sponge Cake**, as above. Spread the lower half with **jam** and then carefully spread **Lemon Buttercream**, as above, over the top of the jam, using a small palette knife. Put the top cake on and sieve **icing sugar** over it.

COFFEE CAKE

This cake is absolutely delicious, but somehow it seems slightly strange to drink tea with coffee cake. You could always make a pot of coffee instead and pretend you are in a coffee shop in Vienna having coffee and cake!

You will need 2 greased 18cm (7in) loose-bottomed sandwich tins.

Preheat the oven to 180°C (fan oven) or equivalent, see below.

Whiz the butter and sugar together in a food processor until light and fluffy. Sieve a couple of spoonfuls of flour carefully over the surface of the butter and sugar and add the eggs, sieve over the rest of the flour with the bicarbonate of soda, cream of tartar and coffee powder and whiz together. Add the milk and whiz until very smooth and glossy and everything is well mixed.

You may need to scrape the mixture down from the sides a couple of times with a flexible spatula. You should now have a dropping consistency.

Pour into the prepared cake tins using a flexible spatula to help all the mixture out.

Bake in the middle of the oven for 18–20 minutes until the cakes are risen and golden and a skewer inserted comes out clean.

Allow the cakes to rest for a few moments and then carefully loosen the edges with a small palette knife. Transfer gently to a cooling rack

To make the Coffee Buttercream
Sieve the combined coffee powder and icing sugar into the softened butter a little at a time, mixing it all together with a wooden spoon. Finally, loosen the mixture slightly with the milk and beat until smooth and glossy.

To make the Coffee Glace Icing
Sieve the icing sugar and coffee powder into a large bowl and stir in the milk and glycerine. Beat with a wooden spoon until smooth and glossy.

Spread the buttercream over one of the sponges and sit the other on top. Spoon the icing carefully over the cake. You may like to decorate with a few strategically placed walnut (or pecan) halves.

175g (6oz) butter
175g (6oz) unrefined
  caster sugar
175g (6oz) plain flour
3 eggs, as fresh as possible
1 teaspoon bicarbonate of
  soda
2 teaspoons cream of
  tartar
2 teaspoons instant
  espresso coffee powder
2 tablespoons milk

Coffee Buttercream
2 teaspoons instant
  espresso coffee powder
75g (3oz) icing sugar
25g (1oz) butter
1–2 tablespoons milk

Coffee Glace Icing (with
  extra sticky properties)
50g (2oz) icing sugar
2 teaspoons instant
  espresso coffee powder
1 tablespoon milk
1 teaspoon glycerine

COFFEE AND WALNUT CAKE

Coffee and walnuts go beautifully together and are a classic cake combination. You can simply decorate the top of the **Coffee Cake** with walnuts or you can actually add some to the cake mixture itself. If you want to do this, make sure the walnuts are very fresh and not at all stale: walnuts are full of oil and can go rancid quite quickly. Chop about **50g (2oz) of walnuts** fairly finely and, once the cake is mixed, remove the processor blade and stir them in.

The flavour is lovely, but the pieces of walnut can be quite sharp and 'poky' and in some ways it's almost a shame to disturb the beautifully soft texture of the sponge! Pecan nuts also go well with coffee cake; again, be sure they are very fresh.

CHOCOLATE CAKE

This is a lovely, easy to make chocolate cake for any occasion and just perfect for a birthday tea.

175g (6oz) butter, softened	You will need 2 greased 18cm (7in) loose-bottomed sandwich tins.
175g (6oz) unrefined caster sugar	
150g (5oz) plain flour	Preheat the oven to 180°C (fan oven) or equivalent.
3 eggs	
1 teaspoon bicarbonate of soda	Whiz the butter and sugar together in a food processor until combined and fluffy. Sieve some of the flour in a layer over the mixture and then add the eggs. Sieve in the rest of the flour, bicarbonate of soda, cream of tartar and cocoa. Whiz again. Add the milk and whiz until smooth and glossy.
2 teaspoons cream of tartar	
25g (1oz) good quality cocoa powder (not drinking chocolate)	You may need to remove the lid a couple of times and scrape the mixture down from the sides with a flexible spatula.
2 tablespoons milk	Turn into the greased sandwich tins and bake for 18–20 minutes or until nicely risen and firm but springy to the touch. A wooden cocktail stick inserted into the cake should come out clean.
	Allow the cakes to rest for a few moments and then carefully loosen the edges with a small palette knife: they should be starting to contract away from the sides of their own accord.

If the tins are too hot to handle, stand the cakes, one at a time, on a jar or something similar. Using both hands, pull the side of the tin down so the cake is left, still on its base, on top of the jar. Move it closer to your cooling rack and loosen from the base using a large palette knife. Transfer gently (you may need a fish slice as well as the palette knife at this stage) onto the cooling rack. Repeat with the other cake.

See Little Chocolate Cakes and Chocolate Butterfly Cakes, in the previous section for Chocolate Buttercream and Chocolate Glace Icing.

Spread some of the buttercream carefully onto one of the sponges with a small palette knife. Put the second sponge on top and spread the rest of the buttercream over it. You might like to grate some chocolate over the top to decorate.

Alternatively, make a half quantity of buttercream and ice the top with chocolate glace icing instead.

Hiding a Birthday Cake

Occasionally, you may find yourself trying to hide a decorated birthday cake in the kitchen for a short time – until the moment comes to produce it with a flourish, candles ablaze. You can screen it from view temporarily with one of those clip boards that opens out like a folder, as it is stiff enough to stand up and big enough to hide an average size cake.

DORSET APPLE CAKE

This is a lovely cake for any time of year but especially in the autumn when there are so many apples around. I's really easy to make and is delicious warm or cold. It goes very well indeed with a dollop of clotted cream.

225g (8oz) plain flour

1½ teaspoons baking powder

110g (4oz) butter

110g (4oz) unrefined granulated sugar, plus a little more for the top

75g (3oz) currants or raisins

225g (8oz) peeled and cored apples, finely chopped (cooking, eating or a mixture of both)

2 eggs, beaten

You will need a greased, loose-bottomed 20cm (8in) cake tin.

Preheat the oven to 160°C (fan oven) or equivalent.

Sieve the flour and baking powder into a bowl and rub in the butter. Stir in the sugar, dried fruit and apple. Mix in the eggs. Turn into the prepared tin and smooth the top with the back of a metal spoon: a wet spoon makes it easier. Sprinkle some more sugar over the top. Cover loosely with greaseproof paper, tucking it underneath the tin to secure and bake for approximately 1¼ hours, until golden on top.

Leave in the tin for a few moments, then remove and cool on a wire rack. Store in an airtight tin.

WARMLY-SPICED AND WHOLESOME APPLE CAKE

Although there is no getting away from the fact that this is a cake, it is a good and wholesome one (and extremely delicious too) made with fresh eggs and butter, wholemeal flour and plenty of apple. Even the cinnamon is good for you: apparently, it may improve digestion, help relieve a blocked nose, ease muscle and joint pain, improve the circulation, help prevent gum disease and tooth decay, and kill certain types of bacteria!

You will need a greased, loose-bottomed 20cm (8in) cake tin.

Preheat the oven to 160°C (fan oven) or equivalent.

Put the flour into a bowl, sieve the baking powder and spices over the top and give it all a good stir to ensure an even distribution. Cut the butter into small dice and rub into the flour mixture and stir in the sugar. Blend in the eggs with a wooden spoon so that all the dry ingredients are moist and coated with egg: it will still look quite rough and crumbly.

Slice the apples in half and place flat side down on a board. Cut into slices of about ½ to ¾ of a centimetre. Save some of the neatest slices for the top of the cake and stir the rest into the cake mixture: some slices will break up but that's fine. (You may find it easier to mix the apple in with your hands: if you wear any rings set with stones and have forgotten to take them off, now could be a very good time to remember!)

Smooth the top of the cake with the back of a metal spoon: wet the spoon to make it easier. Arrange the last of the apple slices over the top and sprinkle with about a teaspoon of sugar. Cover loosely with greaseproof paper, tucking it underneath the tin to secure, and bake in a preheated oven for approximately 1¼ hours, until springy to the touch and a skewer inserted comes out clean.

Leave in the tin for a few moments, then remove and cool on a wire rack. Store in an airtight tin. Eat warm or cold.

225g (8oz) wholemeal flour
1½ teaspoons baking powder
1 teaspoon cinnamon
1 teaspoon mixed spice
110g (4oz) butter
110g (4oz) soft brown sugar, plus a little more for the top
3 eggs, beaten
250g (9oz) peeled and cored apples (cooking, eating or a mixture of both)

APPLE AND SULTANA SPICE CAKE

You will notice that this is a kind of cross between the two previous cakes. It is packed full of goodness with an extra touch of spice, all topped off with a little sprinkling of cinnamon sugar. Note that most of the apple is chopped fairly finely to make the cake nice and moist, but some is cut into bite-sized chunks to add some extra apple-y texture. Again, this cake goes beautifully with clotted cream. A slice is also just the thing to keep you going if you've missed breakfast.

110g (4oz) plain flour
1½ teaspoons baking
   powder
2 teaspoons cinnamon
1 teaspoon mixed spice
110g (4oz) wholemeal
   flour
110g (4oz) butter
110g (4oz) unrefined
   granulated sugar
110g (4oz) sultanas
3 eggs
275g (10oz) peeled and
   cored apples (cooking,
   eating or a mixture of
   both)

Plus, approximately
   another ½ teaspoon of
   cinnamon and 1
   teaspoon unrefined
   granulated sugar for the
   top

You will need a greased, loose-bottomed 20cm (8in) cake tin.

Preheat the oven to 160°C (fan oven) or equivalent.

Sieve the plain flour into a bowl with the baking powder and spices. Stir in the wholemeal flour. Cut the butter into small dice and rub into the flour mixture and stir in the sugar and sultanas. Blend in the eggs with a wooden spoon so that all the dry ingredients are moist and coated with egg: it will still look quite rough and crumbly.

Slice the apples in half and place flat side down on a board. Cut one of the apples into bite-sized chunks and chop the rest fairly finely. Stir into the cake mixture.

Smooth the top of the cake with the back of a metal spoon: wet the spoon to make it easier. Stir the extra sugar and cinnamon together in a small bowl and sprinkle lightly over the top. Cover loosely with greaseproof paper, tucking it underneath the tin to secure and bake in a preheated oven for between 1 and 1¼ hours, depending on the ferocity of your oven, until springy to the touch and a skewer inserted comes out clean.

Leave in the tin for a few moments, then remove and cool on a wire rack. Store in an airtight tin. Eat warm or cold.

BANANA CAKE

As with the apple cakes, previously, banana cake always seems wholesome and full of good things. The bananas for this recipe need to be just over-ripe: the skins should be a bit speckled and the banana should look slightly mealy but still be white. Don't be tempted to add any more banana 'just to use it up' as too much banana will make the cake solid and heavy.

You will need a greased 18cm (7in) loose-bottomed cake tin.

Preheat the oven to 160°C (fan oven) or equivalent.

Whiz the butter and sugar together in a food processor. Add the flours, ground almonds, cream of tartar, bicarbonate of soda and eggs and whiz until combined. Finally, add the banana and whiz that in too.

Spoon into the prepared tin, cover loosely with greaseproof paper and bake for about 1¼ hours, or until a skewer inserted into the cake comes out clean. If you have a fierce oven, test after an hour.

Loosen the sides and bottom with a palette knife, remove from the tin and cool on a wire rack.

110g (4oz) butter, softened
110g (4oz) soft light brown sugar
110g (4oz) wholemeal flour
50g (2oz) plain flour
50g (2oz) ground almonds
2 teaspoons cream of tartar
1 teaspoon bicarbonate of soda
2 fresh eggs
150–175g (5–6oz) ripe bananas (peeled weight), mashed to a puree but not liquidy

BANANA BUNS AND LITTLE LOAVES

You might prefer to make banana buns instead: individual cakes are always popular. All you do is make the mixture as above but spoon it into a greased 12-cup muffin tin or 12 greased mini-loaf tins instead. (There is no need to cover with greaseproof paper.) Bake at the same temperature as above for 20 minutes, or until they are springy to the touch and a skewer comes out clean.

Over-ripe banana alert!
This is a useful recipe if you have a couple of bananas that are well past their best: as long as they are pale brown rather than *actually black* inside, you can still use them, even if the skins are more brown than yellow.

CARROT CAKE

Carrot cake tastes quite indulgent whilst also being packed full of good and healthy ingredients! The cinnamon in this recipe gives a hint of warmth and depth, the orange zest a lovely freshness and the orange buttercream icing a touch of luxury.

110g (4oz) butter, softened
110g (4oz) soft brown
  sugar
110g (4oz) wholemeal
  flour
50g (2oz) plain flour
50g (2oz) ground almonds
2 teaspoons baking
  powder
1 teaspoon ground
  cinnamon
2 eggs
150g (5oz) grated carrot
  (grated weight)
Finely grated zest of 1
  orange

You will need a greased 18cm (7in) loose-bottomed cake tin.

Preheat the oven to 160°C (fan oven) or equivalent.

Whiz the butter and sugar together in a food processor. Add the flours, ground almonds, baking powder, cinnamon and eggs and whiz until combined. Finally, add the grated carrot and orange zest and whiz again.

Spoon into the prepared tin, cover loosely with greaseproof paper and bake for about 1¼ hours, or until a skewer inserted into the cake comes out clean. If you have a fierce oven, test after an hour.

Loosen the sides and bottom with a palette knife, remove from tin and cool on a wire rack.

Carrot Buns and Little Loaves

This recipe also makes brilliant buns. Make the recipe as above but spoon into a greased 12-cup muffin tin or 12 greased mini-loaf tins instead. There is no need to cover. Bake at the above temperature for 20 minutes or until a skewer comes out clean.

Optional icing
Again, both the cake and buns are lovely on their own, but carrot cake is wonderful iced. **Orange Buttercream** makes a delicious change from the usual cream cheese frosting.

Orange Buttercream Icing

Cream the butter in a bowl large enough to give you room to manoeuvre. Use a wooden spoon. Gradually add the icing sugar, passing it through a sieve. When the icing sugar is all combined, stir in the orange juice, just enough to loosen the mixture slightly. Spread onto the top of the cake or buns.	50g (2oz) butter, softened 110g (4oz) icing sugar Squeeze of orange juice

LEMON DRIZZLE CAKE

This is a classic tea-time Lemon Drizzle Cake: not too sweet, and not too sharp, moist and light. This recipe gives you the option to make either a loaf-shaped cake or a round one.

For the cake
110g (4oz) butter, softened
110g (4oz) unrefined
  caster sugar
175g (6oz) plain flour
2 eggs, beaten
1 teaspoon bicarbonate of
  soda
2 teaspoons of cream of
  tartar
Grated zest of 1 lemon
2 tablespoons warm water

For the drizzle
Juice of 2 lemons
2 level tablespoons
  unrefined caster sugar

You will need a greased 450g (1lb) loaf tin (in good condition, preferably anodised) or an 18cm (7in) round, loose-bottomed cake tin.

Preheat the oven to 160°C (fan oven) or equivalent.

Whiz the butter and sugar together until combined and fluffy. Carefully sieve in some of the flour to cover the surface of the butter and sugar and add the eggs. Add the rest of the flour, bicarbonate of soda, cream of tartar, lemon zest and warm water. Whiz until everything is smooth and glossy. You may need to stop the machine a couple of times and scrape the mixture down from the sides.

Pour into the prepared tin and cover loosely with greaseproof paper, tucking it under the tin to secure. You need to have the tension of the paper just right so that it protects the cake from drying out without dipping down onto the surface and sticking to it.

Bake for 45–50 minutes for the loaf cake and 40–45 for the round cake, until risen and golden and a skewer inserted comes out clean.

Whilst the cake is baking, heat the lemon juice and sugar together in a small heavy-bottomed saucepan, stirring frequently until the sugar has dissolved. Put aside to cool.

When the cake is ready, leave it in its tin and prick the surface lightly: if you have a fairly thick needle this won't make such noticeable holes as a cocktail stick or fork. Spoon the drizzle evenly all over the top. If you have one of those Perspex gravy separators with a thin, round spout, this would be ideal for pouring the drizzle over with. Alternatively, spoon it over.

Keep the cake in the tin until it is completely cold and the drizzle has soaked in. Transfer to an airtight tin.

Helpful Note
It is possible to make Lemon Drizzle Buns and Little Loaves as well. They look absolutely perfect and taste delicious, but the considerable downside is they play havoc with your baking tins. The lemon syrup, which is manageable in a large tin, is a nightmare when it comes into contact with all those little baking cups or loaf tins. Consequently, there is a lot of washing up involved: even a dishwasher will struggle.

Plus it is quite a fiddle manoeuvring them all out!

MARMALADE CAKE

There's something about Marmalade Cake and Buns that makes them taste even better in the open air. They are perfect for picnics or a relaxed weekend breakfast in the garden. A lighter, clearer marmalade with thin shreds of peel will give a lovely, light flavour whereas a darker, chunkier marmalade will give a deeper, mellower flavour. If you have any left after a day or two, spread with a little butter.

The zest of an orange gives the cake an extra fresh, zingy flavour but it still tastes good and orangey without.

You will need a greased 450g (1lb) loaf tin or 18cm (7in) round, loose-bottomed cake tin.

Preheat the oven to 160°C (fan oven) or equivalent.

Whiz the butter, sugar and marmalade together until combined and fluffy. Add the orange zest, if using, sieve a tablespoon or two of flour over the top to cover the surface of the mixture and add the eggs. Add the rest of the flour, bicarbonate of soda and cream of tartar. Whiz briefly and add the warm water. Whiz until everything is smooth and glossy but not over mixed.

Ease into the prepared tin, cover loosely with greaseproof paper and bake for approximately 40–45 minutes or until risen and golden and a skewer inserted comes out clean.

Leave in the tin for a few moments and then transfer to a wire rack to cool completely. Store in an airtight tin when cold.

110g (4oz) butter, softened
50g (2oz) unrefined caster sugar
2 tablespoons marmalade
Finely grated zest of 1 orange (optional)
2 eggs
175g (6oz) plain flour
1 teaspoon bicarbonate of soda
2 teaspoons cream of tartar
2 tablespoons warm water

MARMALADE BUNS AND LITTLE LOAVES

If you like, you can make the above recipe in bun form instead. Make the mixture as for the **Marmalade Cake** recipe above and grease a 12-cup muffin tin or 12 mini-loaf tins. Using a dessertspoon, divide the mixture equally between the 12 cups or tins. Bake at 160°C as before, for approximately 12–15 minutes until risen and golden and a skewer inserted comes out clean.

Leave to settle in the tin for a few minutes – they are very fragile at this stage. Then, lever them out very gently and transfer to a wire rack to finish cooling.

Once completely cold, store in an airtight container.

TRADITIONAL ROCK BUNS WITH CURRANTS AND LEMON

These buns are absolutely delicious and so easy to make. Incidentally, they are meant to look *a bit like little rocks: not actually have a rock-like texture! Currants have a nice, citrussy, lemony tang to them anyway, but a little added lemon zest enhances their flavour beautifully. The secret of successful Rock Buns is:* don't overcook them!

You will need a greased baking tray.	MAKES 12 BUNS
Preheat the oven to 180°C (fan oven) or equivalent.	225g (8oz) plain flour
Zest the lemon in very quick, short, up and down movements as nobody wants to end up with long strands of peel dangling from their mouths!	2 teaspoons baking powder or 2 teaspoons cream of tartar
Sieve the flour and raising agents and rub in the butter. Stir in the sugar and currants, the egg and milk. It will look a bit rough and dry to start with but you will soon have a fairly stiff, but pliable, dough.	1 teaspoon bicarbonate of soda
Divide the dough into 12 and roll into balls: you may like to wet your hands first if it seems a bit sticky. Spread them out on the prepared baking tray. Bake for about 12 minutes until they are golden on top and a skewer inserted comes out clean.	110g (4oz) butter 110g (4oz) unrefined caster sugar 110g (4oz) currants Finely grated zest of 1 lemon
Don't overcook them unless you are intentionally aiming for an authentic rock-like consistency! They should be slightly crisp on the outside and light and crumbly on the inside.	1 egg 2 tablespoons milk
Cool on a wire rack and store in an airtight tin when cold. Eat within a couple of days.	

CRANBERRY AND ORANGE ROCK BUNS

These are an extremely yummy version of the above recipe. Instead of currants, use the same amount of **dried cranberries**, and instead of finely grated lemon zest, use **finely grated orange zest**. As with the previous recipe, zest the orange in a quick up and down movement so that you get very short, broken shreds: nobody wants to cope with great long strands in their bun!

Cottage Tea

A Cottage Tea brings to mind quaint little old cottages in quaint old villages with hollyhocks in the gardens and little old ladies on old-fashioned bicycles stopping to talk to the vicar. The tea itself might take place in one of the cottages, or better still in one of the cottage gardens with one of the old ladies – she might even be your grandmother.

There will be a snowy white lacy cloth spread on a gate leg table with a silver teapot and delicate flower-patterned bone china cups and saucers. There will definitely be a tea strainer in its own bowl and most probably a cat rubbing round your ankles.

There will be dainty sandwiches to eat and a choice of cake: light fruit cake, Victoria sandwich or lemon cake, Madeira cake or seed cake and possibly some jam tarts. There might even be scones. Tea will last a long time and afterwards you will go home with some cake in a carrier bag.

COSY CAKE

When I put this recipe together I was trying to recreate a cake I remembered from my childhood. It was known as Granny Cake or Grannies Cake. It was a bought cake and came in a box. This is virtually the same and all the better for being home-baked! If you can, display it on a cake stand with a doily tucked underneath.

It is very simple to make: boiling the fruit beforehand makes it all plump and luscious and the sugar on top is the finishing touch.

110g (4oz) butter
200ml (scant 7 fl oz) water
110g (4oz) light soft brown sugar
225g (8oz) dried fruit: currants, raisins and plenty of sultanas
225g (8oz) self-raising flour
2 eggs, lightly beaten
A teaspoonful or so of unrefined caster sugar for sprinkling

You will need a greased 18cm (7in) loose-bottomed cake tin.

Preheat the oven to 160°C (fan oven) or equivalent.

Cut the butter into small pieces and put into a saucepan with the water, sugar and fruit. Bring to the boil and simmer for 5 minutes, stirring from time to time. Leave until it is completely cold and sieve in half the flour and add the eggs. Sieve the rest of the flour over the top. Mix thoroughly together with a wooden spoon. If you use a fairly roomy saucepan you can use it to mix it all together in and save on washing up!

Pour the mixture into the prepared tin and wrap the tin loosely in greaseproof paper, tucking it underneath to secure. Bake for about 1¼ hours or until it is golden in colour and a skewer inserted comes out clean. Sprinkle with sugar whilst still warm.

Cool on a wire rack and store in an airtight tin.

Madeira Cake and Seed Cake

Here are two really old-fashioned cakes. Madeira cake has actually nothing to do with the Portuguese island of Madeira, as such. It is called Madeira cake because it was the ideal sort of light, plain cake to serve with Madeira wine. Victorian ladies and gentleman would sometimes take Madeira, served in delicate little glasses, as a pick-me-up during the morning with a slice of plain cake. Recipes vary; sometimes it is completely plain, sometimes lightly flavoured with lemon. Sometimes it has a piece of candied lemon peel baked into the top.

Seed cake is another old-fashioned favourite, very similar to Madeira cake but containing caraway seeds, which give it a lovely aniseed-y flavour.

This basic cake mixture is very adaptable and you can also use it to make a classic cherry cake and a classic coconut cake. You can also make a combination cherry *and* coconut cake!

MADEIRA CAKE

The lemon zest gives the cake a lovely freshness, but it is perfectly nice without. This recipe contains less sugar than is often used – more sugar gives a beautiful fine texture – but the texture of this version is still light and delicate. Options are given for both a round version and the more traditional loaf-shaped cake.

You will need a greased 450g (1lb) loaf tin or 18cm (7in) round, loose-bottomed cake tin.

Preheat the oven to 160°C (fan oven) or equivalent.

Whiz the butter and sugar together until combined and fluffy. Carefully sieve in some of the flour and add the eggs. Then add the rest of the flour, bicarbonate of soda, cream of tartar and the lemon zest, if using. Whiz briefly, and add the warm water. Whiz until everything is mixed together but not over mixed. You may need to stop the machine a couple of times and scrape the mixture down from the sides.

Pour into the prepared tin and cover loosely with greaseproof paper, tucking it under the tin to secure. You need to have the tension of the paper just right so that it protects the cake from drying out without dipping down onto the surface and sticking to it.

Bake for 45–50 minutes for the loaf cake and 40–45 for the round cake, until risen and golden and a skewer inserted comes out clean.

Leave in the tin for a while to settle and contract away from the sides.

110g (4oz) butter, softened
110g (4oz) unrefined caster sugar
175g (6oz) plain flour
2 eggs
1 teaspoon bicarbonate of soda
2 teaspoons cream of tartar
Grated zest of 1 lemon (optional)
2 tablespoons warm water

SEED CAKE

The caraway seeds give the cake the most beautiful flavour. Stir them in at the end, as directed, to keep them whole and undamaged. Options are given for both a round and a loaf-shaped cake.

110g (4oz) butter, softened
110g (4oz) unrefined
   caster sugar
175g (6oz) plain flour
2 eggs
1 teaspoon bicarbonate of
   soda
2 teaspoons cream of
   tartar
2 tablespoons warm water
2 teaspoons caraway seeds

You will need a greased 450g (1lb) loaf tin or 18cm (7in) round, loose-bottomed cake tin.

Preheat the oven to 160°C (fan oven) or equivalent.

Whiz the butter and sugar together until combined and fluffy. Carefully sieve in some of the flour and add the eggs. Then add the rest of the flour, the bicarbonate of soda and cream of tartar. Whiz briefly and add the warm water. Whiz until everything is mixed together but not over mixed. You may need to stop the machine a couple of times and scrape the mixture down from the sides.

Remove the blade from the machine and stir in the caraway seeds.

Pour into the prepared tin and cover loosely with greaseproof paper, tucking it under the tin to secure. You need to have the tension of the paper just right so that it protects the cake from drying out without dipping down onto the surface and sticking to it.

Bake for 45–50 minutes for the loaf cake and 40–45 for the round cake, until risen and golden and a skewer inserted comes out clean.

Leave in the tin for a while to settle and contract away from the sides – particularly if you are using a loaf tin – then transfer to a wire rack until completely cold. Once cold, store in an airtight tin.

CHERRY CAKE

If you are fond of glace cherries, you can adapt this mixture for a classic cherry cake recipe. If the glace cherries look a bit syrupy, wash them gently and dry them with a clean cloth before using. If you don't, they can sink and you'll have a kind of cherry layer cake with sunken cherries as the bottom layer! Don't forget to toss them in flour as well, as this also helps to keep them afloat.

If you are not a fan of glace cherries, use dried sour cherries instead: you don't get the classic cherry cake appearance, but the flavour is lovely and tangy. It doesn't hurt to toss the dried cherries in flour as well.

Options are given for both a round and a loaf-shaped cake.

You will need a greased 450g (1lb) loaf tin or 18cm (7in) round, loose-bottomed cake tin.

Preheat the oven to 160°C (fan oven) or equivalent.

Take about a tablespoon of flour from the amount you have measured out and toss the cherries in it. Set aside until the end when you stir them in.

Whiz the butter and sugar together until combined and fluffy. Carefully sieve in some of the flour and add the eggs. Add the rest of the flour, the bicarbonate of soda and cream of tartar. Whiz briefly and add the warm water. Whiz until everything is mixed together but not over mixed. You may need to stop the machine a couple of times and scrape the mixture down from the sides.

Remove the blade from the machine and stir in the floured glace cherries or dried sour cherries.

Pour into the prepared tin and cover loosely with greaseproof paper, tucking it under the tin to secure. You need to have the tension of the paper just right so that it protects the cake from drying out without dipping down onto the surface and sticking to it.

Bake for 45–50 minutes for the loaf cake and 40–45 for the round cake, until risen and golden and a skewer inserted comes out clean.

Leave in the tin for a while to settle and contract away from the sides – particularly if you are using a loaf tin – then transfer to a wire rack until completely cold. Once cold, store in an airtight tin.

- 110g (4oz) butter, softened
- 110g (4oz) unrefined caster sugar
- 175g (6oz) plain flour
- 2 eggs
- 1 teaspoon bicarbonate of soda
- 2 teaspoons cream of tartar
- 2 tablespoons warm water
- 110g (4oz) glace cherries, halved or quartered, or dried sour cherries

COCONUT CAKE

You can also adapt the same mixture again to make a lovely, moist coconut cake.

110g (4oz) butter, softened
110g (4oz) unrefined
  caster sugar
110g (4oz) plain flour
2 eggs
1 teaspoon bicarbonate of
  soda
2 teaspoons cream of
  tartar
2 tablespoons warm water
50g (2oz) desiccated
  coconut

You will need a greased 450g (1lb) loaf tin or 18cm (7in) round, loose-bottomed cake tin.

Preheat the oven to 160°C (fan oven) or equivalent.

Whiz the butter and sugar together until combined and fluffy. Carefully sieve in some of the flour and add the eggs. Add the rest of the flour, the bicarbonate of soda and cream of tartar. Whiz briefly and add the warm water. Whiz until everything is mixed together but not over mixed. You may need to stop the machine a couple of times and scrape the mixture down from the sides.

Finally, add the coconut and whiz briefly to mix it all in evenly.

Pour into the prepared tin and cover loosely with greaseproof paper, tucking it under the tin to secure. You need to have the tension of the paper just right so that it protects the cake from drying out without dipping down onto the surface and sticking to it.

Bake for approximately 40–45 minutes until risen and golden and a skewer inserted comes out clean.

Leave in the tin for a while to settle and contract away from the sides – particularly if you are using a loaf tin.

Even if you are using a loaf tin, provided you have a decent one in good shape (an anodised one is good) and have greased it sufficiently, you shouldn't need to line it. Once the cake has cooled and is starting to pull away from the sides, press gently on the edge of the cake, all the way round the sides, to pull it away further. You may need the very gentlest of help with a small palette knife as well. Shake the tin sideways briskly a couple of times and you should then be able to turn it out.

Transfer to a wire rack until completely cold. Once cold, store in an airtight tin.

COCONUT BUNS

You can adapt any of the recipes in this section to make buns instead. The coconut version is *especially delicious* in bun form and very popular with children.

Make the mixture as for the **Coconut Cake** recipe above and grease a 12-cup muffin tin. Using a dessertspoon, divide the mixture equally between the 12 cups. Bake at 160°C as before, for approximately 12–15 minutes until risen and golden and a skewer inserted comes out clean.

Leave to settle in the tin for a few minutes – they are very fragile at this stage. Then, lever them out very gently, using a small palette knife and transfer to a wire rack to finish cooling. Once completely cold, store in an airtight container.

COCONUT AND RASPBERRY BUNS

These little buns are also fabulous split and spread with raspberry jam. Who would have thought the fruit of the exotic coconut palm, swaying on tropical beaches, and the cool climate raspberry could strike up such a winning partnership? Despite the geographical gulf between them, theirs is a marriage made in heaven.

Slice each bun in half horizontally and sandwich together with **raspberry jam** (use seedless if you don't like the pips). If it is a special occasion, sieve a little **icing sugar** over the top of each bun just before serving: use a tea strainer and stir the icing sugar through with a teaspoon. These are possibly even more popular with children than the plain coconut buns.

CHERRY AND COCONUT CAKE

Cherries and coconut are another classic combination. If you are fond of cherries there is nothing to stop you adding some to your coconut cake. Proceed as before but halve or quarter **50g (2oz) of glace cherries** and toss them in a little of the flour you have measured out. Put aside and, once the cake is mixed, remove the processor blade and gently stir in the floured cherries. Continue as before.

MARIGOLD BUNS

These buns sound a bit quirky but they are really delicious. The marigold flavour doesn't come through very strongly but, if you concentrate hard, there is a faint subtle, almost aniseed flavour. They do look very pretty though. They really capture children's imagination and they are perfect to serve for tea in the garden. The marigolds used in this recipe are the English pot marigold: Calendula officinalis (not the much more pungent French or African marigold: Tagetes).

MAKES ABOUT 10 BUNS

75g (3oz) butter, softened
75g (3oz) unrefined caster
  sugar
175g (6oz) fresh, new self-
  raising flour
2 eggs
2 tablespoons milk
Petals from about 8
  unsprayed, bug-free,
  orange pot marigold
  flowers

You will need a greased 12-cup muffin tin.

Preheat the oven to 180°C (fan oven) or equivalent.

Separate the petals from the flowers as follows: hold each flower in one hand and gather the petals together in the other. Give a sharp tug and they will all come away from the centre together.

Whiz the butter and sugar together in a food processor until combined and fluffy. Sieve in some of the flour and add the eggs. Then sieve in the rest of the flour. Whiz again. Add the milk and whiz until smooth and glossy.

Remove the blade from the machine and stir in the marigold petals.

Spoon into the prepared tin, filling each cup about half to three-quarters of the way up.

Bake for 12–14 minutes until risen and pale golden and a skewer inserted comes out clean. Remove from the tin and cool on a wire rack. Store in an airtight container when completely cold.

Eat warm or cold, as they are or with a little butter.

Orange Buns

If you are not sure about the marigolds, and would like a more traditional bun, these are great made in exactly the same way but with the **finely grated zest of 1 orange** instead of the marigold petals. A lemon zester works best: use a brisk up and down movement to avoid any long shreds of zest in the finished buns.

Lemon Buns

Lemon zest also works well in these buns. Make in exactly the same way as the two previous recipes but add the **finely grated zest of 1 lemon** instead of an orange.

You could also make half a batch of **Lemon Buns** and half a batch of **Orange Buns** and offer them on a plate together.

Crumble Cakes and Crumble Buns

APPLE CRUMBLE CAKE

This scrumptious cake is like eating two favourites at the same time: apple crumble and apple cake! It tastes great served either cold as a cake or warm from the oven with clotted cream as a pudding. It has a denser, moister texture when warm; when cold, the texture is much finer. You make the cake part first and put it in the tin, layer the fruit on next and top everything off with the crumble.

For the cake

110g (4oz) butter, softened

110g (4oz) unrefined caster sugar

50g (2oz) ground almonds

175g (6oz) plain flour

2 eggs

1 teaspoon bicarbonate of soda

2 teaspoons cream of tartar

4 tablespoons milk

For the fruit topping

A couple of dessert apples weighing approximately 225g (8oz) (peeled and cored weight), Cox's are perfect

For the crumble topping

20g (¾oz) butter

50g (2oz) plain flour

¼ teaspoon baking powder

20g (¾oz) unrefined granulated sugar

You will need a greased 18cm (7in) loose-bottomed cake tin.

Preheat the oven to 160°C (fan oven) or equivalent.

Whiz the butter and sugar together thoroughly in the food processor until light and fluffy. Add the ground almonds and whiz to combine. Sieve half of the flour over the top and add the eggs. Sieve the rest of the flour, bicarbonate of soda and cream of tartar over the top and whiz. Add the milk and whiz until everything is fully mixed and smooth. Stop the processor a couple of times and scrape the mixture down from the sides with a flexible spatula.

Cut the peeled and cored apples in half and lay them cut side down on a board. Cut into slices of about half a centimetre.

Make the crumble topping by rubbing the butter, flour and baking powder together and stir in the sugar.

Pour the cake mixture into the prepared tin and layer the apple slices over the surface. Scatter the crumble evenly over the top.

Cover the tin loosely with greaseproof paper, tucking it underneath to secure. Bake for about 1¾ hours until the top is golden and a skewer inserted comes out clean (you may like to remove the greaseproof paper for the last 15 minutes or so). Transfer to a wire rack and store in an airtight container when completely cold.

✔ **Helpful Note**

Don't try to make a crumble mix with the bowl on the worktop – it's too high and you'll feel awkward. Put the bowl on a table instead, it's much more comfortable.

PLUM CRUMBLE CAKE

Make this in exactly the same way as the **Apple Crumble Cake**, above, but instead of apple, use the amount of stoned plums specified below, arranging the plum halves over the top of the cake cut-side down.

Approximately 225g (8oz) or a fraction more plums, Victoria, Marjorie's Seedling, or similar. This will equate to about **7 or 8 plums**.

✓ **Stoning plums**
Removing the stones from plums can be tricky. Cut the plum in half, length-wise (cut along the groove so that stone will be exposed flat) and twist: one half should come away cleanly from the stone. If you are lucky, you can just lift the stone away from the other half. If it proves a bit more stubborn, use a small spoon (an egg or coffee spoon fits more comfortably into the palm of your hand than a teaspoon) to scoop it out.

The success of this operation depends on the plum: a lovely, perfectly ripe, garden-grown Victoria can be separated easily from its stone. Others can be more difficult and the fun can go out of the whole business very quickly!

✓ **Freezing stoned plums**
If you have a glut of plums that you *can* stone easily, it's worth freezing a batch to make a crumble cake or two later in the year. Cut each plum in half, length-wise and stone, as above. Lay the halves, flat side down onto a baking tray or something similar, covered with a piece of greaseproof paper, shiny side up. Put them into the freezer overnight. Remove from the tray and transfer them to freezer bags the next day. Secure the tops tightly. This means you can take the plums out of the freezer singly and they will defrost more quickly. Lay the defrosted plums over the cake as before.

DRIED APRICOT CRUMBLE CAKE

Dried apricots make a fantastic crumble cake. It's useful to have a packet of dried apricots in the cupboard so you can whip up a cake or some buns (see below) at short notice.

225g (8oz) dried apricots Boiling water, to cover	Put the apricots into a pan and cover with boiling water. Leave to soak for the best part of an hour. Bring to the boil and simmer gently, half covered with a lid or covered by a spatter guard, for about three quarters of an hour. Strain and set aside to cool. Make the cake and crumble topping as for Apple Crumble Cake. Pour the cake mixture into the prepared tin. Arrange the apricots over the top and scatter the crumble mixture over the top, as before. Cover the tin loosely with greaseproof paper, tucking it underneath to secure. Bake for about 1¾ hours until the top is golden and a skewer inserted comes out clean (you may like to remove the greaseproof paper for the last 15 minutes or so). Transfer to a wire rack and store in an airtight container when completely cold. Use a sharp non-serrated knife to slice the cake. Put the point of the knife into the centre of the cake first and cut out from the centre to the edge.

CRUMBLE BUNS

These are the same as the crumble cakes above, but in dinky little bun form. They take much less time in the oven and you also have the option of using a selection of toppings, if you would like to offer a mixed plate or have some oddments of fruit left over.

Instead of 225g (8oz), halve the quantity of **fruit** to **110g (4oz)**.

The cakes look good covered completely with a layer of fruit but the buns are better with just a small amount.

You will need to cut the fruit into smaller pieces to allow for the shorter cooking time.

Bake for 15–20 minutes until domed and golden on top.

DRIED APRICOT CRUMBLE BUNS

These are a slight fiddle to make but are so delicious! The tart apricots make a lovely contrast with the fluffy, sweet and buttery bun. If you prefer, make a 50g (8oz) crumble mix, adjusting the other quantities proportionally, take what you need and freeze the rest: you can then whip up a fruit crumble at short notice. Don't leave it in the freezer too long though, or it will start to taste 'airy'.

You will need a greased 12-cup bun tin.

Preheat the oven to 160°C (fan oven) or equivalent.

Put the apricots into a pan and cover with boiling water. Leave to soak for the best part of an hour and then bring to the boil and simmer gently, half covered with a lid or covered by a spatter guard, for about three quarters of an hour.

Strain and set aside to cool.

Whiz the butter and sugar together thoroughly in the food processor until light and fluffy. Sieve half of the flour over the top and add the eggs. Sieve the rest of the flour, bicarbonate of soda and cream of tartar over the top and whiz. Add the milk and ground almonds and whiz until everything is fully mixed and smooth. Stop the processor a couple of times and scrape the mixture down from the sides with a flexible spatula.

Make the crumble topping by rubbing the butter, flour and baking powder together and stir in the sugar. Using a dessertspoon, divide the mixture equally between the 12 cups of the prepared tin.

Snip each apricot into 4 with sharp kitchen scissors. Scatter some apricot pieces on top of each bun.

Sprinkle the crumble evenly over the top. Bake for 15–20 minutes until domed and golden on top and a skewer inserted comes out clean.

Leave the buns to settle for a while until they have begun to cool and contract away from the sides of the tin: they are very fragile when they first come out of the oven.

Transfer to a wire rack and store in an airtight container when completely cold.

For the buns
110g (4oz) butter, softened
110g (4oz) unrefined caster sugar
175g (6oz) plain flour
2 fresh eggs
1 teaspoon bicarbonate of soda
2 teaspoons cream of tartar
4 tablespoons milk
50g (2oz) ground almonds

For the fruit topping
225g (8oz) dried apricots
Boiling water, to cover

For the crumble topping
20g (¾oz) butter
50g (2oz) plain flour
¼ teaspoon baking powder
20g (¾oz) unrefined granulated sugar

CHERRY AND ALMOND CAKE

This cake has the most delicious flavour: it's not over-sweet as the dried cherries used are slightly tart. Flaked almonds on top of a cake always make it look instantly professional.

110g (4oz) butter, softened

110g (4oz) unrefined
caster sugar

175g (6oz) plain flour

2 fresh eggs

1 teaspoon bicarbonate of
soda

2 teaspoons cream of
tartar

4 tablespoons milk

50g (2oz) ground almonds

100–110g (3½–4oz) dried
cherries (sometimes
called dried sour
cherries)

Approximately 25g (1oz)
flaked almonds, to
decorate

You will need a greased 18cm (7in) loose-bottomed cake tin.

Preheat the oven to 160°C (fan oven) or equivalent.

Separate the cherries, and cut any that look a bit big in half with kitchen scissors. Take about a tablespoon of flour from the measured amount and toss the cherries in it: although they are dried, they are still moist enough to have a tendency to sink. Set aside until needed.

Whiz the butter and sugar together thoroughly in the food processor until light and fluffy. Sieve half of the flour over the top and add the eggs. Sieve the rest of the flour, bicarbonate of soda and cream of tartar over the top and whiz. Add the milk and ground almonds and whiz until everything is fully mixed and smooth. Stop the processor a couple of times and scrape the mixture down from the sides with a flexible spatula.

Remove the blade from the food processor and stir in the cherries, distributing them evenly throughout the mixture.

Ease the cake mixture into the prepared tin. Scatter the flaked almonds evenly over the top.

Cover the tin loosely with greaseproof paper, tucking it underneath to secure. Bake for about 45 minutes until the top is golden and a skewer inserted comes out clean.

Transfer to a wire rack and store in an airtight container when completely cold.

Classic Cherry and Almond Cake with Glace Cherries

If you are fond of **glace cherries**, you can use them in the above recipe instead of the dried cherries. The finished cake will taste sweeter, but more traditional. Use the same amount as specified for the dried cherries: **110g (4oz)**.

If the glace cherries look a bit syrup-y, wash them gently and dry them with a clean cloth before using. Too much syrup can make them heavy and they can sink to the bottom of the cake.

Toss them in about a tablespoon of flour from the amount you have measured out as well: this also helps to keep them afloat. Set aside until the end when you stir them into the mixture, in exactly the same way as the dried cherries.

CHERRY AND ALMOND BUNS

*These delicious and tempting little buns are made with a similar mixture to the **Cherry and Almond Cake** but the dried cherries are boiled for a couple of minutes to plump them up and make them even more luscious.*

Buns are slightly fiddlier when you are dividing the mixture into the bun tin, but take much less time to bake and always have a slightly fluffier texture.

Flaked almonds on top always make cakes and buns look instantly lovely and most professional but, if you're not keen on them, leave them out or top half of the buns and leave the rest plain if tastes are divided.

100–110g (3½–4oz) dried cherries (sometimes called 'dried sour cherries')

4 tablespoons water

110g (4oz) butter, softened

110g (4oz) unrefined caster sugar

175g (6oz) plain flour

2 fresh eggs

1 teaspoon bicarbonate of soda

2 teaspoons cream of tartar

4 tablespoons milk

50g (2oz) ground almonds

Approximately 25g (1oz) flaked almonds, to decorate

You will need a greased 12-cup bun tin.

Preheat the oven to 160°C (fan oven) or equivalent.

Put the dried cherries into a small pan with the water, bring to the boil and simmer gently for a minute or two. Strain and set aside to cool, resting on a clean cloth or kitchen paper to dry them as much as possible.

Whiz the butter and sugar together thoroughly in the food processor until light and fluffy. Sieve half of the flour over the top and add the eggs. Sieve the rest of the flour, bicarbonate of soda and cream of tartar over the top and whiz. Add the milk and ground almonds and whiz until everything is fully mixed and smooth. Stop the processor a couple of times and scrape the mixture down from the sides with a flexible spatula.

Remove the blade from the food processor and stir in the cherries.

Using a dessertspoon, divide the mixture equally between the 12 cups of the prepared tin. Scatter the flaked almonds over the top.

Bake for 15–20 minutes until domed and golden on top and a skewer inserted comes out clean.

Leave the buns to settle for a while until they have begun to cool and contract away from the sides of the tin: they are very fragile when they first come out of the oven.

Transfer to a wire rack and store.

Rich, Dark, Moist, Ginger Cake

This dark and sticky ginger cake is not for the faint-hearted. Eat it fresh and fluffy on the first day after baking or leave it in an airtight container for a couple of days to get denser and stickier. Black treacle, incidentally, is good for you as it contains useful amounts of iron.

You will need a greased 450g (1lb) loaf tin, preferably lined.

Preheat the oven to 160°C (fan oven) or equivalent.

Put the butter, sugar, black treacle and water into a roomy pan. Heat fairly gently until everything has melted and the sugar has dissolved.

Put aside to cool a little – but don't let it go completely cold, it should still be warm or the cake won't rise as well.

Once cooler, but still slightly warm, sieve the flour, bicarbonate of soda, cream of tartar and spices over the mixture in several batches, stirring it in as you go, reserving a little of the flour to add with the eggs, at the end.

Mix everything together thoroughly and finally add the eggs and the rest of the flour.

When everything is smooth and glossy, pour into the prepared tin: use a flexible spatula to scrape all the mixture out of the pan. Cover loosely with greaseproof paper and bake for approximately 45 minutes or until a skewer inserted comes out clean.

Leave in the tin for a while to cool slightly and contract away from the sides. Ease out of the tin: you may need to help it along gently with a small palette knife. Finish cooling on a wire rack.

Once completely cold, store in an airtight tin.

- 110g (4oz) butter, cut into small pieces
- 75g (3oz) unrefined caster sugar
- 6 tablespoons black treacle
- 150ml (¼pt) water
- 225g (8oz) plain flour
- 1 teaspoon bicarbonate of soda
- 2 teaspoons cream of tartar
- 2 teaspoons mixed spice
- 3 teaspoons ground ginger
- 2 eggs

✓ **Useful Note**

Be sure to mix the flour in gradually and thoroughly: if you are a bit slap-dash you will end up with the odd little white blob of flour here and there in the finished cake.

GINGER BATTER BUNS

These delectable buns are a must if you are a ginger fan. They are light and fluffy the first day and become denser and stickier after that. The cake mix is very liquidy – like batter – so pour it into a jug with a good pouring spout to transfer the mixture to the bun tin: it can get very, very messy otherwise!

110g (4oz) butter, cut into small pieces

50g (2oz) soft dark brown sugar

2 tablespoons black treacle

4 tablespoons golden syrup

150ml (¼pt) water

225g (8oz) plain flour

1 teaspoon bicarbonate of soda

2 teaspoons cream of tartar

2 teaspoons mixed spice

3 teaspoons ground ginger

2 fresh eggs, beaten

You will need a 12-cup bun tin and 12 muffin-size paper cases.

Preheat the oven to 160°C (fan oven) or equivalent.

Put the butter, sugar, black treacle, golden syrup and water into a roomy pan. Heat fairly gently until everything has melted and the sugar has dissolved.

Put aside to cool a little – but don't let it go completely cold, it should still be warm or the buns won't rise as well.

Once cooler, but still slightly warm, sieve the flour, bicarbonate of soda, cream of tartar and spices over the mixture in several batches, stirring it in as you go, reserving a little of the flour to add with the eggs, at the end.

Stir everything together thoroughly with a wooden spoon and finally add the beaten eggs and stir into the mixture with the rest of the flour. Keep mixing and when everything is fully mixed and smooth and glossy, pour it all into a jug.

Note: If the mixture still appears to have the odd little lump in it, pour it all through a sieve for a completely smooth batter.

Pour into the paper cases in the bun tin. Fill each case to just over half way and try not to let any mixture spill over and down the sides of the cases.

Bake for approximately 18 minutes or until a skewer inserted comes out clean.

Remove from the tin and finish cooling on a wire rack.

Once completely cold, store in an airtight tin.

SMALL GINGER BATTER BUNS

For a smaller bun, bake the above recipe, still in a muffin tin, in fairy cake-size paper cases. The muffin size is more domed in shape and spectacular to look at but the smaller size is very handy for picnics and lunch boxes.

Fill each case to just below the top and try to avoid spilling any down the sides.

Shorten the cooking time to approximately 16 minutes. You will need to bake a second part-batch.

CHOCOLATE BROWNIE BUNS

*These are closely related to the **Ginger Batter Buns**. They have the taste of a brownie and the fluffiness of a bun with a gorgeously sticky top.*

110g (4oz) butter, cut into small pieces

50g (2oz) soft dark brown sugar

6 tablespoons golden syrup

150ml (¼pt) water

200g (7oz) plain flour

1 teaspoon bicarbonate of soda

2 teaspoons cream of tartar

25g cocoa powder

2 fresh eggs, beaten

1 teaspoon vanilla extract or vanilla bean paste

You will need a 12-cup bun tin and 12 muffin-size paper cases.

Preheat the oven to 160°C (fan oven) or equivalent.

Put the butter, sugar, golden syrup and water into a roomy pan. Heat fairly gently until everything has melted and the sugar has dissolved.

Put aside to cool a little – but don't let it go completely cold, it should still be warm or the buns won't rise as well.

Once cooler, but still slightly warm, sieve the flour, bicarbonate of soda, cream of tartar and cocoa over the mixture in several batches, stirring it in as you go, reserving a little of the flour to add with the eggs, at the end.

Stir everything together thoroughly with a wooden spoon and finally add the vanilla to the beaten eggs and stir into the mixture with the rest of the flour. Keep mixing and, when everything is fully mixed and smooth and glossy, pour it all into a jug.

Note: If the mixture still appears to have the odd little lump in it, pour it all through a sieve for a completely smooth batter.

Pour into the paper cases in the bun tin. Fill each case to just over half way and try not to let any mixture spill over and down the sides of the cases. Scrape any mixture from the sides of the jug with a flexible spatula.

Bake for approximately 18 minutes or until a skewer inserted comes out clean.

Remove from the tin and finish cooling on a wire rack.

Once completely cold, store in an airtight tin.

SMALL CHOCOLATE BROWNIE BUNS

For a smaller bun, bake the above recipe, still in a muffin tin, in fairy cake-size paper cases. Fill each case to just below the top and try to avoid spilling any down the sides.

Shorten the cooking time to approximately 16 minutes. You will need to bake a second part-batch.

MOIST MALTED APPLE AND RAISIN BRAN BUNS

There is something decidedly wholesome about these moist little buns! They taste lovely just as they are or split with a little butter once they are day or two old. As well as a delicious tea-time treat they are also great for lunch boxes and picnics, or as a handy quick breakfast.

You will need a greased 12-cup muffin tin.

Preheat the oven to 160°C (fan oven) or equivalent.

Whiz the butter and sugar together until well mixed and fluffy. Add the ground almonds and whiz to mix and then add the wholemeal flour. Whiz again. Sieve half of the plain flour over the mixture, add the eggs and then sieve the rest of the flour and baking powder over the top. Whiz to combine, and add the malt extract and bran. Whiz briefly and add the apple. Whiz until smooth and glossy and well mixed. Remove the blade from the machine and stir in the raisins.

Using a dessertspoon, divide the mixture between the cups in the prepared tin.

Cover loosely with greaseproof paper, tucking it under the tin to secure: keep the tension loose enough to avoid the paper pressing on the buns as they rise. Bake for 20 minutes or until golden brown and a skewer inserted comes out clean.

Leave in the tin for a few moments and then transfer to a wire rack: cover with a clean tea towel to keep them moist as they cool.

Store in an airtight container when cold.

110g (4oz) butter, softened
50g (2oz) unrefined caster sugar
50g (2oz) ground almonds
50g (2oz) wholemeal flour
110g (4oz) plain flour
2 eggs
2 teaspoons baking powder
2 tablespoons barley malt extract
1 generously heaped tablespoon wheat bran
175g (6oz) dessert apple, finely chopped
110g (4oz) raisins

ORANGE AND ALMOND BUNS

These buns are so delicious, and very versatile. Serve with a cup of tea or as part of a tea-time spread. Take them into the garden or on picnics. Alternatively, serve them as a pudding with some natural or Greek yoghurt. They are also wonderful for breakfast. They store well for up to a week, becoming slightly moister and stickier and more flavourful.

2 oranges, not too large:
around about 150g
(5oz) of pulped fruit is
ideal

110g (4oz butter),
softened

110g (4oz) unrefined
caster sugar

110g (4oz) plain flour

110g (4 oz) ground
almonds

2 teaspoons cream of
tartar

1 teaspoon bicarbonate of
soda

2 eggs, beaten

You will need a greased 12-cup muffin tin.

Preheat the oven to 160°C (fan oven) or equivalent.

Take one of the oranges, remove the little green stalk part and put into a pan of cold water. Bring to the boil and simmer, partially covered, for about half to three quarters of an hour or until it is soft. Cool and cut into several pieces. Remove any pips and central pith, and any bits of membrane that will come away easily. Then put the rest into a food processor and whiz until it is an almost smooth, pale, orange-flecked puree.

Peel or grate all the zest from the second orange (a lemon zester works best) and add to the puree. Add the butter and sugar and whiz until smooth. Finally, add the flour, ground almonds, cream of tartar, bicarbonate of soda and eggs and whiz until smooth and thoroughly mixed.

Spoon into the prepared tin. Bake for 12–15 minutes, or until pale golden on top, risen and firm to the touch, and a skewer inserted comes out clean.

Cool on a wire rack and eat warm or cold. The buns will keep in an airtight tin for up to a week.

ORANGE AND ALMOND CAKE

You will need a greased 18cm (7in) loose-bottomed cake tin and some greaseproof paper. Preheat the oven to 160°C (fan oven) or equivalent.

Make the cake mixture in exactly the same way as for the previous recipe, **Orange and Almond Buns**. Pour the mixture into the prepared tin and wrap the whole tin round with greaseproof paper. Bake for about 1¼ hours, or until golden on top, firm to the touch, and a skewer inserted comes out clean.

Cool on a wire rack and eat warm or cold. The cake will keep in an airtight tin for up to a week.

GREEN TEA BUNS

These buns are based on an unusual cake popular in Japan. There are many variations, some rather complicated and some with American-style frosting. This is a very simple version and is light and moist, not too sweet, and comes complete with a useful amount of antioxidants, which, happily, are able to survive the baking process.

Green tea powder, or matcha, *is the best tea to use. This is the tea used in Japanese tea ceremonies, which is made from the very best, fresh green tips of leaves grown in shade and stone-ground into a delicate powder. The tea is brewed in a ceremonial pot and whisked with a special bamboo tea whisk or* chasen, *which is made from a single piece of bamboo.*

Matcha will give the buns a quirky greenish tinge, which fades to a kind of sludgy buff after baking, and an elusive, subtle flavour. The slight downside is that it is rather expensive to buy and can be quite difficult to get hold of.

---

2 teaspoons green tea powder (matcha)

2 tablespoons hot water

110g (4oz) butter

110g (4oz) unrefined caster sugar

175g (6oz) plain flour

2 very fresh eggs

2 teaspoons cream of tartar

1 teaspoon bicarbonate of soda

You will need a greased 12-cup muffin tin.

Preheat the oven to 160°C (fan oven) or equivalent.

Put the green tea powder into a cup. Pour a little boiling water into another cup and transfer 2 tablespoons into the cup containing the tea powder. Set aside to brew and cool.

Whiz the butter and sugar together thoroughly in the food processor until light and fluffy. Sieve half of the flour over the top and add the eggs. Sieve the rest of the flour, cream of tartar and bicarbonate of soda over the top and whiz. Add the cooled (but not completely cold) tea and whiz until everything is fully mixed and smooth. Stop the processor a couple of times and scrape the mixture down from the sides with a flexible spatula.

Using a dessertspoon, divide the mixture equally between the 12 cups of the muffin tin. Bake for approximately 12–15 minutes until risen and golden and a skewer inserted comes out clean.

Leave the buns to settle in the tin for a few minutes – they are very fragile at this stage. Once they have begun to contract from the sides of the tin, lever them out very carefully using a small palette knife and transfer to a wire rack to finish cooling.

Store in an airtight container when completely cold.

HOMEMADE MERINGUES

There is something very appealing about pale, buff-coloured meringues: they just look so deliciously homemade and appetising. Some people can be a bit sniffy about meringues that aren't sparkling white, but although it is very satisfying to pull off a pure white version, it *can* prompt comments like: 'You haven't *made* these, have you?', 'They're bought, aren't they?' In the end it's much less stressful all round to use unrefined caster sugar plus it makes them look and taste absolutely lovely.

Despite what you might think, there is nothing difficult or scary about making a meringue – they are as easy as anything. What is more, they are inexpensive to make and only have two ingredients, they keep for up to six weeks in an airtight container *and* the finished meringues look impressive and taste delicious.

There are a few really simple pointers to bear in mind: after that it's a sure thing!

- The egg whites must be really fresh – not from ancient old eggs lurking at the back of the fridge.

- The bowl, whisk and spoons must be scrupulously clean and grease free: make sure they have all been recently washed, preferably in the dishwasher, and that they are perfectly dry.

- Whisk the egg whites until you can do the classic thing of turning the bowl upside down without them falling out, but equally *don't over beat them either*.

- It's important that the sugar is added *gradually*.

- Bake at a low temperature and line your baking sheet with lightly oiled greaseproof paper (or similar baking paper).

It's surprising how far egg white will go, so the following recipe is for just two egg whites, but you can increase the quantities proportionally. Some people fold the sugar in after the first spoonful, instead of whisking it, and you can do that if you like.

If you want your meringues to be explosively crisp and dry throughout, flatten and spread out the blobs of meringue on the baking tray. If you prefer them to have that dangerously moreish, delectable squidgy centre, then mound them up so they are higher and cover a smaller area.

MAKES ABOUT 12 INDIVIDUAL MERINGUES (OR 1 LARGE ONE)

Very small amount of flavourless oil, such as rapeseed, for greasing
2 very fresh egg whites
110g (4oz) unrefined caster sugar

You will need an electric hand whisk or manual rotary whisk and a large, lined baking sheet.

Preheat the oven to 100°C (fan oven) or equivalent.

Brush a very small amount of oil over the lined baking tray.

Whisk the egg white until stiff – or it might be more accurate to say lightly stiff, see above.

Add a tablespoonful of sugar, whisk it in and continue whisking in a spoonful at a time until all the sugar is incorporated – again, don't over whisk it each time.

Using a dessertspoon, arrange single blobs of meringue on the prepared tray – space them out, not because they will spread, they won't, but you need to give each meringue a bit of room for the hot air to circulate.

Bake for an hour or until you can peel them off the paper easily. Leave them in the oven with the oven door slightly open until the oven has gone cold so they can finish drying out.

Once they are completely cold they will just lift off the tray. Store in an airtight container.

Note on piping meringue
If you prefer, you can pipe the meringue in whirls onto the baking tray, but you may feel it makes the meringues look a bit too formal and creates needless extra washing up!

How to serve the meringues
Eat just as they are or:

- Sandwich two together with whipped cream or clotted cream (even better).

- Pop on top of a lemon curd tart for a Speedy Individual Lemon Meringue Tart.

- Break into smallish pieces and mix with sliced strawberries and whipped or clotted cream in pretty glass dishes for an Eton Mess.

- Break into smallish pieces and mix with sliced mixed fruit (such as strawberries, peaches, kiwi fruit and a few raspberries) and whipped or clotted cream in pretty glass dishes for a kind of Pavlova Sundae.

- Make a Snowball Ice Cream: put a scoop of vanilla ice cream in a bowl, spoon a dollop of whipped or clotted cream over it and arrange a meringue on top at a jaunty angle.

Mrs Simkins' Macaroons: Almond or Coconut

Here are a couple of old-fashioned tea-time favourites. They should be slightly crispy on the outside and moist and chewy on the inside. When you are making and baking macaroons they are a bit like an easy-going meringue: not as fussy, but with certain similarities.

If you can get hold of any rice paper (and it's not easy to find) you can use that to line your baking tray. Once you have allowed the baked macaroons to settle for a while, you can then manoeuvre the whole sheet of rice paper with the macaroons still attached from the baking tray to the cooling rack. Once the macaroons are completely cold, cut each one free and trim the paper neatly with sharp kitchen scissors.

Otherwise, use lightly oiled greaseproof paper to line the tray, leave the macaroons to firm and settle for a while when they first come out of the oven, then peel them away from the greaseproof paper whilst they are still warm. Oil the greaseproof paper by putting it on the baking tray and brushing it very lightly with a mild, flavourless oil, using a pastry brush.

ALMOND MACAROONS

These are beautifully almondy and very traditional looking.

MAKES 9

3 egg whites
½ teaspoon almond
   extract
150g (5oz) unrefined
   caster sugar
175g (6oz) ground
   almonds

Blanched almonds to
   decorate

You will need a baking tray, lined with lightly oiled greaseproof paper (see above).

Preheat the oven to 160°C (fan oven) or equivalent.

Separate the eggs and try to avoid including any stringy parts in the white. If any does slip through, remove it between two teaspoons.

Add the almond extract to the egg whites and whisk with an electric or hand-held rotary whisk until firm, but not too stiff and dry. Whisk in the sugar gradually. Fold in the ground almonds with a tablespoon. The mixture will become quite stiff.

Get yourself a large plate and, using 2 dessertspoons, arrange 9 equal blobs of the mixture on the plate.

Wet your hands and pick up each blob carefully, roll it into a ball and put it on the prepared baking tray. The mixture is quite 'loose' but as long as your hands are wet it's an easy (if slightly messy) operation. Make sure the balls are spaced out on the baking tray, to allow for spreading. Put an almond on the top of each one, pressing it in lightly.

Bake for about 25 minutes, or until they are golden brown and the tops feel firm. Don't overcook them or they will be too dry inside and you will miss out of the lovely moist chewiness.

Don't try to move them as they are very fragile at this stage: leave them to cool and firm up on the tray for a few moments and then peel away from the greaseproof paper.

Transfer to a wire rack to finish cooling and once cold, store in an airtight container.

Coconut Macaroons

These are very light, and very lovely.

You will need a baking tray, lined with lightly oiled greaseproof paper.

Preheat the oven to 160°C (fan oven) or equivalent.

Whisk the egg whites with an electric or hand-held rotary whisk until firm, but not stiff and dry. Whisk in the sugar gradually. Fold in the desiccated coconut with a tablespoon. The mixture will become quite stiff.

Get yourself a large plate and, using 2 dessertspoons, arrange 9 equal blobs of the mixture on the plate.

MAKES 9

3 egg whites
150g (5oz) unrefined
  caster sugar
175g (6oz) desiccated
  coconut
Glace cherries, cut in half,
  to decorate (optional)

Wet your hands and pick up each blob carefully, roll it into a ball and put it on the prepared baking tray. The mixture is quite 'loose' but as long as your hands are wet it's an easy (if slightly messy) operation. Make sure the balls are spaced out on the baking tray, to allow for spreading. Put half a glace cherry on the top of each one, pressing it in lightly.

Bake for about 25–30 minutes, or until they are golden brown and the tops feel firm. As with the previous recipe, don't overcook these.

Don't try to move them as they are very fragile at this stage: leave them to cool and firm up on the tray for a few moments and then peel away from the greaseproof paper.

Transfer to a wire rack to finish cooling and once cold, store in an airtight container.

Chocolate-drizzled Macaroons

Instead of decorating the **Almond** or **Coconut Macaroons** with an almond or a cherry, try drizzling melted dark chocolate over them instead.

Break up **50g good quality, dark chocolate** and put it into a heatproof bowl. Melt the chocolate in the microwave on high, in 30-second bursts: usually, it will take between 1½ and 2 minutes altogether.

Using a spoon, drizzle the chocolate over the now cold macaroons in diagonal lines.

SCRIPTURE CAKE

Here is something a bit different! This cake is made entirely from ingredients that appear in the Bible. In the original scripture cake recipes, none of the ingredients was mentioned by name: you had to find out what each one was by looking up all the references! This is slightly tweaked from an original recipe.

The figs have been replaced with dates, as figs can be a bit too seedy in a cake. (Fig rolls are a different matter!) The dates give a lovely flavour: they should be in keeping as palm trees are mentioned frequently in the Bible. Dates themselves are referred to in Psalm 92, see below. The original finely chopped almonds have been changed to ground almonds, and the set honey to the runny version. Milk has been replaced by water: this is because the original recipe didn't use the boiling technique, which is used here. Boiling the fruit with the butter, sugar and water makes it lovely and succulent and cuts out the arm aching stirring of what was quite a stiff mixture.

Eat it freshly baked and fluffy or wrap it in greaseproof paper and store in an airtight tin for a few days to give it a denser texture and more developed flavour. This is very like a Christmas cake in character: in fact you may like to make it as your Christmas cake one year.

175g (6oz) butter	Judges 5:25, last clause
200g (7oz) soft brown sugar	Jeremiah 6:20
1 tablespoon honey	I Samuel 14:25
350g (12oz) raisins	I Samuel 30:12
175g (6oz) dried, stoned dates	Psalms 92:12–14
2 teaspoons mixed spice	II Chronicles 9:9
5 tablespoons water	Genesis 1:20
150g (5oz) each plain and wholemeal flour	I Kings 4:22
2 teaspoons baking powder	Amos 4:5
3 fresh eggs, beaten	Jeremiah 17:11
50g (2oz) ground almonds	Numbers 17:8
¼ teaspoon salt	Leviticus 2:13

You will need a greased, loose-bottomed 23cm (9in) cake tin.

Preheat the oven to 150°C (fan oven) or equivalent.

Cut the butter into small pieces. Put the butter, sugar, honey, raisins, dates, spice and water into a large, wide saucepan (or wide wok-style pan). Heat gently, stirring to get it started and then occasionally, until the butter has melted, and then turn it up a notch to a simmer. Let it bubble away gently for 5 minutes until the sugar has lost its grittiness and the fruit is plumping up nicely. Stir it frequently.

Leave to cool. Once it is completely cold, sieve in some of the plain flour and baking powder to cover the surface, and add the eggs. Sieve a little more plain flour over the top and stir thoroughly. Add the rest of the flour, the wholemeal flour, ground almonds and salt. Mix everything together really well.

Spoon into the prepared tin. Smooth the top with the back of a wet tablespoon. Wrap the tin loosely in greaseproof paper, tucking it underneath the tin to secure. Bake for 1¼ hours, possibly a fraction longer, depending on your oven, or until firm to the touch and a skewer inserted comes out clean.

Leave the cake in the tin to settle for a while and then remove and cool on a wire rack.

THE THREE BEARS CHRISTMAS CAKE

If the Three Bears were to make their own Christmas cake, they would probably make a great big, generous cake for Daddy Bear, a nice medium-sized cake for Mummy Bear and a teeny, tiny, little one for Baby Bear. It's useful to be able to make different sized Christmas cakes: you can share them around the family and give the smaller ones away as gifts. Options are also given for round, square and bar shaped cakes.

Big, generous cake
This recipe will make one traditional 23cm (9in) round cake, baked in a loose-bottomed tin. If you would prefer to use a square tin for the same amount of mixture you will need a 20cm (8in) one. (The discrepancy in measurement is due to something complicated to do with surface area!)

Medium-sized cake
Alternatively, you can make two medium-sized cakes. There is enough mixture to distribute equally between two 18cm (7in) round, loose-bottomed cake tins or two 450g (1lb) loaf tins. You can use one of each if you prefer: whichever you choose, the two cakes will bake happily side by side.

Miniature cakes
You could also make some dinky round miniature Christmas cakes in a 12-cup muffin tin, or miniature bar cakes in some of those tiny loaf tins you can buy, usually in packs of 4. Since these are quite pricey, you might like to use a combination of the muffin tin and the loaf tins together and make a mixed batch. (You don't actually need cake cases but Christmassy ones can look very festive for the round ones.) The mixture is enough for 30 little cakes, but you may prefer to make 1 medium-sized cake with half the mixture and 15 little cakes with the other half. When filling the medium tin, whether it is round or loaf-shaped, fill the mixture to a depth of 4.5cm (1¾in). Bake the medium and small sizes separately as they will need different cooking times, otherwise by the time you have got the smaller ones out of the oven you have lost too much heat.

Put the raisins, currants and sultanas, and dried cherries if you are using them, into a large saucepan with the butter, sugar, spices and water. Bring it all to the boil and simmer gently for 5 minutes. Leave to cool.

Grease the tin(s) of your choice (line the large and medium ones).

Preheat the oven to 150°C (fan oven) or equivalent *for all cake sizes*.

Once cold, stir in the brandy and cut the glace cherries, if you are using them, into quarters and dust in a little of the flour. Sieve the rest of the flour into the mixture with the eggs. Stir in the floured cherries and candied peel. Stir everything together thoroughly.

Pour the mixture into the prepared tin(s) and tuck a piece of greaseproof paper loosely round the big and medium cakes. (There is no need to do this with the miniature ones.)

Bake the big cake for 1¼ hours until it is firm to the touch and a skewer inserted comes out clean. You may find a square cake will take slightly longer: watch the corners as they can catch and be prepared to turn the cake round if your oven doesn't heat evenly.

Bake the medium cakes together, side-by-side in the oven, for about 1¼ hours. Test earlier if your oven is very fierce. The round and the loaf versions will take about the same time to cook.

If you are baking one medium cake by itself it will still take about 1¼ hours. Again, test earlier if your oven is very fierce.

For the miniature cakes, fill the tins barely half full, as you want them to be fairly flat on top and not too domed. Smooth the top of each little cake gently with a teaspoon and bake for about 20 minutes. You may find the little loaf shapes bake a fraction more quickly. As always, they are ready when firm to the touch and a skewer inserted comes out clean.

Leave the cakes to cool in the tin and contract before turning out onto a wire rack to cool completely. The cakes in the miniature loaf tins should come out very easily. There is no need to poke about with a knife, which may scratch the tins: give them a sharp tap on the bottom if they seem reluctant.

When cold, wrap the cakes in clean greaseproof paper and store in a tin until ready to ice, just before Christmas. (Try not to bake the tiny ones too early, as they can dry out more quickly.)

Useful Notes
• If you are using dried sour cherries rather than glacé cherries, you may also like to try dried cranberries for a change: they are absolutely delicious.

• You may wonder why the large and medium cakes take the same length of time to cook: this is because the tins are filled to a similar depth.

Finally, just to warm you up for all those cracker jokes to come:
What is the best thing to put into a Christmas cake? *Teeth.*

A few days before Christmas cover your cake with marzipan and, if you have time, leave it to dry out slightly for a day or two before icing. You will need to cover the cake with apricot or marmalade glaze before you put on the marzipan. You can buy readymade marzipan and roll-on icing but it is really easy to make the marzipan and icing yourself, and they then become elements of the cake that taste lovely in their own right. You have something you actually want to eat rather than just a bit of decoration.

175g (6oz) raisins
175g (6oz) currants
175g (6oz) sultanas
175g (6oz) butter
225g (8oz) soft dark brown sugar
½ teaspoon each of cinnamon, ground ginger and mixed spice
220ml (7fl oz) water
30ml (1fl oz) brandy
50g (2oz) glacé or dried sour cherries

300g (10oz) fresh self-raising flour
or
300g (10oz) plain flour
2 teaspoons baking powder

3 very fresh eggs, beaten
50g (2oz) candied peel, finely sliced and cut into small pieces

APRICOT OR MARMALADE GLAZE

This helps to stick the almond paste to the cake. Warm **2 tablespoons of apricot jam or marmalade** (you will need to remove any shreds of peel) until it becomes slightly runny. Brush over the top and sides of your cake with a pastry brush if you have one. If not, use a dessertspoon to spoon it over the top of the cake and then use the back of the spoon to smooth it down and over the sides.

HOMEMADE ALMOND PASTE OR MARZIPAN

Almond paste is very simple to make at home and tastes quite different from the bought version: it's fresh and almondy and not at all cloying. You can make this by hand but a food processor makes it easier.

THIS RECIPE IS SUFFICIENT TO COVER A 23CM (9IN) ROUND CAKE OR TWO 18CM (7IN) ROUND CAKES.

110g (4oz) icing sugar
225g (8oz) ground
   almonds
1 very fresh egg yolk
¼–½ teaspoon natural
   almond extract
3 tablespoons lemon juice

Sieve the icing sugar into a bowl and stir in the ground almonds. Tip carefully into the bowl of your food processor. Add the egg yolk, almond extract and lemon juice. Whiz for a few seconds and then stop and scrape the mixture from around the sides into the centre and whiz again. Repeat this a few times. The second the mixture congregates together on the side of the bowl, stop whizzing immediately! If you carry on it will become oily and over-processed.

Take the mixture out of the processor, gathering up any loose crumbs and put it onto a large board or worktop dusted with icing sugar. Knead it gently for a few seconds and then roll it into a ball, dusting with more icing sugar as necessary. Dust your rolling pin with icing sugar and carefully roll it flat until it is just a fraction bigger in circumference than the whole surface area of your cake including the top and sides.

Lift it carefully onto the glazed cake. You might find it easier to lift it by rolling it round your rolling pin and then unrolling it again over the cake. Using both hands, gently and carefully smooth and shape it round the cake and trim the extra from around the bottom of the cake with a knife. Sieve a little more icing sugar over the top and smooth it gently with your rolling pin: if you happen to have a child's rolling pin it will make this bit much easier. Wrap in clean greaseproof paper and keep in a cool dry place for a couple of days before icing.

CHRISTMAS CAKE ICING

If you like to eat a bit of icing with your cake you may have found the ready-roll fondant type icing can be a bit cloying. The more traditional royal icing can go rock hard after a couple of days and you can be in danger of breaking your teeth! A fairly stiff glace icing made with lemon juice is a lot easier on the teeth and tastes good too.

If you aren't very good at fancy icing, don't worry: this is the perfect opportunity to do a bit of 'rough icing' instead. You don't need to do any piping at all, just pile the icing on, rough it up a bit, and pretend the top of the cake is a snow scene! This has several benefits: it's quick and easy, children can have fun helping, and you can use all your favourite decorations!

You will need large palette knife or a flexible 30cm (12in) ruler.

Sieve the icing sugar into a large bowl. Make a well in the middle and pour in the lemon juice. Using a wooden spoon gradually stir the juice into the icing sugar until it is all mixed in: it takes longer than you think, but keep at it. When it is all mixed in keep stirring until it is smooth and glossy. It should be fairly stiff but still just pourable.

Try icing the cake on a large dinner plate, turned upside down. You can leave it there until the icing has set and it is then relatively easy to lift it onto its serving plate, using a couple of fish slices. This saves getting everything too messy.

THIS RECIPE IS SUFFICIENT TO COVER A 23CM (9IN) ROUND CAKE OR TWO 18CM (7IN) ROUND CAKES.

225g (8oz) icing sugar
Approximately 4 tablespoons lemon juice, sieved through a tea strainer

Spoon the icing on top of your cake a little at a time and help it gently over the top and sides with the back of a tablespoon. It helps if the spoon is wet so have a jug of water to hand.

Once the cake is covered, smooth the icing gently with the palette knife or flexible ruler. If you do want to make a snow scene, allow the icing to set slightly and then rough up the surface slightly with the back of a spoon to simulate drifts of snow. If you like, you can make a path across the middle (this may take several attempts) and arrange your decorations on either side of the path. At this stage, it's quite difficult to manoeuvre the cake into a tin, so cover with a large cake dome or cover loosely with foil.

The teeny little Christmas cakes look best if you just ice the tops rather than take the marzipan and icing down the sides as well. Use a 10cm (4in) plain round or fluted cutter to cut out the marzipan for the round cakes and a mini loaf tin to cut out the marzipan to the right size for the loaf-shaped ones. Decorate the little cakes with a single birthday cake candle in white or red – this looks lovely whether the cakes are given away individually or arranged on a plate together for Christmas tea. If you made the bar-shaped cake in a 450g (1lb) loaf tin, again, this shape tends to look better with icing on top only.

SIMPLE SIMNEL CAKE

This is a very simple, straightforward version of Simnel Cake that would be perfect for tea on Easter Sunday. You may like to make the cake a couple of weeks before and top it with the marzipan just before Easter. Simnel Cake was traditionally served on Mothering Sunday but in recent years it seems to have moved on to Easter itself. The 11 balls on top of the cake represent each of the disciples, but without Judas. You can make the cake look even lovelier by filling in the space in the middle with fluffy Easter chicks and coloured eggs or fresh spring flowers from the garden.

200g (7oz) raisins
200g (7oz) currants
200g (7oz) sultanas
175g (6oz) butter
250g (8oz) soft dark
  brown sugar
½ teaspoon each of
  cinnamon, ground ginger
  and mixed spice
250ml (8fl oz) water

300g (10oz) self-raising
  flour
or
300g (10oz) plain flour
2 teaspoons baking
  powder

3 very fresh eggs, beaten

Grease and line a 23cm (9in) loose-bottomed cake tin.

Preheat the oven to 150°C (fan oven) or equivalent.

Put all the raisins, currants and sultanas into a large saucepan with the butter, sugar, spices and water. Bring it all to the boil and simmer gently for 5 minutes. Leave to cool.

Sieve the flour into the mixture and add the eggs. Stir everything together thoroughly.

Pour the mixture into the prepared tin and cover loosely with greaseproof paper, tucking it underneath to secure. Bake for 1¼ hours until it is firm to the touch and a skewer inserted comes out clean.

Leave to cool in the tin slightly before turning transferring to a wire rack to cool completely.

Apricot or Marmalade Glaze
Spread this over the top of the cake before you put on the marzipan. Keep back a little to stick on the marzipan balls.

INDIVIDUAL SIMNEL CAKES AND MINIATURE CAKES

You could also make round miniature Simnel Cakes in a 12-cup muffin tin, or miniature bar cakes in mini-loaf tins. You might like to use a combination of the muffin tin and the loaf tins together and make a mixed batch. The mixture is enough for 30 little cakes, but you may prefer to make one medium-sized cake with half the mixture and 15 little cakes with the other half. When filling the medium tin, whether it is round or loaf-shaped, fill the mixture to a depth of 4.5cm (1¾in). Bake the medium and small sizes separately as they will need different cooking times, otherwise by the time you have got the smaller ones out of the oven you have lost too much heat.

For the miniature cakes, fill the tins barely half full, as you want them to be fairly flat on top and not too domed. Smooth the top of each little cake gently with a teaspoon and bake for about 20 minutes. You may find the little loaf shapes bake a fraction more quickly. As always, they are ready when firm to the touch and a skewer inserted comes out clean.

Leave the cakes to cool in the tin and contract before turning out onto a wire rack to cool completely. The miniature loaf tin cakes should come out very easily. There is no need to poke about with a knife, which may scratch the tins: give them a sharp tap on the bottom if they seem reluctant.

Use a 10cm (4in) plain round or fluted cutter to cut out the marzipan for the round cakes and a mini loaf tin to cut out the marzipan to the right size for the loaf-shaped ones. Decorate the little cakes with a single marzipan ball, a single sugar coated mini egg, a single fresh flower, or vary the batch and have a selection of decorations: you might like to use fluffy chicks on some of the cakes.

Baking a half quantity of cake mixture
If you would like to bake a half quantity of the cake mixture, to make one medium cake, perhaps, halve all the ingredients and use two eggs.

PASTRIES

The very word 'pastries' is enough to make you think of old-fashioned tiered cake stands and silver cake forks. The recipes that follow are for a tempting selection of nostalgic pastry treats.

JAM AND LEMON CURD TARTS

*Instead of using a standard tart tin for these, bake them in a mini-muffin tin. You then get dinky little deep jam tarts that could come straight from a high class patisserie counter. If you prefer, you can make these with sweet shortcrust: see **Apple Crumble Tarts**.*

MAKES ABOUT 16

160g (6oz) plain flour
Pinch salt
40g (1½oz) butter, cold
  and cut into small pieces
40g (1½oz) block vegetable
  shortening, cold and cut
  into small pieces
3 tablespoons cold water

Plus: jam (raspberry,
  strawberry, apricot or
  blackcurrant) or lemon
  curd

You will need a 6cm (2½in) fluted cutter and a greased 12-cup mini-muffin tin.

Preheat the oven to 180°C (fan oven) or equivalent.

Sieve the flour and salt carefully into the bowl of your food processor and add the butter and vegetable shortening. Whiz into fine crumbs. Add the water and whiz until the mixture is starting to come together. Turn it out onto a floured board and knead it lightly until it forms a ball.

Roll it out gently with a floured rolling pin to a thickness of just less than half a centimetre. Cut out circles with the cutter and put them into the prepared tins.

Fill each tart with no more than a slightly rounded teaspoon of jam or lemon curd: they need to be generously filled but not so much that as the jam or lemon curd heats up it boils out of the tarts.

Bake for 12–14 minutes until the pastry is lightly golden. Keep the tart tins level as you take them out of the oven: if you tilt them the practically molten jam or curd can spill out of the tarts at this stage. Remove from the tin with a small palette knife and cool on a wire rack.

Caution: on no account eat the tarts whilst the jam or curd is still liquidy! You will have the roof of your mouth off!

SPEEDY INDIVIDUAL LEMON MERINGUE TARTS

Pop a **Homemade Meringue** on top of a **Lemon Curd Tart** for an instant baby lemon meringue.

LITTLE TREACLE TARTS

Preheat the oven to 180°C (fan oven) or equivalent.

Making the filling
Warm the golden syrup and brown sugar gently in a fairly roomy saucepan over a moderate heat for a couple of minutes until it is of pouring consistency. This will take a little longer in cool weather as the syrup will be firmer to start with.

Remove from the heat and stir in the lemon juice, vanilla and salt. Once the lemon juice is all incorporated, stir in the breadcrumbs, a few at a time, so they are all coated with syrup. Spoon the mixture into the prepared pastry case and smooth into position. Bake for around 30 minutes, until the top is browning very slightly.

Making the pastry
Sieve the flour carefully into the bowl of your food processor and add the butter, vegetable shortening and salt. Whiz into fine crumbs. Add the water and whiz again. Once it is starting to form big crumbs and clump together, turn it out onto a lightly floured board and knead it gently into a ball.

Roll it gently with a lightly floured rolling pin to a thickness of just less than half a centimetre.

Cut out circles of pastry using a 6cm (2½in) fluted cutter and put into the prepared tins, firming them down gently so that the finished tarts will be a good shape rather than just little saucers of pastry. Put a teaspoonful of the treacle mixture into each tart.

Bake for about 15 minutes. Remove from the tin with a small palette knife and cool on a wire rack.

✓ Useful Note: Making the Breadcrumbs
Remove the crusts from the bread and tear the bread into pieces. Whiz briefly in the food processor until fine.

MAKES 16

For the filling
4 tablespoons golden syrup
40g (1½oz) soft dark brown sugar
Juice of 1 lemon, sieved
1 teaspoon vanilla extract
Pinch salt
About 110g (4oz) white or light wholemeal breadcrumbs (no crusts)

For the pastry
160g (6oz) plain flour
40g (1½oz) butter, cold and cut into small pieces
40g (1½oz) block vegetable shortening, cold and cut into small pieces
Pinch salt
3 tablespoons cold water

BAKEWELL TARTS

If you are fond of almonds, there is nothing like a Bakewell Tart or two and a cup of fairly strong tea at tea-time. The crisp pastry and squidgy frangipane matched with the beautiful flavours of almond and raspberry are a terrific combination.

MAKES 15–16

For the pastry
110g (4oz) plain flour
Pinch salt
50g (2oz) cold butter, cut into small pieces
1 rounded dessertspoon unrefined caster sugar
2 tablespoons cold water

For the Bakewell topping (or frangipane)
75g (3oz) butter, softened
75g (3oz) unrefined caster sugar
40g (1½oz) plain flour
1 egg, beaten
½ teaspoon almond extract
110g (4oz) ground almonds
2 tablespoons milk

Plus: about 3 tablespoons raspberry jam, preferably seedless

You will need one or two greased 12-cup tart tins and a 6cm (2½in) cutter, fluted or plain. If you only have one tin you will need to bake a second part batch.

Preheat the oven to 180°C (fan oven) or equivalent.

Making the pastry
Sieve the flour and salt carefully into the bowl of your food processor and add the butter. Whiz into fine crumbs and add the sugar. Whiz again briefly. Add the water and whiz until the mixture is starting to come together. Turn it out onto a floured board and knead it lightly until it forms a ball.

Roll it out gently with a floured rolling pin to a thickness of just less than half a centimetre.

Cut out 12 circles with the cutter. Transfer them to the prepared tart tin and firm them down gently.

Making the Bakewell topping
Whiz the butter and sugar together until light and fluffy. Sieve in the flour and add the egg and almond extract. Whiz briefly and add the ground almonds and milk. Whiz again until thoroughly mixed.

Assembling the tarts
Spoon a little jam into the base of each tart and top with a teaspoonful of the Bakewell mixture. Smooth it gently with the back of the teaspoon, especially round the edges so the jam won't bubble through.

Bake for about 15–18 minutes or until the Bakewell topping is just tinged golden and risen and the pastry is cooked. Leave to settle for a few moments then ease from the tin with a small palette knife and cool on a wire rack. Eat warm (not hot) or cold.

ALMOND TARTS

Bake the **Bakewell Tarts** as in the previous recipe but, instead of leaving them plain, scatter flaked almonds over the top of the tarts and press down lightly before they go into the oven. They look beautiful and taste delicious with a nicely contrasting crunch.

Coconut Tarts

These are made in exactly the same way as the Bakewell Tarts and Almond Tarts but with desiccated coconut for texture and flavour rather than the ground almonds and almond extract.

MAKES 15–16

For the pastry
110g (4oz) plain flour
Pinch salt
50g (2oz) cold butter, cut
  into small pieces
1 rounded dessertspoon
  unrefined caster sugar
2 tablespoons cold water

**For the coconut
  topping**
75g (3oz) butter, softened
75g (3oz) sugar
40g (1½oz) plain flour
1 egg, beaten
110g (4oz) desiccated
  coconut
2 tablespoons milk

Plus: about 3 tablespoons
  raspberry jam,
  preferably seedless

You will need one or two greased 12-cup tart tins and a 6cm (2½in) cutter, fluted or plain. If you only have one tin you will need to bake a second part batch.

Preheat the oven to 180°C (fan oven) or equivalent.

Making the pastry
Sieve the flour and salt carefully into the bowl of your food processor and add the butter. Whiz into fine crumbs and add the sugar. Whiz again briefly. Add the water and whiz until the mixture is starting to come together. Turn it out onto a floured board and knead it lightly until it forms a ball.

Roll it out gently with a floured rolling pin to a thickness of just less than half a centimetre.

Cut out 12 circles with the cutter. Transfer them to the prepared tart tin and firm them down gently.

Making the coconut topping
Whiz the butter and sugar together until light and fluffy. Sieve in the flour and add the egg. Whiz briefly and add the desiccated coconut and milk. Whiz again until thoroughly mixed.

Assembling the tarts
Spoon a little jam into the base of each tart and top with a teaspoonful of the coconut mixture. Smooth it gently with the back of the teaspoon, especially round the edges so the jam won't bubble through.

Bake for about 15–18 minutes or until the coconut topping is just tinged golden and risen and the pastry is cooked. Leave to settle for a few moments then ease from the tin with a small palette knife and cool on a wire rack. Eat warm (not hot) or cold.

LITTLE PICNIC APPLE PIES

These little apple pies are perfect for picnics and are lovely served with cream or ice cream. If you aren't fond of sultanas, leave them out.

You will need two fluted cutters: 7½cm (3in) and 6cm (2½in), and a greased 12-cup tart tin.

Preheat the oven to 180°C (fan oven) or equivalent.

Making the pastry
Sieve the flour and salt carefully into the bowl of your food processor and add the butter. Whiz into fine crumbs and add the sugar. Whiz again briefly. Add the water and whiz until the mixture is starting to come together. Turn it out onto a floured board and knead it lightly until it forms a ball.

Roll it out gently with a floured rolling pin to a thickness of just less than half a centimetre.

Cut out 12 circles with the larger cutter (for the pies) and 12 circles with the smaller cutter (for the lids).

Making the filling
Melt the butter and sugar together over a gentle heat. Cut the apple into small chunks and stir into the melted butter mixture. Try to get all the pieces coated with the butter. Add the sultanas and, again, try to get them all coated in butter too. Put a lid on the pan and cook gently until the apple is just starting to soften and the sultanas are starting to plump up.

Assembling the pies
Divide the apple filling equally between the pastry cases. Try to fill them as generously as you can whilst still being able to get the lids on!

Brush the edge of each lid with water and press them gently onto the pies, sealing the edges. If you would like a nice crispy lid, brush each pie with water and sprinkle a little caster sugar over the top. Make a little hole in each lid with the point of a knife.

Bake for about 12–15 minutes or until pale golden. Remove from the tin and cool on a wire rack.

MAKES 12

For the pastry
160g (6oz) plain flour
Pinch salt
80g (3oz) cold butter
1 dessertspoon unrefined caster sugar
3 tablespoons cold water

For the filling
Generous 10g (½oz) butter
1 rounded teaspoon soft brown sugar
2–3 dessert apples, peeled and cored, approximately 200g (7oz) prepared weight – Cox's are perfect
Generous 10g (½oz) sultanas

A little more caster sugar for finishing (optional)

APPLE CRUMBLE TARTS

These are nice to make for a weekend tea: a winning combination of little apple tarts and well-loved apple crumble. The extra short, sweetened pastry really does make a difference: they are not quite as special made with ordinary shortcrust.

You really only need 12 teaspoons of crumble for this recipe: this equates to a little less than a quarter of a 225g (8oz) mix. Instructions have been given for the full amount, as it is very difficult to mix the very small amount needed successfully. This way, you have enough to make a crumble for lunchtime and the tarts for tea. Alternatively, you could freeze all but 12 spoonfuls of crumble for another day. You can freeze crumble for a short time, but don't leave it in the freezer for weeks and months as it starts to taste a bit stale and 'airy'.

You could make half the amount of crumble if you prefer, as you can make 110g (4oz) successfully, and freeze the rest.

MAKES ABOUT 12

For the pastry
110g (4oz) plain flour
Pinch salt
50g (2oz) cold butter, cut
 into small pieces
1 rounded dessertspoon
 unrefined caster sugar
2 tablespoons of cold
 water

For the crumble (see
 above for note on
 quantity)
225g (8oz) plain flour
1 teaspoon baking powder
75g (3oz) butter, softened
75g (3oz) sugar

You will need a greased 12-cup tart tin and a 7.5cm (3in) fluted cutter.

Preheat the oven to 180°C (fan oven) or equivalent.

Making the pastry
Sieve the flour and salt carefully into the bowl of your food processor and add the butter. Whiz into fine crumbs and add the sugar. Whiz again briefly. Add the water and whiz until the mixture is starting to come together. Turn it out onto a floured board and knead it lightly until it forms a ball.

Roll it out gently with a floured rolling pin to a thickness of just less than half a centimetre.

Cut out 12 circles with the cutter. Transfer them to the prepared tart tin and firm them down gently.

Making the crumble
Sieve the flour and baking powder into a roomy bowl and rub in the butter. Stir in the sugar.

Preparing the apples

Peel and core the apples. Cut each apple in half and lay face down on your chopping surface. Cut length ways into half moon slices about a centimetre thick. Cook them gently for a few moments in a splash of apple juice or water until the juices are starting to run and they are softening slightly. Strain off any surplus juice and set aside.

Assembling the tarts

Lay the apple slices in the base of each tart so that the base is covered. Top each tart with a spoonful of crumble mixture – don't overdo the crumble as too much crumble can be a bit dry in your mouth!

Bake for about 15 minutes or until the crumble is just tinged golden and the pastry is cooked. Ease from the tin with a small palette knife and cool on a wire rack. Eat warm or cold.

For the apple filling

Approximately 225g (8oz) eating apples, 3 or 4 Cox's are ideal

1–2 tablespoons apple juice or, failing that, water

HAPPY CUSTARD TARTS

Here is the classic custard tart: delicate, sweet and quivery egg custard in a crisp pastry case. This recipe involves first baking the pastry cases blind, which makes sure they are crisp with no trace of sogginess. Also, the custard filling can then be baked at a much lower temperature, which ensures it won't be bouncy or rubbery.

Another plus is 'happy tarts' that won't 'weep' clear liquid: something that can happen if the delicate egg custard is cooked at too high a temperature or for too long.

You will need a 10cm (4in) pastry cutter and a 12-cup muffin tin. This is essential to get a good depth of custard. If you don't have a 10cm cutter, a 10cm fluted, individual flan tin or a 10cm plain, round food ring both make excellent alternatives. If you are using a fluted cutter, remove any excess pastry from around it whilst it is still pressed down on the board: if you try to remove it once you pick up the pastry you've cut out, you will stretch it out of shape.

Admittedly, cutting out 10 circles of greaseproof paper is a bit of a fiddle but the result is worth it. When you are drawing your circles before cutting them out you should find that the lid from a 340g jar of jam is the perfect size to use as a template.

Eat these fairly swiftly as the custard won't keep for more than a couple of days.

MAKES 10

For the pastry
160g (6oz) plain flour
Pinch salt
80g (3oz) cold butter
25g (1oz) unrefined caster
    sugar
3 tablespoons cold water

For the custard filling
1 egg
1 egg yolk
½ teaspoon vanilla extract
10g (½oz) unrefined caster
    sugar
4 tablespoons double
    cream
Enough milk to make up
    the quantity to 300ml

Whole nutmeg, for grating

You will need a 12-cup muffin tin with 10 cups greased and a 10cm (4in) fluted or round cutter. Plus baking beans (preferably ceramic) and greaseproof paper.

Preheat the oven to 180°C (fan oven) or equivalent.

Cut out 10 circles of greaseproof paper and put your baking beans into a jug with a good pouring spout for ease of use.

Making the pastry
Sieve the flour and salt carefully into the bowl of your food processor and add the butter. Whiz into fine crumbs and add the sugar. Whiz again briefly. Add the water and whiz until the mixture is starting to come together. Turn it out onto a floured board and knead it lightly until it forms a ball.

Roll it out gently on a very lightly floured board with a lightly floured rolling pin to a thickness of just less than half a centimetre.

Cut out the pastry rounds and using the tips of your first two fingers of each hand press them gently into the prepared muffin tin. Put a little circle of greaseproof paper in each one and fill almost to the brim with baking beans.

Bake for 15 minutes or until crisp and golden.

Leave to settle and cool slightly in the tin.

Reduce the oven temperature to 160°C (fan oven) or equivalent.

Making the custard filling
Whisk the egg and egg yolk and pass through a sieve. A coiled bedspring-type whisk works well. Add the vanilla extract and sugar and whisk in. Whisk in the cream and the milk.

Assembling the tarts
Remove the baking beans from the pastry cases. The easiest way is to pick up each pastry case and tip the beans out carefully into an empty washing-up bowl or something similar. Peel away the greaseproof paper circles.

Pour the filling into the cases and grate nutmeg over the top. Be careful not to fill them too full and try to avoid spilling any between the pastry cases and the tin.

Bake for 12 minutes or until the custard is rising slightly and developing a very light skin. *Don't overcook!*

Leave to rest and cool in the tin for a while and then remove carefully, easing them out with a small palette knife. Transfer to a wire rack to finish cooling.

You are meant to eat custard tarts cold but they are also lovely just a little bit warm!

A Note on Grating Nutmeg
When you are grating nutmeg, make sure you grate some of the outside each time. If you just grate the inside part, once it is exposed, you won't get quite such a characteristic speckled effect – it will be more of a uniform pale brown powder!

Strawberry Tarts and Fruit Tarts

Strawberry tarts and fruit tarts are such a treat. They look elegant and sophisticated and taste delicious. Crisp pastry, creamy and cool vanilla custard, luscious fruit: they are the highlight of a civilised summer tea-time. Incredibly expensive to buy at the patisserie counter, they are much easier to make yourself than you might suppose.

Invest in some 10cm (4in) loose-bottomed, fluted tartlet tins: the kind that come in packs of 6 (also very handy for individual savoury tarts and quiches) and follow the instructions below for baking the tart cases blind. It would be useful to have some proper ceramic baking beans as well, although you can use dried peas.

Next, follow the recipe below for a simple **Confectioner's Custard** or **Crème Patisserie**. After that, it's just a matter of assembling the tarts and making them look pretty!

Planning ahead

If you are planning ahead for a particular occasion you can bake the tart cases and store them in an airtight container for a couple of days: once completely cold they are surprisingly robust. If you are making both sweet and savoury tarts, the **All-Butter Pastry** from the **Garden Tarts** recipe in the **Savouries** section can be used in both sweet and savoury recipes.

If you are planning to serve the tarts over two days for some reason, only assemble the ones you are going to eat straightaway. Assembled tarts still have a beautiful flavour the next day but the contrasting crispness of the pastry with the smoothness of the custard and the succulence of the fruit has gone.

Dedicate your wooden spoons

It's best to keep wooden spoons for sweet and savoury use completely separate. In fact, with something as delicately flavoured as crème patisserie it's not a bad idea to dedicate a wooden spoon specifically for it. You don't want your lovely dainty custard tasting of garlic or curry!

CONFECTIONER'S CUSTARD OR CRÈME PATISSERIE

This is a really useful recipe to have in your repertoire and surprisingly easy to make. Keep it covered and it will last for a couple of days in the fridge. Leftover crème patisserie makes a lovely quick pudding with some fruit: soft fruit or peaches are good, and maybe a shortbread biscuit or something similar on the side. Don't add more cornflour than recommended, though, as this is a light confectioner's custard and not a blancmange!

A coiled bedspring-type whisk works well for this recipe.

Whisk the egg and egg yolk and pass through a sieve. Put the sieved egg into a roomy bowl with the vanilla and sugar and whisk together.

Mix the cornflour to a smooth paste with 3–4 tablespoons of cold milk taken from the measured amount.

Warm the remaining milk and cream in a smallish heavy-bottomed saucepan until it is almost, but not quite, boiling. Pour it into the cornflour paste, whisking gently all the time. Now whisk the milk and cream and cornflour mixture gently into the eggs, sugar and vanilla.

Wash out the saucepan and put the mixture back. Return to the heat and cook gently, stirring constantly, but lightly, with a wooden spoon to start with, and then change to the whisk as the mixture starts to thicken.

Once the mixture is thickening, turn off the heat and whisk until smooth and creamy. Don't worry if the mixture seems to turn alarmingly gloopy: keep whisking and it will soon become smooth.

Pour into a non-metallic jug or bowl. Allow to cool. A piece of greaseproof paper cut to fit and resting on the surface of the custard will prevent a skin forming. Store covered in the fridge until needed.

1 egg
1 egg yolk
½ teaspoon vanilla extract
40g (1½oz) unrefined caster sugar
2 level tablespoons cornflour
150ml (¼pt) milk
150ml (¼pt) double cream

✓ Cornflour Warning

Cornflour can sometimes act up a bit when you are trying to mix it into a paste. The amount of liquid should be double the amount of cornflour and the liquid should always be cold when mixing with the dry cornflour. If you find yourself with what seems like unmanageable gloop that veers weirdly between wet and dry, even though you have added the correct amount of liquid, pour it through a sieve: it will soon calm down.

STRAWBERRY TARTS

These are the classic elegant tea-time treat.

MAKES 8

For the pastry
160g (6oz) plain flour
Pinch salt
80g (3oz) cold butter
25g (1oz) unrefined caster
 sugar

Quantity of **Crème
 Patisserie**, see above

To finish
Fresh strawberries

Redcurrant Glaze
4 tablespoons redcurrant
 jelly
4 tablespoons water

You will need 8 greased, fluted, loose-bottomed, 10cm tartlet tins, and a baking tray, plus baking beans (preferably ceramic) and greaseproof paper.

Preheat the oven to 180°C (fan oven) or equivalent.

Cut out 8 circles of greaseproof paper using one of the loose bottoms as a template, and put your baking beans into a jug with a good pouring spout for ease of use.

Making the pastry
Sieve the flour and salt carefully into the bowl of your food processor and add the butter. Whiz into fine crumbs and add the sugar. Whiz again briefly. Add the water and whiz until the mixture is starting to come together. Turn it out onto a floured board and knead it lightly until it forms a ball.

Divide the pastry into 8 equal pieces. Working with one piece at a time, form it into a ball and roll out gently, keeping it circular, on a very lightly floured board with a lightly floured rolling pin, to a thickness of just less than half a centimetre.

Drape the pastry circle over the prepared tin and lower gently into position. Firm the pastry lightly into the fluted sides and coax it into shape. Smooth your hand carefully over the top of the tin so the fluted edges cut through the excess pastry and trim it away, or roll your rolling pin across the top.

It is really important that you don't stretch the pastry: if you do it will ping back down the sides of the tins during baking like overstretched elastic!

For ease of use, arrange the tartlet tins on a baking tray. Put a little circle of greaseproof paper in each one and fill almost to the brim with baking beans.

Bake for 12–15 minutes or until crisp and golden. Leave to settle and cool in the tin.

Once cool, remove the baking beans from the pastry cases. The easiest way is to pick up each pastry case and tip the beans out carefully into an empty washing-up bowl or something similar. Peel away the greaseproof paper circles.

Making the Redcurrant Glaze
Melt the redcurrant jelly in a small saucepan with the water, pass through a sieve and allow to cool.

Assembling the finished tarts
Spoon enough Crème Patisserie into each tart to cover the bottom to a depth of about a centimetre to a centimetre or so. Smooth into position with the back of a teaspoon.

Slice the strawberries in half and place cut-side down on top of the crème patisserie: try to cover the whole surface of the tart as much as possible.

Spoon a small amount of the redcurrant glaze over the top: just enough to give the strawberries a very light coating and carry it to the sides of the tart to cover the crème patisserie.

If you own any silver cake forks, now is the time to give them an airing!

Using the pastry trimmings
Re-roll the trimmings and use to make some little jam tarts. The re-rolled pastry is fine for small tarts but a little bit over-worked for anything larger.

FRUIT TARTS

Make these in exactly the same way as the **Strawberry Tarts** but instead of strawberries, arrange a selection of different fruits on top of the **Crème Patisserie**. Ideal fruits to use are: black or green grapes cut in half and arranged cut-side down, sliced or halved strawberries, sliced kiwi fruit, sliced peaches, raspberries and blueberries.

Instead of using redcurrant jelly, make an **Apricot Glaze** from apricot conserve, in the same way as the **Redcurrant Glaze** in the **Strawberry Tart** recipe.

STORE CUPBOARD PEACH TARTS

These tarts are absolutely delicious and perfect for a special tea at any time but this is also a useful recipe to turn to when you haven't had time to go shopping.

If you have guests arriving at short notice, providing you have the pastry ingredients, some cream and eggs, and a tin of sliced peaches (preferably in natural juice) in the cupboard you can whip up some very impressive Peach Tarts. If you don't have any cream, see **Emergency Crème Patisserie**, below.

Put the recipe together in the same way as the **Strawberry Tarts** and **Fruit Tarts**, previously. Make a glaze with apricot conserve (or marmalade, at a pinch) and juice from the tin of peaches instead of water. Three slices of peach, fanned round in a circle look attractive. Carry the apricot glaze to the sides of the tart to cover the crème patisserie.

EMERGENCY CRÈME PATISSERIE

Even if you have no cream, you can still make a very good crème patisserie. Your guests will be hard-pressed to tell the difference between this version and the one made with half milk, half cream!
Don't overdo the cornflour or it will be too thick and not 'silky' enough.

Whisk the egg and egg yolk and pass through a sieve. Put the sieved egg into a roomy bowl with the vanilla and sugar and whisk together.

Take 3–4 tablespoons of the cold milk and mix with the cornflour to a smooth paste.

Warm the remaining milk in a smallish heavy-bottomed saucepan until it is almost, but not quite, boiling. Pour it into the cornflour paste, whisking gently all the time. Now whisk the milk and cornflour mixture gently into the eggs, sugar and vanilla.

Wash out the saucepan and put the mixture back. Return to the heat and cook gently, stirring constantly, but lightly, with a wooden spoon to start with, and then change to the whisk as the mixture starts to thicken.

Once the mixture is thickening, turn off the heat and whisk until smooth and creamy. Don't worry if the mixture seems to turn alarmingly gloopy: keep whisking and it will soon become smooth.

Pour into a non-metallic jug or bowl. Take the cube of butter and spear it onto an ordinary dinner fork. Whisk and stir the fork briskly through the custard until the butter has all melted and is evenly distributed throughout the custard.

Allow to cool. A piece of greaseproof paper cut to fit and resting on the surface of the custard will prevent a skin forming. Store covered in the fridge until needed.

1 egg
1 egg yolk
½ teaspoon vanilla extract
40g (1½oz) unrefined caster sugar
2 level tablespoons cornflour
300ml (½pt) milk – full cream or semi-skimmed
10g (½oz) cube of butter – preferably unsalted if possible

SMALL STRAWBERRY TARTS

You can make smaller strawberry tarts by baking the pastry cases in a muffin tin: see the recipe for **Custard Tarts**. Prepare the **Crème Patisserie** and assemble in the same way as the **Strawberry Tarts**.

ECCLES CAKES

Some people put spices into Eccles Cakes but there is really no need: it's a shame to detract from the flavour of the currants. Currants have a naturally light citrussy flavour and it's nice to enhance that a bit more with a little finely grated lemon zest, but leave it out if you prefer. Have one of these with a strong cup of tea tucked up in front of the fire on a wintry afternoon, or take one with you 'to keep the cold out' on a bracing winter walk.

MAKES 8

8 dessertspoons currants
25g (1oz) soft brown sugar
25g (1oz) butter
1 tablespoon water
Very finely grated zest of half a lemon
1 sheet of all-butter, ready-rolled, frozen puff pastry, defrosted in the fridge until pliable
1 egg, beaten
Caster sugar to finish

You will need a greased baking tray.

Preheat the oven to 200°C (fan oven) or equivalent.

Put the currants with the sugar, butter, water and lemon zest into a pan and cook gently until the butter has melted, the sugar has lost its grittiness and the currants are plumping up nicely. Turn off the heat and put a lid on the pan. Leave to cool.

Working on an average size of about 230mm x 400mm for your sheet of pastry, put it on a lightly floured board and cut into 8 equal squares with straight, decisive movements, using a sharp, non-serrated knife.

Take a square at a time and brush round the edges with beaten egg. Put a dessertspoonful of the currant mixture in the middle.

Starting with the corners, draw them into the middle and press them down. Use kitchen scissors to snip away any excess overhang, so the bottom doesn't become too 'wodgy' with too many layers of overlapping pastry that might not cook through properly. Use another dab of beaten egg to stick it down where necessary.

You should now have an approximately round shape. Flip it over so the sealed part is underneath, and smooth the sides with the flat of your hands, keeping your hands vertical to the board, and turning the cake round, as you do so. Pat the top gently with your middle three fingers. You should now have a neat round cake.

If the pastry has become a little warm during handling, put the shaped cakes in the fridge for 10–15 minutes before the next stage.

Add a drop of water to the beaten egg and use it to brush over the cakes. Sprinkle with caster sugar and make several holes with a skewer or the prongs of a carving fork.

Lay the cakes on the prepared baking tray and bake for 12–15 minutes or so until they are crisp and golden.

There may be a little 'seepage' from the currants on the baking tray when you take them out of the oven, but this is quite normal. Lift them off the tray with a fish slice and transfer to a cooling rack.

Eat slightly warm or cold – but not boiling hot as the currants retain the heat for quite a while after they come out of the oven.

Once cold, store in an airtight container.

SIMPLE CUSTARD SLICES

*These are a 'light as a whisper' version of the old favourite from the baker's shop. All you need is a roll of all-butter, ready-rolled puff pastry, preferably Dorset Pastry, some **Crème Patisserie** (see recipe above), and a little icing sugar to finish. They are very easy as you bake the individual pastries separately, then split and fill them.*

MAKES 8

You will need half a roll of all-butter, ready-rolled, frozen puff pastry (working on an average size of about 230mm x 400mm), defrosted in the fridge until pliable.

Make up a quantity of Crème Patisserie, upping the quantity of cornflour very slightly from 2 level tablespoons to 2 gently rounded tablespoons. Pour the crème patisserie into a plastic sandwich box with a lid – the box should be the right size to give the custard a depth of about 1cm (½in) or a fraction more. Once cool, store in the fridge.

You will need a greased baking tray.

Preheat the oven to 200°C (fan oven) or equivalent.

Lay your pastry on a lightly floured board and cut into 4 equal squares with straight, decisive movements, using a sharp, non-serrated knife. Cut each square into 2 equal rectangles.

Bake for 10 minutes until risen and golden.

Transfer to a cooling rack, using a fish slice, and allow to cool.
Once cold, cut each rectangle into two horizontally, using a sharp knife, and sandwich with a 'slice' of custard cut from the box of crème patisserie. Dust the tops with a little icing sugar stirred through a tea strainer before serving.

Useful Puff Pastry Box for Sweet or Savoury Fillings

This is a useful technique for making an impressive looking pastry really easily! You can use the resulting 'box' for sweet or savoury fillings. Vary the size of the box if you prefer.

You will need a roll of all-butter, ready-rolled, frozen puff pastry (working on an average size of about 230mm x 400mm), defrosted in the fridge until pliable.

You will need a greased baking tray.

Preheat the oven to 200°C (fan oven) or equivalent.

Lay your pastry on a lightly floured board and cut into 8 equal squares with straight, decisive movements using a sharp, non-serrated knife.

With the point of a sharp knife, lightly score a border all the way round each square approximately 1–2 centimetres away from the edge. Don't cut all the way through.

Bake for 10 minutes until risen and golden.

Transfer to a cooling rack, using a fish slice, and allow to cool.

Once cool, remove the rectangular 'lid' from the middle of each box with the point of a sharp knife and trim away any of the layers or 'laminations' of pastry underneath to make a clear space for your filling.

Filling suggestions
Try Salmon or Tuna Fish Paste as a savoury filling idea or Crème Patisserie with some fruit for a sweet one.

MAKES 8

MINCE PIES

If you are making your own mince pies, it's important that both the components are really good: the pastry should be short and delicious, a bit like shortbread in fact, and the mincemeat should be fresh and fruity, with maybe just a little hint of brandy.

This recipe is for an all-butter pastry, with a bit more butter and a bit less water than usual. It's easier to make sweet pastry extra nice as the sugar adds to the crumbly texture. If you have made your own mincemeat (see next recipe) then they should be really special!

MAKES 12

180g (6oz) plain flour
Pinch salt
120g (4oz) cold butter
25g (1oz) unrefined caster
   sugar
1 tablespoon cold water
12 teaspoons mincemeat
   (preferably homemade,
   see next recipe)
A little more caster sugar
   for finishing

You will need 2 fluted cutters: 7.5cm (3in) and a 6cm (2½in), and a greased 12-cup tart tin.

Preheat the oven to 180°C (fan oven) or equivalent.

Sieve the flour and salt carefully into the bowl of your food processor and add the butter. Whiz into fine crumbs and add the sugar. Whiz again briefly. Add the water and whiz until the mixture is starting to come together. Turn it out onto a floured board and knead it lightly until it forms a ball.

Roll it out gently with a floured rolling pin to a thickness of just less than half a centimetre.

Cut out 12 circles with the larger cutter (for the pies) and 12 circles with the smaller cutter (for the lids). As you put the larger circles into the tart tins, firm them down gently so that the finished pies will be a good shape rather than just little saucers of pastry!

Put about a teaspoon of mincemeat into each: don't overfill as the mincemeat can boil out. Brush the edge of each lid with water and press them gently onto the pies. If you would like a nice crispy lid, brush each pie with water and sprinkle a little caster sugar over the top. Make a little hole in each lid with the point of a knife.

Bake for about 12 minutes or until pale golden. Remove from the tin and cool on a wire rack.

HOMEMADE MINCEMEAT

Homemade mincemeat is far better than anything you can buy readymade. It needs a good two weeks for the flavours to develop properly, so if you are making it for Christmas, aim to make it in good time so it will be ready for your first batches of mince pies. It's very easy: just a bit of weighing, chopping and stirring.

Put everything into a large bowl, a casserole dish with a lid is ideal. When you add the apples, grate them on to a clean board and make sure you include all their juice. Strain the orange and lemon juice through a sieve and zest the peel into short pieces rather then long strands.

Mix everything together thoroughly and leave overnight in a cool place for the flavours to amalgamate.

The next day, give everything a stir and spoon into sterilised jars. Try to avoid leaving any air pockets: keep turning the jars round to check and push the mincemeat down with a dinner knife if you see any.

Sterilising jars
Wash the jars in hot soapy water and rinse thoroughly. Shake off any excess water and stand on a baking tray. Put into the oven for 10 minutes or so at 160°C or equivalent. Alternatively, you can put them through the hottest cycle of your dishwasher if you have one.

MAKES APPROXIMATELY
1.5 KG (A LITTLE OVER
3LBS)

225g (8oz) raisins
225g (8oz) sultanas
225g (8oz) currants
225g (8oz) soft dark
  brown sugar
225g (8oz) firm dessert
  apple such as Cox's,
  peeled and cored
  (prepared weight)
175g (6oz) shredded suet
110g (4oz) candied peel,
  cut into fine pieces
Finely grated zest and juice
  of 1 orange
Finely grated zest and juice
  of 1 lemon
2–3 teaspoons mixed spice
150ml (¼pt) brandy

LITTLE CHRISTMAS-SPICED APPLE PIES

These are just like mince pies, but instead of mincemeat they are filled with Christmassy spiced apple, very similar to an apple strudel filling. They are lovely in their own right but also very handy to offer as a festive alternative to mince pies for those who aren't fond of mincemeat. (They also make a great pudding – serve one or two with a little cream.)

If you are offering mince pies and apple pies together, it's useful to be able to tell the difference between the two – you could top one set of pies with caster sugar (see recipe) and leave the others plain.

MAKES 12

For the pastry
180g (6oz) plain flour
Pinch salt
120g (4oz) cold butter
25g (1oz) unrefined caster
   sugar
1 tablespoon cold water

For the filling
Generous 10g (½oz)
   butter
1 rounded teaspoon soft
   brown sugar
½ teaspoon mixed spice
½ teaspoon powdered
   ginger
½ teaspoon powdered
   cinnamon
2–3 dessert apples, peeled
   and cored,
   approximately 200g
   (7oz) prepared weight –
   Cox's are perfect
Generous 10g (½oz)
   sultanas

A little more caster sugar
   for finishing

You will need 2 fluted cutters: 7.5cm (3in) and a 6cm (2½in) and a greased 12-cup tart tin.

Preheat the oven to 180°C (fan oven) or equivalent.

Making the pastry
Sieve the flour and salt carefully into the bowl of your food processor and add the butter. Whiz into fine crumbs and add the sugar. Whiz again briefly. Add the water and whiz until the mixture is starting to come together. Turn it out onto a floured board and knead it lightly until it forms a ball.

Roll it out gently with a floured rolling pin to a thickness of a little less than half a centimetre.

Cut out 12 circles with the larger cutter (for the pies) and 12 circles with the smaller cutter (for the lids). As you put the larger circles into the tart tins, firm them down gently so that the finished pies will be a good shape rather than just little saucers of pastry.

Making the filling
Melt the butter and sugar together over a gentle heat and then add the spices. Cut the apple into small chunks and stir into the melted butter mixture. Try to get all the pieces coated with the butter. Add the sultanas and, again, try to get them all coated in butter too.

Cook gently until the apple is just starting to soften, the sultanas are starting to plump up and everything is smelling lovely and Christmassy.

Assembling the pies

Divide the apple filling equally between the pastry cases. Try to fill them as generously as you can whilst still being able to get the lids on!

Brush the edge of each lid with water and press them gently onto the pies, sealing the edges. If you would like a nice crispy lid, brush each pie with water and sprinkle a little caster sugar over the top. Make a little hole in each lid with the point of a knife.

Bake for about 12–15 minutes or until pale golden. Remove from the tin and cool on a wire rack.

TEA AND BISCUITS

There's a lot to be said for tea and biscuits. Tea and biscuits add up to instant hospitality: if someone drops in unexpectedly, you can have the kettle on and the biscuit tin open in seconds.

There is something very British about tea and biscuits, so much so that the phrase has actually become part of the language as a kind of a metaphor for something totally inactive and non-challenging. As in:

'So what do you *think* happened? We all sat around having *tea and biscuits*?'

Packet Biscuits and Homemade Biscuits

There's a definite distinction between packet biscuits and homemade ones: they are a different type of thing altogether. One is generally speaking, drier, smaller and plainer (apart from the chocolate ones, obviously); the other bigger, bouncier and more extravagant.

Many packet biscuits hold a special place in people's hearts. Even the names act as a kind of password to a gentle, soothing world of reviving hot drinks and reaching into the cupboard or nipping to the corner shop for your favourites: Rich Tea, Morning Coffee, Marie, Arrowroot (if you are feeling a bit seedy), Nice (prompting the perpetual question: do you say *Neece*, as in the town in France, or *nice*, as in very pleasing?), Bourbon, Custard Creams, Ginger Nuts, Malted Milk, and best of all, Digestives.

Sometimes only packet biscuits will do, it depends on the occasion, but homemade biscuits are such a treat, it is well worth taking the trouble when you can.

What Is the Difference between a Biscuit and a Cake?

There have been occasions when this has been the topic of fervent debate. Here are a couple of definitions that settle matters fairly succinctly.

A cake rises significantly as it cooks; a biscuit remains flat. A cake becomes harder as it goes stale; a biscuit becomes softer. A cake is soft to bite into; a biscuit is crisper.

Making Biscuits

Biscuits are simple to make. Just be careful not to over cook them as they can burn very easily. It only takes a minute to overdo it by mistake: always use a timer so you know when to check.

When biscuits first come out of the oven they are still soft and you might be tempted to put them back for a minute or two. Just don't: they will soon harden as they cool down.

Some biscuits are meant to have a slightly chewy cookie consistency rather than being crisp and brittle.

Get to know your oven and make notes of cooking times and temperatures that work for a particular recipe in your oven and refer back to them.

VANILLA BISCUITS

It's very difficult to eat just one of these light, crisp biscuits as they are very moreish indeed. They have a beautiful flavour – half a teaspoon of vanilla extract is exactly right, so don't be tempted to add a bit more 'for luck' or anything!

You will need a large, greased baking tray and a plain 6cm (2½in) cutter.

Preheat the oven to 180°C (fan oven) or equivalent.

Put the butter and sugar in the bowl of your food processor and whiz until light and fluffy. Add the vanilla to the egg. Sieve about half the flour and baking powder carefully over the mixture. Add the egg and vanilla and sieve the rest of the flour on top. Whiz until the mixture is just starting to come together and then stop and scrape any mixture down from the sides. Whiz until the mixture starts to clump together, then stop the machine. You may have to do this in stages as the mixture is quite dense, removing the lid and scraping the mixture down from the sides three or four times, particularly at the beginning.

Scoop the mixture out of the machine and knead it lightly together on a floured board. It's quite soft and delicate to work with so keep everything lightly floured and treat it gently. It is easier to manage if you divide it into two pieces and make the biscuits in two batches. Roll the first piece out to a thickness of about half a centimetre. Cut out rounds with the cutter.

Transfer to the prepared baking sheet: use a palette knife to help you, as the mixture is quite delicate. Leave space between the biscuits as they spread out a bit during baking.

Bake for 5–7 minutes until they are pale golden, but not at all brown. Repeat for the second batch. If you prefer, you can store the dough in the fridge for a few days or freeze it. Defrost frozen dough overnight in the fridge and take dough out of the fridge 20 minutes or so before you need to use it.

Leave to cool and harden for a couple of minutes, no more, on the tray and then transfer to a cooling rack, using a palette knife. (If you leave them on the tray for too long they can become stuck fast and you will have to practically chisel them off, breaking them in the process!)

The biscuits are very soft when they come out of the oven, but will harden as they cool. Once they are completely cold, store in an airtight tin.

MAKES APPROXIMATELY
34 BISCUITS

150g (5oz) butter, slightly
    softened
110g (4oz) unrefined
    caster sugar
½ teaspoon good quality
    vanilla extract (not
    vanilla flavouring)
1 egg, beaten
200g (7oz) plain flour
2 teaspoons baking
    powder

ALMOND BISCUITS

If you like almond you will love these scrumptious biscuits. The recipe is based on the one above but these biscuits are flavoured with almond extract and have ground almonds added to the mixture. The ground almonds firm up the mixture slightly and stop it spreading too much during baking so you can use a fluted cutter which gives a nice professional look. These biscuits are perfect for afternoon tea and are also good to serve with ice cream or a light mousse or fool.

MAKES APPROXIMATELY 34 BISCUITS

150g (5oz) butter, slightly softened

110g (4oz) unrefined caster sugar

½ teaspoon natural almond extract

1 egg, beaten

150g (5oz) plain flour

2 teaspoons baking powder

50g (2oz) ground almonds

You will need a large, greased baking tray and a fluted 6cm (2½in) cutter.

Preheat the oven to 180°C (fan oven) or equivalent.

Put the butter and sugar in the bowl of your food processor and whiz until light and fluffy. Add the almond extract to the egg. Sieve about half the flour and baking powder carefully over the mixture. Add the egg and almond extract and sieve the rest of the flour on top. Whiz briefly and add the ground almonds. Whiz until the mixture is just starting to come together and then stop and scrape any mixture down from the sides. Whiz until the mixture starts to clump together, then stop the machine. You may have to do this in stages as the mixture is quite dense, removing the lid and scraping the mixture down from the sides three or four times, particularly at the beginning.

Scoop the mixture out of the machine and knead it lightly together on a floured board. It's quite soft and delicate to work with so keep everything lightly floured and treat it gently. It is easier to manage if you divide it into two pieces and make the biscuits in two batches. Roll the first piece out to a thickness of about half a centimetre. Cut out rounds with the cutter.

Transfer to the prepared baking sheet: use a palette knife to help you as the mixture is quite delicate.

Bake for 5–7 minutes until they are pale golden, but not at all brown.

Repeat for the second batch. If you prefer, you can store the dough in the fridge for a few days or freeze it. Defrost frozen dough overnight in the fridge and take dough out of the fridge 20 minutes or so before you need to use it.

Leave to cool and harden for a couple of minutes, no more, on the tray, and then transfer to a cooling rack, using a palette knife. (If you leave them on the tray for too long they can become stuck fast and you will have to practically chisel them off, breaking them in the process!)

The biscuits are very soft when they come out of the oven, but will harden as they cool. Once they are completely cold, store in an airtight tin.

COCONUT BISCUITS

If you are fond of coconut, you will love these gorgeous, slightly crumbly, melt-in-the-mouth biscuits. A round, fluted cutter works perfectly well but if you have a similar size square one it looks really effective. You can mix the dough by hand but it's a bit easier in a food processor.

You will need a large, greased baking tray and a fluted 6cm (2½in) cutter.

Preheat the oven to 180°C (fan oven) or equivalent.

Put the butter and sugar in the bowl of your food processor and whiz until light and fluffy. Sieve about half the flour carefully over the mixture. Add the egg and sieve the rest of the flour and baking powder on top. Whiz briefly and add the coconut. Whiz until the mixture is just starting to come together and then stop machine. (You may have to stop and scrape the mixture down from the sides a couple of times.)

Take the mixture out of the machine and gently finish kneading it together on a floured board.

Once the dough is ready it is easier to manage if you divide it into two pieces and make the biscuits in two batches. Roll the first piece out to a thickness of about half a centimetre.

Cut out the biscuits and transfer to the prepared baking tray: you may find a palette knife is useful to help you move them across.

Bake for 5–7 minutes until they are pale golden, but not at all brown.

Repeat for the second batch. If you prefer you can store the dough in the fridge for a few days or freeze it. Defrost frozen dough overnight in the fridge and take dough out of the fridge 20 minutes or so before you need to use it.

MAKES APPROXIMATELY 34 BISCUITS

150g (5oz) butter, slightly softened
110g (4oz) unrefined caster sugar
150g (5oz) plain flour
1 egg, beaten
2 teaspoons baking powder
50g (2oz) desiccated coconut

EASTER BISCUITS

Traditionally, Easter Biscuits are a fairly large, round biscuit with fluted edges. You may like to keep to tradition or you may prefer to make them a bit smaller. Alternatively, if you are making them with, or for, children, you can use novelty cutters instead: chicks, bunnies and egg shapes are popular for Easter. A little caster sugar sifted over these biscuits is a nice finishing touch.

MAKES APPROXIMATELY 24 BISCUITS, DEPENDING ON CUTTER SIZE

110g (4oz) butter, softened
75g (3oz) unrefined caster sugar
200g (7oz) plain flour
¼ teaspoon mixed spice, optional
1 whole egg and 1 egg yolk, beaten

You will need a large, greased baking tray.

Preheat the oven to 180°C (fan oven) or equivalent.

Put the softened butter and sugar in a large bowl and cream together with a wooden spoon until completely mixed together and fluffy.

Sieve the flour (and spice, if using) over the mixture and add the egg and egg yolk. Stir together with the wooden spoon until it is fairly well mixed and most of the flour has been absorbed. It will be quite stiff.

You will need to get your hands in now to finish the mixing: the warmth from your hands will help bind everything together. Put the mixture onto a floured board and continue to knead the mixture until you have what looks (and feels) like a large ball of marzipan.

Roll out with a floured rolling pin to a thickness of a bit more than a pound coin. Cut out with your chosen cutters and transfer to the prepared baking tray.

Bake for 7–8 minutes or until very pale golden. Remove fairly swiftly from the baking tray with a small palette knife, and cool on a wire rack. Sprinkle with caster sugar, if liked. Once cooled, they will keep in an airtight tin for several days.

MALTED MILK BISCUITS

Children love making and eating these simple biscuits. They taste very like the malted milk biscuits you can buy in packets: the ones with the bobbly bits and pictures of cows stamped on them. You can cut them out in any shape you like, but a cow-shaped cutter would be perfect. Just a dessertspoonful of malt extract is all you need for a subtle, mild, child-friendly flavour and 50g of sugar is plenty, as the malt extract is naturally sweet.

You will need a large, greased baking tray and a biscuit cutter.

Preheat the oven to 180°C (fan oven) or equivalent.

Whiz the butter and sugar together and sieve in the flour and salt (if using). Whiz again. Add the malt extract and milk and whiz until the mixture starts to form large clumps and begins to gather on one side of the bowl. Remove the blade, scoop out the mixture and transfer to a lightly floured board. Knead the mixture gently together with your hands.

Roll out using a lightly floured rolling pin to about a centimetre thick. Cut out and arrange on the greased baking tray. Re-roll the trimmings until you have used up all the dough.

Bake for about 7–8 minutes, until the biscuits have the very faintest golden brown tinge around the edges. Leave them on the tray for a minute or so and then remove with a small palette knife and cool on a wire rack. Store in an airtight container when cold.

These are great served with a glass of cold milk. (Or a cup of tea!)

✓ **Useful Note**
As well as storing any biscuits in an airtight container, it's a good idea to wrap them in foil first as well, particularly if the container is very roomy. It's also best not to store a selection of different biscuits together, unless each kind is closely wrapped in foil, otherwise all the biscuits taste of each other, instead of distinctly of themselves.

MAKES ABOUT 30, DEPENDING ON CUTTER SIZE

110g (4oz) butter, softened
50g (2oz) unrefined caster sugar
225g (8oz) plain flour
Tiny pinch salt, optional
1 dessertspoon barley malt extract
4 dessertspoons semi-skimmed milk

MALTED MUESLI BISCUITS

These scrummy little biscuits are just the thing to keep you going if energy is flagging a little. They are also great for picnics and lunch boxes or to offer with a sociable cup of tea on a free afternoon. They don't contain much sugar as the malt extract is naturally sweet.

MAKES ABOUT 22 BISCUITS

110g (4oz) butter, softened
50g (2oz) soft brown
  sugar
1 level tablespoon barley
  malt extract
1 tablespoon milk
110g (4oz) wholemeal
  flour
110g (4oz) unsweetened
  muesli (any large nuts
  should be chopped into
  smaller pieces)

You will need a greased baking tray.

Preheat the oven to 180°C (fan oven) or equivalent.

Instructions are given here using the food processor as it's slightly quicker but you can easily make these biscuits by hand.

Whiz the butter and sugar together until combined and fluffy and add the malt extract. Whiz again to combine. Add the milk and wholemeal flour and whiz until thoroughly mixed.

Remove the blade from the machine and stir in the muesli, making sure it is evenly distributed throughout the mixture.

Take teaspoons of the mixture and roll into balls about the size of a walnut. Space these out evenly on the prepared baking tray. Use a fork to flatten each ball into a disc shape (you are not making fork biscuits as such: the biscuits will spread slightly during baking).

Bake for 7–8 minutes until they are just starting to go golden brown around the edges.

Leave to settle for a moment or two and then transfer to a wire cooling rack, using a small palette knife. They will still be soft at this stage but will firm up as they cool.

Once cool, store in an airtight container. Wrap them closely in foil inside the container to keep them extra fresh.

You can eat these warm if you like, once the outside has firmed but the middle is still soft. Also, unfortunately, the uncooked dough is very appealing to the adult palate, so if you thought your days of licking mixing bowls were safely behind you, be on your guard!

MALTED GINGER OAT BISCUITS

There is something very yummy and appealing to the taste about anything malted. Here, a spoonful is added to these little oaty biscuits.

You will need a greased baking tray.

Preheat the oven to 180°C (fan oven) or equivalent.

Instructions are given here using the food processor as it's slightly quicker but you can easily make these biscuits by hand.

Whiz the butter and sugar together until combined and fluffy and add the malt extract. Whiz again to combine. Add the wholemeal flour, salt, ginger and milk and whiz until thoroughly mixed.

Remove the blade from the machine and stir in the oats, a few at a time, making sure they are evenly distributed throughout the mixture.

Take teaspoons of the mixture and roll into balls about the size of a walnut. Space these out evenly on the prepared baking tray.

Use a fork to flatten each ball into a disc shape (you are not making fork biscuits as such: the biscuits will spread slightly during baking). Aim for each disc to measure roughly 4.5cm across. You may find it easier if your hands, and the fork, are slightly wet.

Bake for 7–8 minutes until they are just starting to go golden brown around the edges.

Leave to settle for a moment or two and then transfer to a wire cooling rack, using a small palette knife. They will still be soft at this stage but will firm up as they cool.

Once cool, store in an airtight container. Wrap them closely in foil inside the container to keep them extra fresh.

MAKES ABOUT 22 BISCUITS

110g (4oz) butter, softened
50g (2oz) soft brown
  sugar
1 level tablespoon barley
  malt extract
110g (4oz) wholemeal
  flour
Pinch salt
1–2 teaspoons ground
  ginger
1 tablespoon milk
110g (4oz) porridge oats

GINGERBREAD BISCUITS

These delicious, spicy biscuits have the most lovely flavour. If you like, you can eat these warm from the oven, or you can wait until they are cooled and crispy. Either way, they are fabulous with a cup of tea!

MAKES APPROXIMATELY 30 BISCUITS

150g (5oz) butter, softened
150g (5oz) soft, dark brown sugar
225g (8oz) plain flour
1 egg, lightly beaten
Pinch salt
2 teaspoons baking powder
1½ teaspoons each of ground mixed spice, ginger and cinnamon

You will need a large, greased baking tray and a 6cm (2½in) cutter.

Preheat the oven to 180°C (fan oven) or equivalent.

Whiz the butter and sugar together in the food processor. Sieve half of the flour over the top and add the egg. Then sieve the rest of the flour over the top with the salt, baking powder and spices and whiz until the mixture begins to gather together. (You may need to stop the machine a couple of times and scrape the dough down from the sides of the bowl with a flexible spatula.) Stop the processor, remove the blade and finish gently kneading the dough together on a lightly floured board.

Roll out the dough with a lightly floured rolling pin to roughly half a centimetre thick or a fraction more. There is quite a bit of dough so you may want to work in two batches and, unless your oven is enormous, you will probably need to bake in two batches.

Cut out the biscuits and transfer to the prepared baking tray: a small palette knife makes the job easier as the dough is quite soft. Bake for about 7 minutes or until pale golden and very, very, slightly brown at the edges. Leave to settle for a few moments then remove from the tray with a small palette knife and cool on a wire rack. Once cold, store in an airtight container.

Variation
You can make a slightly plainer version of this recipe by using 2 tablespoons of milk instead of the egg.

GINGERBREAD PEOPLE

If you need to double the quantity, make two batches rather than one big one: it's easier for the food processor to cope, plus you need quite a lot of work surface space to roll out a double batch all at once.

You will need a large, greased baking tray and cutters.

Preheat the oven to 180°C (fan oven) or equivalent.

Whiz the butter and sugar together in the food processor. Add the flour, salt and spices and milk, and whiz until the mixture forms large clumps and begins to gather together. Stop the processor, remove the blade and finish gently kneading the dough together by hand on a lightly floured board.

Roll out the dough with a lightly floured rolling pin to roughly half a centimetre thick or a fraction more. Cut out the biscuits, you may need a small palette knife to transfer them to the prepared tray without mishap, and bake for about 7 minutes or until pale golden and very, very, slightly brown at the edges.

Remove from the tray with a small palette knife and cool on a wire rack. Once they are cold, store in an airtight container.

MAKES ABOUT 12
SMALL GINGERBREAD
PEOPLE (USING
APPROXIMATELY 8CM
TALL CUTTERS)

60g (2¼oz) butter,
 softened
60g (2¼oz) soft brown
 sugar
110g (4oz) plain flour
Pinch salt
½ teaspoons each of
 ground mixed spice,
 ginger and cinnamon
1 tablespoon milk

Boots, Buttons, Gloves and Faces
If you feel like melting some chocolate, your gingerbread people could soon be wearing smart chocolate boots and a lovely big smile!

You will need **50g chocolate, dark or milk and 10g butter**. Break the chocolate into pieces and put in a heatproof bowl. Cook in the microwave on high for a total of 1½ –2 minutes in 30-second bursts. Cut the butter into small dice and stir very gently into the melted chocolate: it will dissolve in the heat of the chocolate.

Dip the gingerbread men's feet into the melted chocolate; you could dip the hands in as well, if you like. You may find it easier (and less messy) to scoop some chocolate into a spoon and dip the biscuits into the spoon. Next, snip the end off a cocktail stick, dip it into the chocolate, and draw in the eyes and a great big smile.

You could also dab on some chocolate buttons, using the end of a teaspoon handle. Alternatively, if you fancy a bit of colour, stick some mini chocolate bean sweets on top of the melted chocolate. Lay the biscuits carefully on some greaseproof paper until the chocolate has set.

PICNIC BISCUITS

These scrumptious biscuits are practically a picnic in themselves. A couple of these, a crisp apple and a flask of something and you are all set. You can mix them by hand if you like, but it's easier in the food processor even though the mixture is quite stiff.

MAKES ABOUT 28–30

150g (5oz) butter, softened
110g (4oz) soft light
 brown sugar
150g (5oz) plain flour
2 teaspoons baking
 powder
1 egg, beaten
50g (2oz) porridge oats
50g (2oz) desiccated
 coconut
75g (3oz) raisins and dried
 cranberries, mixed

You will need a large, greased baking tray.

Preheat the oven to 180°C (fan oven) or equivalent.

Whiz the softened butter and sugar together until soft and fluffy. Sieve in half of the flour and baking powder over the surface of the mixture and add the egg. Sieve in the rest of the flour and baking powder and whiz briefly.

Add the oats and coconut and whiz until thoroughly mixed. You may have to stop the machine a couple of times and scrape the mixture down from the sides with a flexible spatula. You may also want to stir the mixture slightly with a dinner knife as it is quite stiff.

Remove the blade from the machine and stir in the raisins and cranberries; a dinner knife works better than a spoon for this.

Take generous teaspoons of the mixture and roll into balls about the size of a walnut. Space these out evenly on the prepared baking tray. Use a fork to flatten each ball into a disc shape (you are not making fork biscuits as such: the biscuits will spread slightly during baking). It helps if the fork is wet, so have a jug of water handy.

You may need to bake the biscuits in two batches. Bake for 7–8 minutes until they are just starting to go golden brown around the edges.

Leave to settle for a moment or two and then transfer to a wire cooling rack, using a small palette knife. They will still be soft at this stage but will firm up as they cool.

Once cool, store in an airtight container: wrap them closely in foil inside the container to keep them extra fresh. The finished biscuits are more of a cookie than a crisp biscuit in consistency.

TOTALLY OATY PICNIC BISCUITS

These are very similar to the original **Picnic Biscuits**, but leave out the desiccated coconut and make up the quantity of **oats** to **110g (4oz)**.

✓ **Using Vacuum Flasks for Tea**
If you take both tea and coffee out and about in vacuum flasks, make sure you have dedicated flasks for each. Tea quickly picks up a coffee taste from a flask that has previously been used for coffee: coffee doesn't take long to permeate the seals round the stopper and won't wash away completely. This applies to vacuum-type mugs as well.

HIKING BISCUITS

Stir in **50g (2oz) dark chocolate chips** along with the cranberries and raisins to either of the above recipes for extra energy.

✓ **Using a small palette knife to remove biscuits from baking trays**
When your biscuits first come out of the oven they will be very soft and delicate. Leave them on the baking tray for a couple of minutes to firm up slightly. If you try to move them now they will crumble into pieces.

After a couple of minutes, they still won't be hard, but will be firm enough to move. If you leave them on the tray for too long, some biscuits can become stuck fast and you will have to practically chisel them off, breaking them in the process!

To remove the biscuits press as much of the blade of the palette knife as you can down flat against the surface of the baking tray, next to the biscuit. Use a sideways sweeping motion, and still keeping the blade pressed down, sweep it under the biscuit.

You'll soon get the hang of it!

Transfer the biscuits to a cooling rack to cool and harden completely. As soon as they are cold, store them in an airtight container to keep them fresh – for extra insurance, wrap them closely in foil first.

HEART-SHAPED SHORTBREAD BISCUITS

These are just the thing to serve with tea served in delicate bone china cups. You don't have to use heart-shaped cutters but they do look very appealing. If you have two sizes of heart cutters it's a good idea to use both sizes: then you can cut out more biscuits each time without re-rolling too much, as well as being able to offer a choice of sizes.

MAKES ABOUT 20 BISCUITS, DEPENDING ON CUTTER SIZE

110g (4oz) butter, softened
50g (2oz) unrefined caster sugar – plus a little more for rolling and sifting
175g (6oz) plain flour

You will need a greased baking tray.

Preheat the oven to 140°C (fan oven) or equivalent.

Put the softened butter in a bowl and half stir, half beat, with a wooden spoon until it is soft and creamy. Add the sugar and continue until creamed and fluffy.

Start adding the flour, a tablespoonful at a time, and beat and stir until it is incorporated. By the time you get to the last couple of spoonfuls of flour it will be a mass of large lumps: finish binding it together with your hands, there is no need to flour them. It will take a couple of minutes to work it all together but the warmth from your hands will help it along.

Divide the dough into two batches: it's easier to deal with a smaller amount.

Spread the board with a little extra caster sugar, and roll the rolling pin in sugar: there is no need for flour as well.

Roll the dough out to the thickness of two pound coins, one on top of each other.

Bake for 15–18 minutes or until very pale golden but not at all brown. Leave for a couple of moments then remove fairly swiftly with a small palette knife and cool on a rack.

Sprinkle with a little caster sugar whilst still warm.

Once cold, store in an airtight container.

LAVENDER SHORTBREAD BISCUITS

These are a little bit different and lovely with a cup of tea in the garden on a summer's day. You just want the merest hint of lavender so don't overdo it, or the shortbread will taste more like a bar of soap than a biscuit!

You will need about **5–10 sprigs of lavender**. Pick the lavender when it is still in bud and deep purple in colour. Once the buds open the flowers are a bit too 'bristly' in the mouth and the colour isn't as good.

Lay the lavender sprigs on kitchen paper for a while to allow any small passengers to leave. Remove all the florets from the stalks and shake them lightly in a sieve to remove any debris.

Make the shortbread as for the **Heart-shaped Shortbread Biscuits** recipe, above, adding the lavender florets after the first spoonful of flour. You can use any shaped cutter but they are particularly appealing cut into heart shapes.

LEMON SHORTBREAD BISCUITS

The lemony tang contrasts well with the rich buttery taste of the shortbread. Follow the **Shortbread Biscuits** recipe, above, but **add the finely grated zest of 1 lemon** when you add the sugar to the mix. Bake as above. Sprinkle with caster sugar, cool on a wire rack and store in an airtight tin. The lemon flavour will be more pronounced the next day.

CRANBERRY AND LEMON SHORTBREAD BISCUITS

Cranberries and lemons just go together so beautifully! Make this in the same way as the **Lemon Shortbread**, above, but knead **25–50g (1–2oz) of dried cranberries** into the mix once you have taken it out of the processor and it still hasn't quite come together.

SHORTBREAD BISCUITS WITH DRIED SOUR CHERRIES

Make as above, but use **dried sour cherries** instead of cranberries and leave out the lemon zest.

SIMPLE AND SNEAKY MILLIONAIRE'S SHORTBREAD IN A BOX

Making Millionaire's Shortbread is quite an elaborate process. Ideally, you would make the shortbread base yourself, and also the caramel by boiling condensed milk, in its tin, until it has thickened and darkened. However, if you are pressed for time and nervous about boiling a can for several hours, *there is another way!* You can still achieve the fabulous layers of shortbread, caramel and chocolate by a much easier route.

This recipe uses a crushed shortbread base, very much the same idea as a crushed digestive biscuit base for a cheesecake. A few spoonfuls of dulce de leche, which is milk condensed and reduced commercially, provides the caramel.

Use good quality, actual chocolate, not chocolate coating, for the topping: it should have around 70% cocoa solids. The small amount of butter added to the chocolate helps give a shiny, glossy finish.

If you prefer, for a more child-friendly version, you can use milk chocolate, but again use good quality: around 30% cocoa solids. Alternatively, you could use half dark, half milk.

This recipe is light on actual preparation time but you do need to leave time in between the stages for chilling. Be precise about the butter measurement for Stage 1 – not enough and the base won't hold together; too much and it will be too rich and buttery.

There is often a price to pay for a shortcut, and the price here is that the caramel layer is not quite as firm as the conventional method. It can squidge out a bit when you bite into it – but it is still *completely* irresistible!

Stage 1
225 (8oz) all-butter
   shortbread, homemade
   or bought
105g (2¼oz) butter

Stage 2
Approximately 3
   tablespoons dulce de
   leche

Stage 3
100g good quality dark
   chocolate
25g (1oz) butter

You will need a lightly greased plastic sandwich box of roughly 23 x 18cm (9 x 7in) with a lid or, if you prefer, an 18cm (7in) brownie tin.

Crush the shortbread: the easiest way is to put it in a large plastic bag and bash it and roll over it with a rolling pin.

Cut the butter into small pieces and melt it gently over a low to moderate heat. Stir in the crushed shortbread until it is fully coated.

Pile the mixture into the box and smooth it down firmly with the back of a metal spoon. Make sure the edges are smooth. Once it is cool, put the lid on the box and refrigerate for a couple of hours.

Spread the dulce de leche fairly thinly over the chilled shortbread base.

Put the lid back on and refrigerate for another couple of hours.

Break up the chocolate and put it into a heatproof bowl. Melt the chocolate in the microwave on high, in 30-second bursts: usually, it will take between 1½ and 2 minutes altogether. (Alternatively, melt the chocolate in a bowl over a pan of barely simmering water. Choose a bowl that will fit comfortably in the top of the saucepan but without the bottom touching the hot water.)

Cut the butter into tiny pieces and stir gently into the melted chocolate – don't stir too vigorously. Microwave for another 30 seconds if necessary.

Allow the chocolate to cool down a little. Pour the chocolate carefully over the top of the chilled dulce de leche and case into the corners with the back of a tablespoon. Use a flexible spatula to get the last of the chocolate from around the sides of the bowl.

Leave it to cool for 20 minutes or so and then put the lid on (this avoids a build up of condensation) and chill it in the fridge for a few hours.

Once it's starting to chill, you can mark it into smallish squares before the chocolate has completely set, otherwise it can tend to crack. Use a dinner knife, or a strong plastic picnic knife if you are worried about scratching your box. Loosen the sides and bottom as well. Rest a plastic ruler on the top of the box to guide you as you cut: this will give you clear straight lines.

Store in the fridge.

CHOCOLATE BISCUIT FRIDGE CAKE IN A BOX

Here is an old favourite: straightforward and yummy. If you prefer, you can make this more traditionally in an 18cm (7in) brownie tin or an 18cm (7in) round, loose-bottomed cake tin. It's quite handy to make it in a sandwich box, though, as then it can stay in there once it has set and it's ready to go if you are taking it somewhere.

250g (9oz) digestive biscuits

3 tablespoons golden syrup

75g (3oz) butter, cut into small pieces

110g (4oz) raisins (or sultanas and raisins, mixed)

100g bar milk chocolate

Variations

You can use **dark chocolate** instead of milk chocolate, if you prefer, or half dark, half milk. For extra crunch and goodness, **25g (1oz) chopped blanched almonds** (not flaked) are a nice addition to the biscuit mixture.

You will need a lightly greased, plastic sandwich box roughly 23 x 18cm (9 x 7in) with a lid.

Crush the digestive biscuits: spread them out on a piece of greaseproof paper or a clean tea towel and roll over them a few times with a rolling pin. Take it easy: don't crush them to a fine powder as you want some biscuity texture!

Melt the golden syrup gently in a fairly roomy pan and stir in the butter. Keep stirring over a gentle heat until the butter has just melted – this avoids overheating the butter until it is split and oily. Stir the biscuit crumbs, raisins and sultanas into the melted butter and syrup and mix thoroughly.

Pile the mixture into the box and smooth it down firmly with the back of a metal spoon – it's easier if the spoon is wet. Make sure the edges are smooth and there isn't a hump in the middle!

Break up the chocolate and put it into a heatproof bowl. Melt the chocolate in the microwave on high, in 30-second bursts: usually, it will take between 1½ and 2 minutes altogether. (Alternatively, melt the chocolate in a bowl over a pan of barely simmering water: choose a bowl that will fit comfortably in the top of the saucepan but without the bottom touching the hot water.)

Spread the chocolate carefully over the biscuit mixture: it's a bit of a fiddle but a flexible spatula and a dinner knife will make the job easier.

Leave it to cool down for 20 minutes or so and then put the lid on (this avoids a build up of condensation) and chill it in the fridge for a few hours. Once it's starting to chill, you can mark it into squares or slices: use a dinner knife, or a strong plastic picnic knife if you don't want to scratch your box. Loosen the sides and bottom as well.

Store in the fridge.

Tea and Ices

It's funny how only a slight change of word can create such a different picture in your mind. Tea and ice cream doesn't sound quite right, but 'tea and ices' sounds beautifully quaint, instantly transporting you back to a gentle age of relaxed pots of tea and real dairy ice cream, served in an English country garden or a lovely old-fashioned tea shop.

As a child, I used to be taken to such a tea shop with my Mum and Grandma as a special treat. It was on the third storey above a small department store, and you could go upstairs in one of those old lifts with folding metal gates. I would always have vanilla ice cream in a little silver dish and the grown-ups would have a pot of tea *and* ice cream. If you are sitting down at a table, a cup of hot tea goes surprisingly well alongside a scoop or two of ice cream and maybe a delicate biscuit or wafer.

Alternatively, and particularly for children, you might like to serve your homemade ice cream in a cornet. If you do, make sure you buy the crunchy waffle cones, they are a treat in themselves and complement the ice cream beautifully. Also, treat yourself to a proper metal ice cream scoop rather than risk bending all your spoons: a scoop of ice cream *always* looks more professional.

Removing Ice Cream from an Ice Cream Machine without Scratching

It's important not to scratch the metal bowl of your ice cream maker so don't try to get the ice cream out with anything metal. A robust, plastic, picnic spoon – the kind that comes in a set with knives and forks – works well and is particularly good for filling individual tubs.

HONEY AND VANILLA ICE CREAM

Honey and vanilla together make a glorious ice cream: the honey has a greater depth of flavour than sugar and a more mellow sweetness.

Separate the eggs using two dessertspoons or an egg separator, rather than passing them between the two halves of the shell, as the mixture is only going to be cooked very lightly.

Put the egg yolks into a roomy bowl with the vanilla and honey and whisk together.

Warm the milk in a smallish, heavy-bottomed saucepan until it is almost, but not quite, boiling. Pour it into the egg mixture, whisking gently all the time.

Wash out the saucepan and put the mixture back. Return to the heat and cook gently, stirring all the time until the mixture coats the spoon very lightly; you might notice a very slight deepening of colour when it's ready. Take it off the heat immediately and pour into a Pyrex measuring jug. If you leave it in the metal pan it will carry on cooking slightly and may start to scramble and curdle. (If the mixture does curdle a bit, the sieving should sort it out.)

Leave to cool and stir in the cream.

The next stage is much easier if you have an ice cream machine. If you do, follow the maker's instructions from this stage.

If you don't, stir the mixture thoroughly or, better still, whisk it, and then pour it into a lidded plastic freezer box and put it into the freezer. After an hour or so, take it out of the freezer and stir it through, beating it quite vigorously with a wooden spoon: this is to break up any large ice crystals that will be forming. Return to the freezer. Repeat after another 30 minutes to an hour, and then again after another 30 minutes to an hour.

It's best to eat homemade ice cream within a couple of days of making if you can, as it does tend to get very hard when it has been in the freezer for a while. Take it out of the freezer for 20 minutes or so before you want to serve it.

6 very fresh egg yolks
½ teaspoon vanilla bean paste or vanilla extract (not vanilla flavouring)
3 tablespoons runny honey
275ml (½pt) milk, semi-skimmed is fine
275ml (½pt) double cream

HONEY AND VANILLA ICE CREAM WITH CRUSHED MALTESERS®

This is a delicious and moreish version of the **Honey and Vanilla Ice Cream** with added crushed Maltesers®. Make the ice cream as above. You will need **approximately 100g Maltesers®**.

Once you have stirred the cream into the ice cream and before you put it into the machine, crush the Maltesers® with a pestle and mortar *very slightly*. This is really just to break them open a bit. Alternatively, put them inside a plastic bag and run over them very briefly with a rolling pin. Stir the lightly crushed Maltesers® into the ice cream: take care to keep them in recognisable pieces and not crush them into powder. Put it into the ice cream machine and proceed as above.

STRAWBERRY ICE CREAM

If you like strawberries and cream, you will love this! It is so simple to make: just fruit puree, sugar and cream stirred together. The volume of strawberry puree is great enough to make sure you don't feel you are just eating mouthfuls of frozen cream. You don't have to sieve the mixture before you put it in the ice cream machine, but it does give a more professional result and the ice cream isn't full of those pesky little seeds!

450g (1lb) strawberries
75g (3oz) unrefined caster sugar
2 tablespoons lemon juice
300ml double cream

Puree the strawberries in a food processor or blender. Once they start to break up add the sugar and lemon juice. Once they are completely smooth add the cream and whiz briefly to incorporate it into the puree.

Pour the mixture through a sieve (a nylon one is usually finer and better at catching the teeny little seeds than a metal one) into a jug with a good pouring spout and pour into the ice cream machine. Follow the maker's instructions.

If you are making the ice cream without a machine, follow the instructions in the Honey and Vanilla Ice Cream recipe.

RASPBERRY ICE CREAM

*Strawberries are fabulous but, as my grandmother often remarked, raspberries 'can knock them into a cocked hat'! If you have your own home-grown raspberries the flavour will be even more intense and fragrant. This is perfect with chocolate ice cream, or as a little trio of scoops of raspberry, vanilla and chocolate. It's also good with a few freshly picked raspberries, still warm from the sun, a little cream and a **Homemade Meringue**.*

If you do grow your own and also have loganberries and tayberries, there is nothing to stop you mixing them in with the raspberries. Keep to the overall weight of fruit as suggested, though.

Puree the raspberries and sugar in a food processor or blender until smooth. Once the mixture is completely smooth add the cream and whiz briefly to incorporate it into the puree.

Pour the mixture through a sieve into a jug with a good pouring spout and pour into the ice cream machine. Follow the maker's instructions.

If you are making the ice cream without a machine, follow the instructions in the Honey and Vanilla Ice Cream recipe.

450g (1lb) raspberries

75g (3oz) unrefined caster sugar

300ml double cream

CHOCOLATE ICE CREAM

This has a wonderful deep chocolate flavour. Use a little less cocoa if you feel it is a bit too powerful and dark-chocolatey for children. A scoop of this goes beautifully with either a scoop of the strawberry, the raspberry or the honey and vanilla ice cream.

6 very fresh egg yolks
½ teaspoon vanilla bean
  paste or vanilla extract
  (not vanilla flavouring)
75g (3oz) unrefined caster
  sugar
2 tablespoons cocoa
  powder
275ml (½pt) milk
275ml (½pt) double cream

Put the egg yolks into a roomy bowl with the vanilla and sugar and whisk together.

Mix the cocoa to a smooth paste with a little of the milk. Warm the rest of the milk in a smallish, heavy-bottomed saucepan until it is almost, but not quite, boiling. Pour it into the cocoa mix and stir thoroughly. Next pour the warm milk and cocoa into the egg mixture, whisking gently all the time.

Wash out the saucepan and put the mixture back. Return to the heat and cook gently, stirring constantly until the mixture coats the back of the spoon very lightly. Take it off the heat immediately and pour into a Pyrex measuring jug. Leave to cool and stir in the cream when completely cold.

Pour into an ice cream maker, and follow the maker's instructions from this stage. If you are making this without an ice cream maker, see Honey and Vanilla Ice Cream for full instructions.

BLACKBERRY RIPPLE ICE CREAM WITH HONEY AND VANILLA

This is the most gorgeous ice cream: the fragrant and delicious blackberry syrup goes beautifully with the creamy vanilla. If you are picking your own blackberries, you may want to pick them before Michaelmas Day on the 29th of September: the old tale is that after that the devil spits on them! It can be tricky doing the ripple part manually at home but you can have a fair crack at it if you use the method below. Here's to the last taste of summer!

Whisk the egg yolks, vanilla and honey together. Warm the milk in a smallish, heavy-bottomed saucepan until it is almost, but not quite, boiling. Pour it into the egg mixture, whisking gently all the time.

Wash out the saucepan and put the mixture back. Return to the heat and cook gently, stirring constantly until the mixture coats the back of the spoon very lightly. You might notice a very slight deepening of colour when it's ready. Take it off the heat immediately and pour into a Pyrex measuring jug. If you leave it in the metal pan it will carry on cooking slightly and may start to scramble and curdle. Leave to cool and stir in the cream when completely cold.

The next stage is much easier if you have an ice cream machine. If you do, follow the maker's instructions from this stage.

If you don't, stir the mixture thoroughly or, better still, whisk it, and then pour it into a lidded, plastic freezer box and put it into the freezer. After an hour or so, take it out of the freezer and stir it through, beating it quite vigorously with a wooden spoon: this is to break up any large ice crystals that will be forming. Return to the freezer. Repeat after another 30 minutes to an hour, and then again after another 30 minutes to an hour.

6 very fresh egg yolks
½ teaspoon vanilla bean paste or vanilla extract (not vanilla flavouring)
3 tablespoons runny honey
275ml (½pt) milk, semi-skimmed is fine
275ml (½pt) double cream

For the blackberry syrup
175g (6oz) blackberries
1½ tablespoons water
1 gently rounded tablespoon unrefined caster sugar

To make the ripple, cook the blackberries, water and sugar together over a medium to high heat until the blackberries are completely soft and the liquid is starting to look a little syrupy. Keep stirring once the mixture starts to bubble. Push them through a sieve and discard the pulp. Cool the syrup and chill.

Once the ice cream is ready, spoon about a third of it into a lidded, plastic freezer box (or another freezer box if you are making it by hand) and drizzle about a third of the blackberry syrup in lines over it. Spoon another layer of ice cream over that and drizzle more syrup on top. Repeat with the last of the ice cream and syrup. Finally, with a cocktail stick, feather the top layer of syrup into swirls and freeze.

Serve using an ice cream scoop for best effect.

RASPBERRY RIPPLE ICE CREAM WITH HONEY AND VANILLA

This is a version of the classic fruit ripple ice cream and virtually identical to the **Blackberry Ripple Ice Cream** above. Instead of blackberries, use the same quantity of raspberries and proceed in the same way.

LAVENDER AND HONEY ICE CREAM

If you are fond of lavender: this is so nice! Although you can make it without an ice cream machine, it is much easier with, if you do have one. The lavender flavour is quite ethereal but it's definitely there. The honey has a more subtle sweetness than sugar and the flavour can vary with the type of honey you use. Pick the lavender flowers whilst they are still in bud: the deep purple colour is better and they are soft and not 'bristly' like the smoky-tinged open flowers.

A Word of Warning

As with the other lavender recipes in this book: be sure to use only the more common English lavender: Lavandula *angustifolia*, sometimes called Lavandula *officinalis* or Lavandula *spicata*. The tufty French lavender: Lavandula *stoechas* can be toxic.

10–12 sprigs of lavender flowers (this will equate to a couple of teaspoons)

6 very fresh egg yolks

½ teaspoon vanilla bean paste or vanilla extract (not vanilla flavouring)

3 tablespoons runny honey

275ml (½pt) of milk, semi-skimmed is fine

275ml (½pt) double cream

Lay the lavender sprigs on kitchen paper for a while to dry out and allow any small creatures to escape. Remove all the florets from the stalks and shake them lightly in a sieve to remove any debris.

Separate the eggs using two dessertspoons or an egg separator, rather than passing them between the two halves of the shell, as the mixture is only going to be cooked very lightly.

Whisk the egg yolks, vanilla and honey together. Warm the milk in a smallish, heavy-bottomed saucepan until it is almost, but not quite boiling. Pour it into the egg mixture, whisking gently all the time.

Wash out the saucepan and put the mixture back. Return to the heat and cook gently, stirring all the time until the mixture coats the spoon very lightly. You might notice a very slight deepening of colour when it's ready. Take it off the heat immediately and pour into a Pyrex measuring jug. If you leave it in the metal pan it will carry on cooking slightly and may start to scramble and curdle. (If the mixture does curdle a bit, pour it discreetly through a sieve.) Leave to cool and then stir in the cream and lavender.

The next stage is much easier if you have an ice cream machine. If you do, follow the maker's instructions from this stage.

If you don't, stir the mixture thoroughly or, better still, whisk it, and then pour into a lidded, plastic freezer box and put it into the freezer. After an hour or so, take it out of the freezer and stir it through, beating it quite vigorously with a wooden spoon: this is to break up any large ice crystals that will be forming. Return to the freezer. Repeat after another 30 minutes to an hour, and then again after another 30 minutes to an hour.

It's best to eat homemade ice cream within a couple of days of making if you can, as it does tend to get very hard when it has been in the freezer for a while. Take it out of the freezer 20 minutes or so before you want to serve it.

✓ Helpful Note (if your ice cream maker is the kind with a bowl you put in the freezer)
When you put the bowl of your ice cream maker back in the freezer, put it inside a large plastic bag. This helps to keep it clean and stops any stray frozen peas and the usual freezer debris from getting inside. Once the bowl is frozen it is very difficult to wipe it clean as the cloth sticks to the surface: clearly you can't just wash it in hot water at this stage as it would start to unfreeze! Keep the motor part, the paddle and central piece all together in another bag as you don't want to lose the smaller parts and render the entire machine completely useless!

✓ Individual Ice Cream Tubs
The first time you serve ice cream, it's relatively easy to scoop it out. Once it's been in the freezer for a couple of days it can become very hard and you need a lot of strength and energy to prise it out of the container. What you can do is to freeze the ice cream in individual portions to start with. This avoids those moments when your child would like ice cream for pudding, or during a sudden hot spell, but you just feel too exhausted to wrestle with it all!

Some of the more robust yoghurt cartons are good for this. Fill to within a centimetre from the top and cover tightly with cling film: they need to be covered otherwise they will taste 'airy'. If you are freezing several, a large shallow plastic freezer box is useful to store them in.

Do remember, though, that homemade ice cream is at its best freshly made, so don't store it for too long.

MILK LOLLIES

These light milky lollies are just the thing for small children, but don't let that stop you if you fancy one yourself: they are just the thing to cool down a frazzled adult on a hot day!

It is absolute simplicity itself to make them but you do need an ice cream machine: nothing complicated, just one of those where you have to pre-chill the bowl in the freezer.

The lollies are made with semi-skimmed milk and no cream. Regular ice cream contains more fat which keeps a check on too many ice crystals forming, therefore a little oil has been added to this recipe to smooth things along a bit. You won't be able to stir it into the milk but it will all be incorporated once it gets into the ice cream machine.

Start off with 75g of sugar, as specified, but if you find this a little sweet, cut down slightly next time you make them.

MAKES ABOUT 8, DEPENDING ON THE SIZE OF YOUR LOLLY MOULDS

570ml (1pt) semi-skimmed milk

75g (3oz) unrefined caster sugar

1 teaspoon vanilla extract

1 tablespoon mild flavourless oil (such as rapeseed)

You will need a lolly mould and wooden lolly sticks.

Heat the milk to almost, but not quite, boiling point. Remove from the heat and stir in the sugar until it has dissolved. Leave to cool completely: it will cool faster if you pour it into a non-metal bowl or jug.

Stir in the vanilla extract and add the oil. Pour into the ice cream machine (it will be easier if you have it in a jug at this stage). Follow the ice cream manufacturer's instructions.

Once the machine stops, spoon the mixture (it will be frozen to a loose slush) into the lolly moulds. Now you can put the lolly sticks in: you don't have to use the lids, as the mixture is stiff enough for you just to stand the sticks upright. (This is a very useful recipe if you have lost or broken some of your lids!)

Freeze for 12–24 hours. When you want to get them out of the moulds, put a washing-up bowl in the sink and hold the lolly mould under the hot tap for a few moments. If they don't work loose straight away, you can dip them in the bowl of hot water briefly. Don't overdo it or they will start to melt too much.

If you are leaving the lollies in the freezer for longer and haven't used lids, wrap the whole thing closely in a freezer bag to avoid that stale freezer after-taste.

Once you have cracked these, you can move on to the following equally simple chocolate version below. Honestly, talk about child's play!

CHOCOLATE MILK LOLLIES

These are very similar to the above recipe: the ingredients differ only slightly in that this recipe contains 2 tablespoons of cocoa powder as well as vanilla extract. Please don't feel these have to be restricted to the children either!

You will need a lolly mould and wooden lolly sticks.

Combine the cocoa in a bowl or jug with about 4 tablespoons of the cold milk and stir to a smooth paste.

Heat the rest of the milk to almost, but not quite, boiling point. Remove from the heat and stir in the sugar until it has dissolved. Pour the sweetened milk gradually into the cocoa and milk paste, stirring as you go. Leave to cool completely.

Stir in the vanilla extract and add the oil. Pour into the ice cream machine (it will be easier if you have it in a jug at this stage). Follow the ice cream manufacturer's instructions.

Once the machine stops, spoon the mixture into the lolly moulds, as for Milk Lollies, and put in the sticks. Freeze for 12–24 hours.

MAKES ABOUT 8, DEPENDING ON THE SIZE OF YOUR LOLLY MOULDS

2 level tablespoons good quality cocoa powder (not drinking chocolate)
570ml (1pt) semi-skimmed milk
75g (3oz) unrefined caster sugar
1 teaspoon vanilla extract
1 tablespoon mild flavourless oil (such as rapeseed)

Sundries

PROPER OLD-FASHIONED LEMONADE

A summer's day in the garden, bees buzzing, flowers blooming, birds singing, a relaxing chair and an ice-cold glass of lemonade: bliss!

5 large plump fresh
   lemons (try to buy
   unwaxed)
110–150g (4–5oz)
   unrefined granulated
   sugar
1litre (1¾pt) cold water
Small amount of boiling
   water

If you suspect the lemons are waxed, wash and scrub them thoroughly in hot soapy water, rinse and pat dry. Peel 4 of the lemons very thinly: a swivel peeler works well. Try to avoid cutting into the white pith as it's very bitter and will taint the finished lemonade.

Put the sugar into a saucepan with just enough water to cover and simmer gently until the sugar has completely melted and lost its grittiness. Cool slightly and pour into a heatproof jug. Add the lemon peel and leave to infuse and cool.

Once cool, squeeze the juice from the 4 peeled lemons and pour into the jug – don't sieve it yet. Add the water, stir well, cover and chill for a couple of hours.

Finally, cut the fifth lemon in half, squeeze half into the jug and slice the other half thinly. Check for sweetness, adding a little more sugar if necessary (use caster sugar at this point as it will dissolve more quickly). Strain into a serving jug and decorate with the lemon slices. You may like to add some ice, but pour the lemonade out quickly if you do: otherwise the ice will melt and the lemonade will be too diluted!

Add a few sprigs of fresh lemon balm if you have any in the garden. If you have any lemon verbena, you could add a few of the precious sherbet-lemon tasting leaves.

LEMON AND LIMEADE

This is even zingier than the lemonade and seems more exotic! It is just as thirst quenching and is something a bit different.

Make the recipe as for Proper Old-fashioned Lemonade, above, reserving 1 lemon and 1 lime for the final stage. As before, cut the lemon in half, squeeze half into the jug and slice the other half thinly. Do the same with the lime.

Check for sweetness and strain and serve as before.

3 large plump fresh
    lemons (try to buy
    unwaxed)
3 fresh limes
110–150g (4–5oz)
    unrefined granulated
    sugar
1litre (1¾pt) cold water
Small amount boiling
    water

STEAMIES AND FROTHIES

If you have a coffee machine that steams milk for a cappuccino, you can use it to heat and froth some plain milk for a child's drink. Shake a little **cocoa powder** or **drinking chocolate** over the froth for the finishing touch.

For a **honey and cinnamon** version, stir in a small spoonful (not too much) of runny honey and a little pinch of cinnamon. You may like to sprinkle a tiny amount of cinnamon on top of the froth as well.

If you have a jar of **malt extract** in the house, a small amount stirred into warm milk is delicious. A teaspoonful for an average size mug of milk is about right or half a teaspoon or a little egg or coffee spoon for a tiny child's mug.

Alternatively, warm the milk and froth the milk manually with one of the hand-held milk whisks or frothers you can buy.

These milky drinks are so lovely and soothing that you may like to make one for yourself as well!

STRAWBERRY JAM

Homemade strawberry jam is just the thing to set off a cream tea in the garden or to spread on hot buttered toast for a taste of summer in the depth of winter. Once you have mastered the basics and got your confidence up, it's not at all difficult to make.

You can buy thermometers for testing when jam is at the correct temperature to set, but in practice they can confuse matters. They have a tendency to steam up so you can't read them very easily, and you can be so preoccupied with trying to see what the thermometer says, you can miss what is actually happening to the jam itself – and before you know it you have a pan full of strawberry toffee!

Some commercial jams can be rather stiff and jellified; what you are aiming for with homemade jam is more of a 'soft-set' or 'continental' jam – not runny, obviously, but not solid either. Once you detect a slight wrinkle on your testing plate, remove from the heat immediately. If you get to the 'thread' stage (*very* unlikely with strawberry) it's gone too far!

Choose a good proportion of slightly under-ripe strawberries as strawberries don't contain huge amounts of pectin, which is what helps the jam to set, and over-ripe strawberries contain even less. The lemon juice and the peel and pips will help to boost the pectin content.

THIS RECIPE MAKES APPROXIMATELY 6 X 370G (12OZ) JARS OF JAM.

- 1.8kg (4lb) hulled strawberries, preferably slightly under-ripe
- 2 large plump lemons (nothing wizened or shrunken)
- 1.35kg (3lb) granulated sugar

A stainless steel jam funnel and a ladle make transferring the jam into the jars much easier.

Before you start, put a few small plates or saucers in the fridge to test the jam for setting later.

You will need a small square of muslin and some string, sterilised jars, wax discs and jam pot covers or lids, a long-handled wooden spoon plus a clock or timer that shows minutes clearly.

Put the strawberries into a preserving pan or large stock pot-sized saucepan. Copper-bottomed pans work well as they conduct the heat so efficiently.

Squeeze the juice from the lemons and pour it through a sieve onto the strawberries. Tie the lemon peel and pips and bits from the sieve into a piece of muslin. Tie it to the handle of your pan and suspend it in the strawberries.

Simmer the fruit over a medium heat, stirring from time to time, until the fruit is completely cooked and soft, but still a recognisable shape. This should take roughly half an hour.

Remove the pan from the heat and stir in the sugar. Keep stirring, gently, and the sugar should dissolve. If not, return it to the hob on a gentle heat until it does.

Once the sugar is dissolved, turn up the heat and bring to the boil. Remove the bag of peel, pips and pith and boil rapidly, stirring more or less constantly.

It should take around 7 minutes or so to come to the boil and a further 20–30 minutes to get a set. Strawberry jam is notoriously reluctant to reach setting point but start testing after 20 minutes, and once every minute after that.

To test for a set
Put a teaspoonful of jam onto a cold plate and push it with your finger. If it wrinkles slightly, it's ready.

When the jam is ready, remove from the heat and leave to settle for 10–15 minutes. Remove any persistent scum from the surface with a tablespoon: it should more or less 'peel away' cleanly.

Ladle the jam into the warm, sterilised jars using a jam funnel. Cover the jam with the wax discs and lids.

Wait until the jars are cold before labelling. Store in a cool, dry and preferably dark place.

Helpful Notes
- **To sterilise jars:** Wash the jars in hot soapy water and rinse thoroughly. Shake off any excess water and stand on a baking tray. Put them into the oven for 10 minutes or so at 160°C or equivalent. Alternatively, you can put them through the hottest cycle of your dishwasher if you have one.
- Rather than stirring furiously, just push the boiling jam gently around the pan. As the jam reaches setting point it will bubble and spit wildly so keep at arm's length (this is why you need a long-handled spoon!). It's not a bad idea to have a damp cloth handy and wipe up spits and spatters as they happen.
- You can use home-frozen strawberries for this recipe. Weigh them before bagging so they will be the right weight for the recipe. Secure the tops tightly and defrost almost completely before using.

Take Care
Always keep small children and excitable pets out of the kitchen when making jam. Once the fruit and sugar are boiling it can be very dangerous indeed and the jam retains the heat for quite a while after the hob has been turned off.

BREAD AND MILK

This is a really old-fashioned thing that you never hear of these days, except between the pages of a children's storybook. It used to be given to children and invalids and is quite literally just bread soaked in milk, preferably warm milk, which you eat with a spoon just as it is, or with a little sugar. It tastes very bland – you are not sure whether you are eating bread or baby porridge but it is strangely soothing and some young children really like it!

You must make it with a decent white bread with a proper crumb structure, nothing over processed and 'wodgy' otherwise it will be like wallpaper paste! This may well be why it fell out of favour.

You don't really need precise quantities but as a general rule approximately **75g (3oz) of two or three day old decent white bread, preferably with crust removed, to 140ml (¼pt) of milk, or a fraction less** is about right. This will give two child-sized portions.

Warm the milk and crumble the bread into a bowl. Pour the milk on top and let the bread soak it up. Give it a bit of a stir and eat sprinkled with a little sugar. If you would like it a bit warmer, you can heat the bread and milk together gently in a saucepan – but you mustn't let it burn or catch or it will taste disgusting and be ruined! You can also make it in the microwave if you prefer.

LEMON CURD

Lemon curd is quick and easy to make and only *ever so* slightly nerve-wracking (just at the end when you are trying to thicken it without scrambling). It tastes absolutely delicious: fresh, light and lemony. It's fabulous on fresh white bread and butter, on toast, in delicate little crustless sandwiches and for filling tarts and cakes.

Sometimes bought lemon curd can be fairly solid; homemade lemon curd has more of a 'soft set', which means it is a bit like the consistency of thick cream.

If you happen to have a big enough heavy-bottomed saucepan you can make the lemon curd directly in that – it must have a thick heavy bottom, though, or the heat from the hob will be too fierce.

Otherwise, make the curd in a heatproof bowl on top of a pan of simmering water. Make sure the bowl fits snugly and securely into the top of the pan and doesn't wobble about. Also, the water shouldn't come up as far as the bottom of the bowl.

If you have a double boiler, that would be perfect for the job.

If the lemons are very large, zest them all but just use the juice of 2½. If you suspect they have been waxed, scrub them in hot soapy water, rinse and pat dry.

Cut the butter into small pieces and put into the pan (or bowl or double boiler) with the sugar. Heat gently until the butter has melted and the sugar has dissolved. Stir in the lemon juice and zest. Use a wooden spoon to stir.

Gently stir in the eggs. Keep the heat low, stirring carefully throughout, until the mixture has thickened enough to coat the back of the spoon lightly. Be steady: you want lemon curd not lemon curdle! (If by any chance you do overdo it a fraction and it curdles slightly, just sieve it discreetly and remember not to heat it quite so much next time!)

Sieve to remove the zest, which has now done its job: the finished curd should be completely smooth. Pour into sterilised jars, leave to cool and put in the fridge to set. (See the Strawberry Jam recipe, above, for instructions for sterilising jars.)

Eat within a couple of weeks.

THIS RECIPE MAKES ENOUGH TO FILL ABOUT 1½ STANDARD JAM JARS.

110g (4oz) butter
225g (8oz) unrefined caster sugar
3 lemons – grated zest and juice
3 eggs, beaten and sieved (discard the very gloopy white left in the sieve)

CHOCOLATE BLANCMANGE

You can make this in a traditional-type jelly mould or pour it into individual serving dishes. It also makes a great 'chocolate bunny' if you can get hold of a rabbit-shaped jelly mould, which is especially nice for young children and anyone feeling a bit nostalgic.

SERVES 4–6

40g (1½oz) cornflour
10g (½oz) cocoa powder
40g (1½oz) unrefined
  granulated sugar
570ml (1pt) milk
½ teaspoon vanilla extract
  or vanilla bean paste

You will need a heavy-bottomed milk saucepan.

Sieve the cornflour and cocoa powder carefully into a bowl. Add the sugar and stir together. Take sufficient milk from the measured pint and mix to a smooth paste with a metal spoon. Stir in the vanilla.

Put the rest of the milk to heat on the hob until it is almost, but not quite, boiling. Pour it on to the cocoa mixture, stirring constantly with a wooden spoon. Wash out the saucepan and pour the mixture back.

Return to the hob and cook on a medium heat, stirring all the time until the mixture is thick and glossy. Cool slightly and pour into the mould or individual serving dishes to cool and set completely.

This is lovely on its own or with any kind of cream: a spoonful of whipped or clotted cream is especially nice.

Turning Blancmange out of a Mould
If you are using a mould, it helps with the turning out process later if the mould is wet. Rinse it out with a little water and shake out the surplus before you pour in your mixture. When the blancmange is ready to turn out, pull it gently away from the sides of the mould with your fingertip, invert the serving plate over the top, give it a brisk shake, and turn over and out onto the plate.

BUNNY CUSTARD

Custard made from custard powder makes a perfect blancmange if it is allowed to go cold and set. You can make it a bit more special by making it in a rabbit mould. This is perfect for serving with jelly for traditional 'jelly and custard'. Sometimes, it seems that nostalgic adults are a lot more enthusiastic about jelly and custard (or indeed jelly and ice cream) than children: who have been brought up on yoghurt and fromage frais and find the textures a bit too wobbly and slippery!

You will need a heavy-bottomed milk saucepan.

Put the custard powder and sugar into a bowl and stir together. Add sufficient milk taken from the measured pint and mix to a smooth paste with a metal spoon.

Put the rest of the milk to heat on the hob until it is almost, but not quite, boiling. Pour it onto the custard mixture, stirring constantly with a wooden spoon. Wash out the saucepan and pour the mixture back.

Return to the hob and cook on a medium heat, stirring all the time until the mixture is thick and glossy.

Cool slightly and pour into the mould to cool and set completely.

✓ **Refrigerating Blancmange**
If you are going to refrigerate the blancmange, be sure it has cooled down before you put it into the fridge and also cover it: if you don't, the blancmange may pick up flavours from other foods stored with it.

SERVES 4–6

35g (1½oz) custard powder
25–35g (1–1½oz) unrefined granulated sugar
570ml (1pt) milk

ORANGE JELLY

This is a lovely, fresh-tasting jelly. You can make it in a traditional jelly mould, a novelty animal-shaped one or in individual serving dishes. You can also make it in a plain dish and serve it 'chopped'. You can chop the jelly up and serve it surrounding your custard or chocolate bunny blancmange if you like.

MAKES 570ML (1PT):
SERVES 4–6

2 sachets powdered
   gelatine
150ml (¼pt) hot water
420ml (¾pt) juice
   squeezed from 3–4
   oranges
1 level dessertspoon
   unrefined caster sugar,
   or to taste

Pour the hot water into a measuring jug and sprinkle the gelatine over the top. Stir briskly with a dinner fork.

Once the gelatine is dissolved make up to 570ml (1pt) with the orange juice. Taste and add sugar as needed.

Pour into a mould or serving dish or dishes, cover and leave in a cool place to set.

Orange Juice Jelly
If you don't actually have any oranges to hand you can make the jelly with orange juice from a carton: freshly squeezed or from concentrate. If you use juice from concentrate, the jelly will be cloudy rather than clear but it still looks nice and tastes good.

RASPBERRY AND CRANBERRY JELLY

Sometimes the occasion calls for a classic red jelly, jewel bright and glowing. Raspberry and cranberry juice drink makes a beautifully flavoured one with a good colour. Look for a top quality juice drink sweetened with actual sugar rather than anything artificial and with as few additives as possible: the quality and flavour of the finished jelly will depend entirely on the quality of the juice.

Measure the hot water into a measuring jug and sprinkle the gelatine over the top. Stir briskly with a dinner fork until the gelatine has melted. Pour in the cranberry juice and stir.

Pour into the serving dish or dishes, cover and leave to set in a cool place.

2 sachets powdered gelatine
150ml (¼pt) hot water
150ml (¼pt) raspberry and cranberry juice drink (see above)

Adding Sugar
If the juice is a little tart, you may need to add some sugar. Test once you have added the juice and add a little sugar to taste if necessary. Use caster sugar as it will dissolve more easily and stir briskly.

✓ **Turning Jelly Out of a Mould**
Rinse the mould out with a little water and shake out the surplus before you pour in your mixture, as with blancmange. When the jelly is ready to turn out, loosen the sides at the top very carefully with a knife and stand the mould in very hot water for about 30 seconds. Invert your serving plate over the top, give it a decisive shake, and turn over and out onto the plate. Good luck!

Bread, Rolls, Fruit Loaves and Buns with the Aid of a Bread Machine

Your trusty bread machine can help you bake a loaf from start to finish on an everyday basis but for special tea-time occasions you can use it to make the dough and bake something a bit different in the oven.

HALF AND HALF HOVIS® LOAF

One of my earliest memories is of my Grandma (my Mum's Mum) standing at the tea table cutting bread for us all.

She had this really unusual, incredibly dangerous *way of buttering and slicing bread (it was always Hovis®). She would tuck the loaf into her waist with one hand, and with the other she would spread it with butter and then cut a slice, slicing upwards towards herself! The slices were thin and delicate but every so many slices a kind of tuft would develop on the upper side. She would cut this tuft off and give it to me. This recipe tastes to me, at least, very like the Hovis® I remember from my childhood. I wouldn't recommend slicing it like Grandma did, though!*

The recipe uses the bread machine's Quick Loaf or Rapid Bake program. The water should be warm to activate the yeast properly. One way to warm the water is to put it in the microwave for 30–40 seconds on high.

1 teaspoon quick yeast
1 teaspoon salt
1 tablespoon unrefined granulated sugar
190g (7oz) strong white bread flour
190g (7oz) Hovis® Strong Wholemeal bread flour
300ml warm water
2 tablespoons mild flavourless oil, such as mild olive, sunflower, or rapeseed

Put the yeast, salt and sugar into the bread pan of your machine and put the flour on top. Pour in the warm water and the oil.

Set the machine to the Quick Loaf program and select the Medium size setting. In some machines, the sizing is M, L and XL: in which case, select L.

Once the loaf is ready, take it out of the machine and slide it out, on its side, onto a wooden board. Pick it up and stand it upright on a cooling rack. Once it is completely cold, store it in an airtight plastic box or a sealed plastic bag. If you are going to slice it by machine wait a few hours, as it is difficult to slice it properly when it is very fresh.

✓ Removing the loaf

Never ease a loaf out with a knife or anything metal or you will damage the inside of your bread pan. Sometimes, the mixing blade can get stuck in the loaf. Once the loaf is cool it's easy to get it out with your fingers. Again, don't use anything metal as you will scratch the blade. Incidentally, if you leave the loaf in the machine for too long once it is ready, it will become damp and wrinkly. It will dry out but it's best to avoid this happening if you can!

HALF AND HALF HOVIS® MINI LOAVES

*These are something else I remember from my childhood. You can still buy them, but with the aid of your bread machine, a bag of Hovis® flour and some dinky little loaf tins, you can make your own. See also **Mini-Milk Loaves**.*

You will need 12 greased mini-loaf tins (the kind you can buy in packs of 4).

The ingredients for the dough are as for the Hovis® Loaf recipe. Select the Dough setting: this should take around 45 minutes.

Once the dough is ready, take it out of the machine and flour your hands well before removing it from the bread pan. Put the dough onto a floured surface and cut into 12 equal pieces. There is no need to shape the pieces.

Put a piece into each prepared mini-loaf tin or bun tin cup and leave to rise in a warm place for around three quarters of an hour, until almost doubled in size.

Bake in a preheated oven at 180–200°C (fan oven) or equivalent until golden. Bake at the lower temperature if your oven is very fierce.

Once baked, leave in the tin to cool and contract for a few minutes. You should then be able to just lift them out of the tins.

Makes 12 mini loaves

CRUSTY FARMHOUSE LOAF

Make the dough for this old fashioned-looking crusty loaf in a bread machine and bake it in a loaf tin in the oven.

1 teaspoon quick yeast

1 tablespoon unrefined granulated sugar

1 teaspoon salt

385g (14oz) strong white bread flour

300ml warm water

2 tablespoons mild flavourless oil, such as mild olive, sunflower, or rapeseed

You will need a greased 450g (1lb) loaf tin.

Put the yeast, sugar and salt in separate corners of the bread pan. Add the flour and the warm water on top and spoon in the oil.

Select the Dough setting: this should take around 45 minutes.

Once the dough is ready, turn it out onto a floured board and turn it lightly in the flour. There is no need to knead it further. Pick it up and ease it gently into the prepared loaf tin.

Leave it to rise for 30–40 minutes until it has almost doubled in size and looks like the right size for the finished loaf. It's difficult to be precise about how long this will take as it depends on the temperature of the room: it will rise faster in a warm spot than in a cold one.

Once it has risen sufficiently, dust the top with a little flour stirred through a tea strainer and with your sharpest, non-serrated knife make a deep cut length-wise across the top.

Turn the oven on to 210–220°C or equivalent and leave the loaf until the oven has come to temperature.

Put the loaf in the oven and, as soon as you have shut the door, turn the temperature down to the temperature you would normally use to bake bread and pastry: 180–200°C or equivalent.

Bake for approximately 30 minutes until browned and ready.

Remove from the oven and leave for a few minutes for the loaf to cool and contract slightly before you turn it out. Cool on a wire rack.

LARGE FLAT BREAD BUN

This uses exactly the same dough as the **Crusty Farmhouse Loaf**, above, but is baked as a flat round on a baking tray and comes out with a much softer and more delicate crust. It's really simple to make *and* easy to slice! If you make bread regularly, this might be one you'll make again and again.

Make the dough as above and once it is ready, ease it out of the bread pan with floured hands onto a lightly floured board. Shape into a round, flat disc and ease onto a greased baking tray. You may need to smooth it out a bit more. At this stage it should measure roughly 20cm (8in) across (if you make it too deep and round the middle won't cook through properly). Leave it in a warm place to rise until it is practically half as big again and, although still fairly flat, more domed in appearance.

Bake in a preheated oven at your usual bread temperature: 180–200°C (fan oven) or equivalent for approximately 20–25 minutes or until light brown all over.

Leave on the tray for a few moments and transfer to a wire rack to cool. A clean tea towel over the top will keep it moist as it cools.

You may like to dust the bun very lightly with flour (stir a little through a tea strainer with a teaspoon) before you serve it.

✓ Helpful Note

If you make bread often, you might find it easier to transfer your yeast (see below) to a screw-top jar that you can keep it in the fridge: this makes it a bit handier for spooning out than the original packaging. A clean Marmite jar is ideal: the glass is dark and doesn't let much light in, and the lid is plastic and won't rust. If you don't make bread very often then once the yeast is open, reseal the packet, with tape if necessary, and keep it in the fridge.

Yeast Type: Be sure to buy actual quick yeast for bread machines for use in your bread machine.

LAVENDER AND HONEY BREAD

The lavender makes this quite an unusual loaf that tastes wonderful! The lavender flavour is very gentle but you can tell it is there. The honey flavour comes through subtly as well. This is great for a relaxed tea in the garden: serve with a little butter, thin slices of cheese and a fresh garden salad enhanced with a homemade honey dressing. (This is equally good at lunchtime.)

The Lavender Bread is also delicious buttered with a creamy set honey or a good jam or jelly: bramble or crab apple jelly is especially good.

! A Word of Warning
Be sure to use only the more common English lavender: Lavandula *angustifolia*, sometimes called *Lavandula officinalis* or *Lavandula spicata*. The tufty French lavender: *Lavandula stoechas*, can be toxic.

15–20 sprigs of lavender flowers still in bud (this will equate to 2–3 teaspoons) 1 teaspoon quick yeast 1 teaspoon salt 385g (14oz) strong white bread flour 300ml warm water 1 tablespoon runny honey 2 tablespoons mild flavourless oil, such as mild olive, sunflower, or rapeseed	Lay the lavender sprigs on kitchen paper for a while to dry out and allow any small creatures (if there are any) to leave. Remove all the florets from the stalks and shake them lightly in a sieve. Put the yeast and salt into separate corners of the bread pan of your machine and put the flour on top. Add the lavender. Pour in the warm water, honey and oil. Select the Quick Loaf setting. Once the loaf is ready, remove from the machine and cool on a wire rack. This is best eaten fresh but if you do have any over it is good toasted, spread with butter and honey for breakfast: the lavender scent really comes through as it warms up in the toaster!

GARDEN SALAD

*Try this with your **Lavender Bread** and cheese.*

Spoon the mustard and honey into the screw-top jar. Add the oil and vinegar, screw the top on firmly and shake vigorously.

Drizzle over your salad at the table.

For the salad
Lettuce or other salad leaves
Celery, very thinly sliced
Cucumber, peeled and very thinly sliced
Unsprayed and bug-free edible flowers such as: nasturtium, borage, viola, marigold petals, fennel flowers (snip the little yellow individual flowers from the large flat heads)
Tomatoes, fresh from the garden, if available
Handful of podded peas, fresh from the garden, if available
Thinly sliced radishes, fresh from the garden, if available

For the homemade salad dressing
You can use this to dress all kinds of salad. Make it in a screw-top jar with a plastic lid, if possible (metal will react with the vinegar).

1 heaped teaspoon Dijon mustard
1 teaspoon runny honey
3 tablespoons oil (mild olive, rapeseed or sunflower)
1 tablespoon cider vinegar

COTTAGE LOAF

Here is a version of the classic cottage loaf, which you can start in the bread machine.

1 tablespoon sugar
1¾ teaspoons quick yeast
1 teaspoon salt
500g (1lb 2oz) strong
 white bread flour
275ml (½pt) lukewarm
 water or milk
3 tablespoons mild oil

You will need a large, greased baking tray.

Put the sugar, yeast and salt in separate corners of the bread pan. Add the flour and the warm water on top, and then pour in the oil. Set your machine to the Dough setting: normally this takes about 45 minutes.

When the dough is ready, flour your hands and ease it out onto a lightly floured board.

Divide the dough into two pieces: one piece should be about two thirds of the mixture or a fraction more and the other about one third or a fraction less.

Roll the larger piece into a ball and put it towards one end of your prepared tray, but so it has sufficient room all round to rise. Roll the smaller piece into a ball and put on the tray as far away from the other piece as you can, again, still leaving enough space all the way round for it to rise. If they won't both fit on the tray, you will need to use a second greased baking tray for this stage. Leave the dough in a warm place for 40 minutes or so until it has doubled in size. (If you assemble the loaf *before* it has risen, you won't have the two clear parts to the loaf – it will all merge into one big amorphous mass!)

When the dough has risen, manoeuvre the smaller piece on top of the larger one.

Grease the handle of a wooden spoon and plunge the greased handle through the centre of the ball on top of the loaf right through until it touches the baking tray. Ease it out again gently. This will leave you with a nice little dimple on top and anchor the 'topknot' securely onto the loaf.

Alternatively, you can use your finger or, for a flatter loaf that looks more 'of a piece', you can use the thumb and forefinger of both hands at the same time, positioned on either side of the loaf and work round, making quite a large hole.

Leave it to rise a little longer whilst you preheat your oven to 210–220°C (fan oven) or equivalent.

When the oven has come to temperature, put in your loaf, turn the oven down to 180–200°C and bake for 30 minutes or so until golden brown.

Cool on a wire rack. A clean tea towel over the top will keep it moist as it cools.

NOVELTY DUCK ROLLS

You can make these for a children's tea or party. The duck part is really simple to put together: if you aren't normally very artistic you will stun yourself with your expertise! Be careful though: it's very easy to make them look too cute *– and then nobody will have the heart to actually eat them! Admittedly, they look more like a bath duck than the real thing but they are very appealing.*

You will need a large, greased baking tray and a second tray: this will not go into the oven so does not need to be oven-proof.

Make the dough as above. Flour your hands and transfer the dough to a lightly floured board. Divide the dough into two pieces: one piece should be about two thirds of the mixture or a fraction more and the other about one third or a fraction less.

MAKES 12 ROLLS

Dough as for the Cottage
  Loaf
24 currants
A carrot or 2, peeled

Divide the larger piece into 12 equal pieces and shape gently into flattish rounds, as if you were making baps, and space them out in their final positions on the prepared baking tray.

Divide the smaller piece into 12 and shape into round balls. Space them out well on the second well-greased tray – you will need enough room between them when they are fully risen to manoeuvre them off the tray with a palette knife.

Leave them all in a warm place for 40 minutes or so until they have risen and virtually doubled in size. If you can cover the round balls with an upturned bowl or something similar, it will stop them drying out.

Position the round balls on top of the flatter rolls. Put them in the middle: they will drift of their own accord whilst baking to more of a 'head' position.

Leave them to rise a little longer whilst you preheat your oven to 180–200°C (fan oven) or equivalent.

When the oven has come to temperature, put the loaves in and bake for 8 minutes or so until golden brown.

Leave on the tray for a few moments before transferring to a wire rack to cool. A clean tea towel over the top will keep them moist as they cool.

Once they are cool, make tiny slits either side of the 'head' for eyes and wedge the currants into position. Make a longer slit where the beak will be and cut beak shapes from the peeled carrot. Wedge into position.

MINI MILK LOAVES

A milk loaf isn't massively different from a regular white loaf but it does have a lovely extra soft and fine texture. Use skimmed milk as it gives the softest and finest texture. Milk loaves keep well but they are at their most soft and delicious when fresh.

Milk loaf dough makes lovely little rolls, which you can make in a bun tin or set out on a baking tray. Best of all, though, are mini loaves baked in mini loaf tins. These are really popular with children, both to eat at meal times or to cut into dinky little slices for dolls and teddy bears' tea parties.

MAKES 12 MINI LOAVES	You will need 12 greased, mini-loaf tins.
1 teaspoon quick yeast 1 teaspoon salt 1 tablespoon unrefined granulated sugar 385g (14oz) strong white bread flour 300ml skimmed milk, warmed 2 tablespoons mild flavourless oil, such as mild olive, sunflower or rapeseed	Put the yeast, salt and sugar into the bread pan of your machine and put the flour on top. Pour in the warm milk and the oil. Set the machine to the Dough program. This should take about 45 minutes. Once the dough is ready, take it out of the machine and flour your hands well before removing it from the bread pan. Put the dough onto a floured surface and cut into 12 equal pieces: there is no need to shape the pieces. Put a piece into each prepared mini loaf tin and leave to rise in a warm place for around three quarters of an hour, until almost doubled in size. Bake in a preheated oven at 180–200°C (fan oven) or equivalent until golden. Bake at the lower temperature if your oven is very fierce. Once baked, leave in the tin to cool and contract for a few minutes. You should then be able to just lift them out of the tins.

MILK LOAF

Alternatively, use the same dough as for the **Mini Milk Loaves**, above, but make a full size loaf entirely in the bread machine. Set the machine to the Quick Loaf program and select the Medium size setting (in some machines, the sizing is M, L and XL, in which case, select L).

Once the loaf is ready, take it out of the machine and slide it out, on its side, onto a wooden board. Pick it up and stand it upright on a cooling rack. Once it is completely cold, store it in an airtight plastic box or a sealed plastic bag. If you are going to slice it by machine wait a few hours, as it is difficult to slice it properly when it is very fresh.

MILK SPLITS

This is the same dough as for the milk loaves, above, but baked like this they are very like Devonshire or Cornish Splits and are perfect split and eaten with clotted cream and jam as a change from scones. Eat them with savouries if you prefer.

You will need a greased, 12-cup muffin tin.

Put the sugar, yeast and salt in separate corners of the bread pan. Add the flour and the warm milk on top and pour in the oil. Set your machine to the Dough setting: normally this will take about 45 minutes.

Once the dough is ready, turn it out onto a lightly floured board and cut it into 12 fairly even pieces (there is no need to shape them further). Put a piece into each cup of the prepared muffin tin. Leave them in a warm place for an hour or so until doubled in size.

Bake in a preheated oven at 180–220°C (fan oven) or equivalent for 8–10 minutes until golden brown. Leave on the baking tray for a few moments to cool and contract and then remove and finish cooling on a wire rack. A clean tea towel over the top will keep them fresh and moist as they cool.

Dust each roll with a little flour: stir it through a tea strainer for a light, even distribution.

MAKES 12 ROLLS

- 1 tablespoon unrefined granulated sugar
- 1 teaspoon quick yeast
- 1 teaspoon salt
- 385g (14oz) strong white bread flour
- 300ml warm skimmed milk
- 2 tablespoons mild flavourless oil, such as mild olive, sunflower or rapeseed

BRIDGE ROLLS

Who knows why bridge rolls are called 'bridge rolls'? Is it because they are shaped like a bridge or maybe because they are sometimes served at card parties? Whatever the origin of the name, they are a really useful shaped roll to be able to make. You can serve them at tea time filled with cheese, ham, egg, potted meats or fish pastes and so on, and they are also perfect for accommodating a sausage. A hot sausage in a bridge roll is great for children's parties or take them filled with a cold sausage for picnics.

MAKES 12 ROLLS

1 tablespoon unrefined granulated sugar
1 teaspoon quick yeast
1 teaspoon salt
385g (14oz) strong white bread flour
300ml warm water
2 tablespoons mild flavourless oil, such as mild olive, sunflower or rapeseed

You will need a greased baking tray.

Put the sugar, yeast and salt in separate corners of the bread pan. Add the flour and the warm water on top and pour in the oil. Set your machine to the Dough setting: normally this will take about 45 minutes.

Once the dough is ready, turn it out onto a lightly floured board and cut into four equal pieces. You may need to add a little more flour as you go along, but try to keep it to a minimum.

Working with one piece on the board at a time, to give yourself elbow room, roll it into a long cylinder shape. Cut the cylinder into three equal pieces.

Take one of the pieces and roll it on the board with the flat of your hand. Roll with your three middle fingers, lightly backwards and forwards, tucking in the ends of the roll as you do so with your thumb and forefinger. Do this a few times, gently and quickly. Repeat with the others.

Lay the rolls on the prepared baking tray in two rows of six, fairly close together so that they will touch each other as they spread out and you'll have two joined rows of six rolls each.

Leave them in a warm place for an hour or so until doubled in size.

Bake in a preheated oven at 180–220°C (fan oven) or equivalent for 8–10 minutes or until golden brown. Leave on the baking tray for a few moments to cool slightly and then remove and finish cooling on a wire rack. A clean tea towel over the top will keep them fresh and moist as they cool.

Eat fresh.

ICED BUNS

These are very simple to make, inexpensive and popular with most people but especially with small children. It's nice to colour half the icing pink and have half the batch with pink icing and half with white. There's no need to resort to food colouring: just use a dab of raspberry jam. Iced Bun icing needs to have that extra sticky, slightly stretchy quality: the glycerine provides that effect. The lemon juice prevents the icing from tasting overpoweringly sweet.

Sieve the icing sugar into a roomy bowl and stir in 2 tablespoons of lemon juice and the glycerine. Work the icing sugar into the liquid with a wooden spoon and add the rest of the lemon juice as necessary: it shouldn't be too runny.

Once the rolls are completely cold, spoon half of the icing onto six of the rolls. Use a teaspoon and spread and smooth the icing along the length of the roll with the back of the spoon.

Stir the jam into the rest of the icing and ice the other six rolls.

Eat very fresh.

✓ **Helpful Note**
Sometimes, you might want to make up a half quantity of icing and ice half the batch, leaving the rest as plain rolls.

MAKE THE BRIDGE ROLLS FROM THE PREVIOUS RECIPE AND THEN TURN THEM INTO ICED BUNS.

Glace Icing (with extra
   sticky properties)
175g (6oz) icing sugar
2–3 tablespoons lemon
   juice
3 teaspoons glycerine
Small spoonful of seedless
   raspberry jam: enough
   to tint the icing the
   exact shade you want

POPPY SEED ROLLS

These yummy little rolls are perfect for tea with butter and a really good jam but they are also great for breakfast, packed lunches or to serve with soup. You'll feel very pleased with yourself as you take them from the oven as they look like something from an exclusive baker's! The beaten egg gives a shiny golden finish and the poppy seeds, which stay on surprisingly well, have a nice nutty crunch.

You can buy special poppy seeds for baking: they are usually sold in the spice section. These seeds are from the Hungarian Blue Breadseed Poppy, which is a variety of the opium poppy Papaver somniferum, *and they have a distinctive, beautiful, blue sheen. Theoretically, you could use seeds from the ordinary opium poppy if you have any in your garden, and know for certain that is what they are. The seeds themselves are edible, although they don't have the lovely blue sheen. Don't eat the rest of the plant, though, and certainly don't use other varieties, as some, such as the oriental poppy* Papaver orientale, *are poisonous.*

MAKES 12 ROLLS

For the rolls
1 teaspoon quick yeast
1 teaspoon salt
1 tablespoon unrefined
   granulated sugar
385g (14oz) strong white
   bread flour
300ml skimmed milk,
   warmed
2 tablespoons mild
   flavourless oil, such as
   mild olive, sunflower or
   rapeseed

For the glaze and
topping
1 egg, beaten with a drop
   of water
About 2 dessertspoons of
   poppy seeds

You will need a large, greased baking tray.

Put the yeast, salt and sugar into the bread pan of your machine and put the flour on top. Pour in the warm milk and the oil. Set the machine to the Dough program. This should take about 45 minutes.

Once the dough is ready, take it out of the machine and flour your hands well before removing it from the bread pan. Put the dough onto a floured surface and knead it for a few moments.

Divide it into four pieces and divide each of those into a further three pieces. Roll each of these pieces into a long cylindrical tube about 30cm (12in) long.

You can make at least four different shapes from the long cylinders. Here are the main ones but you may come up with others:

- Plait: Plait three of the pieces together and cut the plait into three equal pieces.

- Twist: Twist two of the pieces together and cut the twist into three equal pieces.

- Coil: Cut a long cylinder into three sections and coil each section round on itself so that it looks a bit like a snail shell.

- Knot: Cut a long cylinder into three sections and tie each section carefully into a knot.

Put the finished shapes onto the prepared baking tray and leave in a warm place for about an hour until they have almost doubled in size and look about the right size for the finished rolls. Once they are at this stage, brush them carefully with the beaten egg and sprinkle with the poppy seeds.

Bake in a preheated oven at 180°C (fan oven) or equivalent for 8–10 minutes until the tops are golden. Cool on a wire rack. A clean tea towel laid over them will keep them moist as they cool.

MALTED MILK AND HONEY BUNS

These delicious squidgy buns are a bit like little, round, golden malt loaves. Eat them split with butter. It's really easy to make the dough in the bread machine and then bake them in the oven. If you have any left after a couple of days they are gorgeous toasted: cut them in half and toast them lightly on both sides under the grill – they are too fat to go in the toaster! You can buy jars of barley malt extract in most health food shops.

You will need to select the Raisin Dough setting for this recipe. This means either the machine will beep after most of the kneading has been done so you can rush at breakneck speed back to it and add your dried fruit then, or, if you have a newer model, you will have put the fruit into a special compartment in the lid which will release it into the dough at the correct time. This is because if you add the fruit at the beginning it will be kneaded into an unappetising brown sludge with no discernible separate fruits!

The raisin dough program usually takes around 2 hours, 20 minutes or so in most machines.

This will look like a 'rare old mixture' when it's sitting in the bread pan, as if it will never mix together, but it will.

MAKES 12 BUNS

1½ teaspoons yeast
1 teaspoon salt
500g (1lb 2oz) strong
    white bread flour
300ml milk, warmed
1 generous tablespoon
    runny honey
3 tablespoons barley malt
    extract
1 egg
2–3 tablespoons mild oil
110g (4oz) raisins and
    sultanas, mixed

About 2 tablespoons
    runny honey to glaze

You will need a greased 12-cup muffin tin.

Put the yeast and salt in separate corners of the bread pan. Add the flour and the warm milk on top, then the honey, malt extract and egg, and spoon in the oil. Put the dried fruit in the raisin compartment and select the Raisin Dough setting.

Once the dough is ready, turn it out onto a floured board and cut into 12 fairly even pieces. There is no need to knead it further. Roll each piece lightly and put into the greased 12-cup muffin tin.

Space them out evenly on the baking tray and leave them in a warm place for an hour or so until risen and practically doubled in size.

Bake in a preheated oven at 180°C (fan oven) or equivalent for 8–10 minutes until golden brown.

Whilst the buns are baking, warm the extra honey for glazing, either in a saucepan or for about 20 seconds on high in the microwave until it becomes more liquidy.

Once the buns are baked, leave them in the baking tray for a few moments and then remove to a wire rack. Brush the warmed honey over the tops of the buns and leave to cool.

They will be very squidgy indeed whilst they are still warm, but once they are cool they will have the right balance of squidginess and fluffiness.

Extra fibre
If you feel you are a bit lacking in fibre, add 1 generously heaped tablespoon of wheat bran to the mixture along with the flour.

Alternative glaze
Instead of honey, try 2 tablespoons of malt extract mixed with 1 teaspoon of hot water.

Soothing bedtime milk
If you are fond of warm milk at bedtime, try stirring in a teaspoon of malt extract for a lovely soothing flavour and a bit of extra goodness.

Malt extract is a sugar
Don't overdo it though as maltose is a sugar just like sucrose, glucose, dextrose and fructose, and any other 'ose' most likely!

PLUM BREAD

This is a lovely, old-fashioned fruit loaf. It doesn't actually contain any plums or even prunes: the plum part actually refers to the drying process known as plumming, and so plums came to mean any kind of dried fruit. In this version, you make the dough in a bread machine and bake it in a loaf tin in the oven. Serve it sliced thinly and spread with butter for a delicate afternoon tea or slice it thickly for a more substantial meal. It is also lovely toasted the following day and great with thin slices of cheese.

½ teaspoon quick yeast
1 tablespoon unrefined
 caster sugar
1 teaspoon salt
300g (11oz) strong bread
 flour
140ml (scant ¼pt) warm
 water
1 egg
1–2 tablespoons mild oil
110g (4oz) raisins, currants
 and sultanas, mixed
25g (1oz) candied peel,
 finely chopped
 (optional)

You will need a greased (450g) 1lb loaf tin.

Put the yeast, sugar and salt into the bread pan and add the flour, warm water, egg and oil. Put the dried fruit and candied peel, if using, into the raisin compartment and set the machine to Raisin Dough. This should take a couple of hours or so.

Once the dough is ready, flour your hands and turn it onto a floured board. Roll it gently around the board until it has a light coating of flour all over and put it into the prepared tin. Don't worry about shaping it, as it will expand to fit the tin as it rises.

Leave it to rise for 30–40 minutes until it has almost doubled in size and looks like the right size for the finished loaf. It's difficult to be precise about exactly how long this will take as it depends on the temperature of the room: it will rise faster in a warm spot then in a cold one.

Once it has risen sufficiently, preheat the oven to 180–200°C (fan oven) or equivalent. Bake for approximately 30 minutes until browned and ready.

Remove from the oven and leave it in the tin for a few minutes for the loaf to cool and contract slightly before you turn it out. Cool on a wire rack. Cover with a clean tea towel to keep it moist as it cools.

No Loaf Tin?
If you don't have a suitable loaf tin you can still make a lovely round version of this loaf. Roll it into a round shape, put it on a greased baking tray, leave it to rise and bake as above. This looks so appealing: you might actually prefer to make this version even if you do have the right tin!

BARA BRITH (WELSH TEA BREAD)

This is a bread-type version of the popular Welsh tea bread. Bara brith means 'speckled bread', that is to say, bread speckled with dried fruit: it was made originally by adding dried fruit to the usual bread dough. There is also a cake type version made with self-raising flour and recipes for both types vary tremendously. Both versions are an established part of the traditional Welsh tea table. The cake versions have better keeping qualities, but the bread versions have a longer tradition and the added advantage of being very toastable, which is a big plus as it is very good toasted.

Eat it sliced fairly thickly and spread with butter for tea. Eat it fresh the first day and, after that, eat it lightly toasted: it's lovely for breakfast.

The honey glaze is a nice touch, but it's not essential. If you are not fond of candied peel or don't have any to hand, leave it out and make the total weight of currants and raisins up to 110g (4oz) instead.

You will need a greased 450g (1lb) loaf tin.

Put the yeast, sugar and salt into the bread pan and add the flour, warm water, egg and vegetable shortening or lard. Put the dried fruit and candied peel into the raisin compartment and set the machine to Raisin Dough.

Once the dough is ready, flour your hands, turn it onto a lightly floured board, and then ease it into the prepared loaf tin. Leave it in a warm place until it has almost doubled in size.

Once the dough has nearly risen sufficiently, turn on your oven to 180–200°C (fan oven) or equivalent and, once it has come to temperature, bake for approximately 30 minutes until browned and ready.

Remove from the oven and leave for a few minutes for the loaf to cool and contract slightly before you turn it out. Brush with the honey whilst still warm, and cool on a wire rack.

1 teaspoon quick yeast
2 tablespoons unrefined granulated sugar
1 teaspoon salt
385g (14oz) strong bread flour
300ml (10fl oz) warm water
1 egg
50g (2oz) block vegetable shortening or lard, diced
75g (4oz) currants and raisins, mixed
25g (1oz) candied peel, finely chopped
Plus approximately 2 tablespoons clear honey to glaze

✓ Helpful Note

If you have difficulty getting your Bara Brith or a similar shaped loaf (where the top can overhang the sides of the tin very slightly, if you have left it to prove a bit too long) out of the tin, try this. Always leave the baked loaf in the tin for a few minutes as it will contract slightly as it cools and start to pull away naturally from the sides of the tin. Once it has rested for a few moments, protect the hand holding the tin with an oven glove or wodge of tea towel and with your other hand gently press the sides of the loaf and ease it away from the tin. Do this on all four sides and it should then slip out quite easily.

BATH BUNS

One of the very nicest places to have a cup of tea or coffee in England is the Pump Room at the Roman Baths in Bath. You can have a cup of tea or coffee, morning or afternoon, accompanied by a delicious Bath bun with cinnamon butter. If it is afternoon, you may want to go mad and have the full afternoon tea. Whichever you choose, you will be sitting in the most beautiful room whilst helpful waiters and waitresses attend to you solicitously. As if this weren't enough, you are treated to the loveliest classical music played by a trio of talented musicians. You can while away a happy hour in wonderful surroundings straight out of the pages of a Jane Austen novel.

Obviously, you won't be going there very often but you can make a very good version of a Bath bun at home. There's nothing to stop you tuning in your radio to some atmospheric classical music and dreaming whilst you eat your bun!

MAKES 12 BUNS

½ teaspoon quick yeast
2 tablespoons unrefined
   caster sugar
1 teaspoon salt
300g (11oz) strong bread
   flour
140ml (scant ¼pt) warm
   water
50g (2oz) cold butter,
   diced
1 egg
1 egg yolk
75g (3oz) raisins and
   sultanas, mixed
25g (1oz) candied peel,
   finely chopped

Plus 1 beaten egg and 1
   dessertspoon water, to
   glaze
And several white sugar
   lumps, crushed in a
   pestle and mortar

You will need a large, greased baking tray.

Put the yeast, sugar and salt into the bread pan and add the flour, warm water, egg, egg yolk and butter. Put the dried fruit and candied peel into the raisin compartment and set the machine to Raisin Dough.

Once the dough is ready, turn onto a floured board. Divide it into 12 pieces, shape gently into rounds and put them onto the prepared baking tray: the dough will be quite rich and soft to the touch. Leave them in a warm place until they are practically half as big again.

Brush gently with the egg and water mix and sprinkle with the crushed sugar lumps.

Bake in a preheated oven at your normal bread baking temperature: 180–200°C (fan oven) or equivalent, for approximately 8–10 minutes or until golden brown. They will rise a little more in the oven.

These are fabulous eaten fresh and warm, just as they are, or with a touch of butter or Cinnamon Butter. They are still lovely the next day but that nice little contrast has gone between the ever so slightly crisp firmness of the outside of the bun and the squidgy softness inside. In any event, eat within a couple of days.

A Note on the Sugar Topping

If you have had a genuine Bath bun you will have noticed the special sugar on top. It must be a closely guarded bakers' secret as it doesn't seem to be available in the shops! Sugar lumps crushed in a pestle and mortar are a good alternative; if you can get hold of the more irregular shaped cane sugar lumps, these work better. White sugar on top of the buns seems more traditional, but brown sugar lumps are appealing too.

CINNAMON BUTTER

Stir a little **icing sugar** and a similar amount of **cinnamon** into **softened butter**. Don't add too much: just enough to flavour the butter slightly without being over powering.

BIG BATH BUN

This is exactly the same dough but, instead of forming it into little buns, shape it into one big bun. It does look quite comical, as it looks exactly the same as the regular ones but 12 times as big! It's a bit like looking at one of those outsize versions of yellow plastic bath-time ducks: you are so used to the smaller ones, the large ones are strangely unexpected.

Make the dough as for the **Bath Buns**, above, and once it is ready, ease the dough out of the bread pan with floured hands onto a lightly floured board. Shape into a flattish round and ease onto a greased baking tray. You may need to smooth it out a bit more. At this stage it should measure roughly 20cm (8in) across: if you make it too deep and round the middle won't cook through properly. Leave it in a warm place to rise until it is practically half as big again and, although still fairly flat, more domed in appearance.

Once it has risen sufficiently, brush the top gently with beaten egg and water as before and sprinkle with crushed sugar lumps: two or three lumps are plenty.

Bake in a preheated oven at your normal bread baking temperature: 180–200°C (fan oven) or equivalent for 20–25 minutes until golden brown.

Slice it thickly and eat on its own or spread with butter or **Cinnamon Butter**. If you have any left the next day you can eat it with butter and apricot conserve or toast it under the grill.

Bit of buttered big Bath bun, anyone?

CURRANT BUNS

This classic currant bun is very versatile. Eat them buttered for tea when they are fresh or split and toast under the grill the day after baking. They are perfect for picnics and lovely with a bit of jam or some thin slices of cheese.

*You can leave out the spice and candied peel for a more everyday bun, and use the full recipe to make your own **Hot Cross Buns** at Easter time.*

MAKES 12 BUNS

1 teaspoon mixed spice (optional)
450g (1lb) strong white bread flour
1½ teaspoons quick yeast
1 teaspoon salt
25g (1oz) unrefined caster sugar
1 egg
210ml (8fl oz) warm water
2–3 tablespoons of mild oil
110g (4oz) currants, raisins, sultanas, mixed
25g (1oz) candied, not mixed peel, diced (optional)

You will need a large greased baking tray or 12-cup muffin tin.

Put the spice, if using, into the bread pan and then the flour. Add the yeast, salt and sugar into separate corners on top. Add the egg, warm water and oil. Put into the machine, setting it to Raisin Dough. Measure the dried fruit and candied peel, if using, and put them into the raisin compartment, if you have one, see below.

Once the Raisin Dough program has finished, take the dough out and put it onto a lightly floured board. Divide into 12 pieces and lightly shape each one into a ball and place on a greased baking tray. Alternatively, put each piece into the cups of a 12-cup muffin tin. Cover lightly with greaseproof paper and leave in a warm place for about an hour or until the dough has just about doubled in size, that is to say, is the size the finished buns will be.

Towards the end of this time, preheat the oven to 180–220°C (fan oven) or equivalent.

Bake for 8–10 minutes or until golden brown. Remove from the oven and cool on a wire rack.

STICKY GLAZE

You can turn your buns into 'sticky buns' with this delicious easy glaze. Heat **2 tablespoons of caster sugar** and **2 tablespoons of water** together in a small heavy-bottomed pan until all the sugar is melted and bubbling. Brush the glaze over the buns and allow them to cool slightly before serving.

HOT CROSS BUN CROSSES

If you are feeling ambitious and want to put crosses on your buns for Easter, make up a simple pastry by rubbing **50g (2oz) plain flour, a pinch of salt** and **25g (1oz) of cold, diced butter** together into fine crumbs. Bind with **2 tablespoons of cold water** and roll onto a floured board. Cut into strips.

Beat **1 egg** with a **drop of water** and brush over the buns: this will give the buns a good gloss *and* help to secure the crosses. Lay the strips across each bun to make the crosses.

Bake for 8–10 minutes or until golden brown. Remove from the oven and cool on a wire rack.

TEA CAKES

Toasted Tea Cakes and a pot of tea are the perfect tea-time combination for a winter's afternoon. These are also lovely eaten fresh and untoasted on the day of baking.

You will need a large, greased baking tray.

Put the yeast, sugar and salt into the bread pan and then add the flour and lard or vegetable shortening. Pour in the warm water.

Put the dried fruit into the raisin compartment and set the machine to the Raisin Dough program.

Once the program has finished, put the dough onto a floured board and divide it into 10 pieces. Shape into balls and flatten gently with your hands or a floured rolling pin. Space them out onto the greased baking tray, and leave to rise in a warm place for an hour or so until they have doubled in size.

Bake in a preheated oven at 180–220°C (fan oven) or equivalent for 8–10 minutes until golden brown. Cool on a wire rack.

1 teaspoon quick yeast
1 tablespoon sugar
1 teaspoon salt
450g (1lb) strong bread flour
35g (1½oz) lard or vegetable shortening
300ml (½pt) warm water
110g (4oz) mixed currants, raisins and sultanas

INDEX